Population, Public Policy, and Economic Development

edited by
Michael C. Keeley
foreword by
Mark Perlman

Published in cooperation
with G. E. TEMPO, Center for
Advanced Studies

The Praeger Special Studies program—
utilizing the most modern and efficient book
production techniques and a selective
worldwide distribution network—makes
available to the academic, government, and
business communities significant, timely
research in U.S. and international economic, social, and political development.

Population, Public Policy, and Economic Development

Praeger Publishers   New York   Washington   London

PRAEGER SPECIAL STUDIES IN INTERNATIONAL ECONOMICS AND DEVELOPMENT

Library of Congress Cataloging in Publication Data
Main entry under title:

Population, public policy, and economic development.

   (Praeger special studies in international economics and
development)
   Bibliography: p.
   CONTENTS: The economic consequences of demographic change:
Economic-demographic modeling: Enke, S. Economic consequences
of rapid population growth. Keeley, M. C. A neoclassical analysis
of economic-demographic simulation models. Applications of
economic-demographic simulation models: Herrick, B. H.
Economic effects of Chilean fertility decline. Maxwell, D. L.
and Brown, R. Developed and developing countries. [etc.]
   1. Demography—Mathematical models—Addresses, essays,
lectures.   2. Economic development—Mathematical models—
Addresses, essays lectures.   3. Population policy—Mathematical
models—Addresses, essays, lectures.   I. Keeley, Michael C.
II General Electric Company. Technical Military Planning
Operation. Center for Advanced Studies.
HB885.P66   301.32   75-23975
ISBN 0-275-55670-0

PRAEGER PUBLISHERS
111 Fourth Avenue, New York, N.Y. 10003, U.S.A.

Published in the United States of America in 1976
by Praeger Publishers, Inc.

© 1976 by Praeger Publishers, Inc.

Printed in the United States of America

Dedicated to Stephen Enke (1916–1974)

whose intellectual and entrepreneurial efforts
made this book possible.

Stephen Enke's pioneering research in the field of economic development and population policy provides the foundations upon which many of the papers in this volume are based. From the beginning, his writings reflected considerable interest in the interplay between economic theory and international economics. As time went on (by the mid-1950s) his attention turned increasingly to discussions of the international economic problems of less developed countries, in particular the interrelated problems of population growth and economic development, and it is these issues which are the primary concern of this book.

Stephen Enke was born in Victoria, British Columbia (Canada) on July 15, 1916. He received a baccalaureate degree in Economics at Stanford in 1937 and a master's degree in 1939. He went on for further education at Harvard University where he received a master's degree in Public Administration in 1940 and a doctorate in Economics in 1943. At the time of his death he was Manager of technical programs, General Electric/TEMPO in Washington, D.C. Previously he had held a variety of positions including several in academia. These were at the University of California, Los Angeles (1942-47), a visiting professorship at Yale (1959-60), and a professorship at Duke University in 1961-62. He was associated with the Rand Corporation where he was ultimately the chief of the logistics division, from 1949 to 1958. From 1961 until 1962 he was with an organization now known as the Center for Naval Analyses, and from 1962 until 1965 he was assistant to the president of the Institute for Defense Analysis. He held a variety of governmental positions including Deputy Assistant Secretary of Defense under Robert McNamara, assistant administrator of the Agency for International Development and numerous consulting positions. In the last decade of his life he was repeatedly involved in studies of the defense policy of the United States and in studies pertaining to economic growth and population policy of less developed countries.

Enke published four major books: Intermediate Economic Theory (Prentice-Hall, New York, 1950); International Economics (with Dr. V. Salera) (Prentice-Hall, New York, 1957, third edition); Economics for Development (Prentice-Hall, Englewood Cliffs, N.J., 1963), and Defense Management (editor) (Prentice-Hall, Englewood Cliffs, N.J., 1967). In addition, he published over 100 articles and papers as well as writing about a score of classified research papers in the economics of defense area.

Enke was very much in the tradition of neoclassical (particularly Austrian) economic theory. He had a talent for developing a priori models. He was not averse to empirical research, but his was a fertile mind accustomed to creating and manipulating logical arguments.

He occasionally expressed a tendency toward slashing verbal exchange. But he could receive criticism as well as offer it, and those who did not mind verbal battles invariably found him an exhilarating person to be around. He had an original eye and a passion for debunking facile social reform suggestions.

His work on economic development and population policy manifests the quality which his friends particularly valued. It had vigor, originality, and independence. His was an independent mind which appreciated integrity and intellectual courage. He was not always (as the record shows) correct in his theory or his predictions; but he was always interesting, even optimally stimulating. His TEMPO growth models are, for this decade, among the more frequently employed by neoclassical economists. His research in the area of economic development and population policy has had very important influences on shaping public policy, especially U.S. foreign aid policy.

Enke, dying suddenly on the 22nd of September in 1974, was not granted the Biblical span of 70 years. The quantity and quality of his output, however, was a multiple of that normally produced. The record clearly indicates that he managed to do far more than is asked of most in somewhat less than the appointed period.

There are few among us who believe that anyone can now actually construct a personal permanent monument like the Pyramids. We realize that the impact of our ideas is, by reason of the scientific nature of our work, limited. But Stephen Enke's work serves to shape today's thinking; I venture to suggest that its influence will still be felt for more than a decade or two. This is a real achievement. This volume bears witness to the fact that others doubtless share my opinion; it also, thus, becomes part of a significant self-fulfilling prediction.

Concern about rapid population growth is one of the most important issues on the world's agenda. Changes in fertility, mortality, and migration have many important long-term economic, social, and political consequences. Although there is considerable debate regarding what rate of population growth is socially optimal, there are few who would argue that the current rapid rates of population growth of the less developed countries (LDCs) can or should continue indefinitely. The real questions are what are the economic and social consequences and causes of such high rates of population growth, when will these rates decline, and how can public policy affect these rates?

The current rates of population growth in LDCs are without historical precedent, averaging approximately 2.5 percent per year, which implies a doubling of the population every 28 years. These high rates of population growth are due largely to declines in mortality (within the last 20 years) brought about largely by public health measures such as sanitation and inoculation against contagious diseases. Fertility is only slightly higher than it was prior to the declines in mortality. Because these very high rates of population growth have existed for some time, most LDCs are characterized by very young age distributions. This means that even if fertility rates were to fall to replacement levels, population would continue to grow fairly rapidly for a substantial period of time. Thus, it seems likely that rapid population growth rates could continue to characterize LDCs for at least the near future. It is evident that this demographically unique situation has many long-term implications for the social welfare and economic well-being of the majority of the world's population living in LDCs and could, in addition, have important consequences for the economies of the more developed countries.

This volume presents a collection of articles that provide analyses of both the causes and long-term economic implications of rapid population growth. The articles presented are policy oriented in that they provide a variety of analytical tools and methodological devices, within an economic framework, that are useful to policy makers and planners. Economic theory and public decision making are mutually reinforcing activities in the sense that public policy problems partially dictate what sorts of theories are useful, and good theory increases the usefulness and success of policy formulation and public decision making. Accordingly, the choice of research topics included in this volume, in part, is determined by their relevance to the important policy questions regarding population growth and economic development.

The articles have bearing on the importance of population policy, the choice between alternative policies, and the choice of methodologies that are relevant to the public decisions that are facing planners in the great majority of LDCs. To quote Stephen Enke (in Economics for Development, 1963, p. ix):

> Many officials who make economic policy, although they may have a great deal of factual and necessary knowledge, are largely unaware of the economic principles essential to their work. Economics is not a simple subject. True relations are often the opposite of what at first they appear to be. There must be more economics in economic development if there is to be more development.

Accordingly, the articles contained in this book stress the principles, theory, and analytical techniques that are relevant to policy formulation and public decision making.

Most of the articles presented in this volume are the results of research carried out by persons associated with the Population Studies group at TEMPO, General Electric Company's Center for Advanced Studies. In part, these studies represent a general program of research at TEMPO that has been supported financially by the United States Agency for International Development, Office of Population, since 1968. However, the policies and views presented represent those of the authors only and should not be attributed to AID or to TEMPO.

Stephen Enke, who was the founder and first manager of TEMPO's population studies group, did the pioneering research on which many of the papers presented in this volume are based. Enke was one of the first scholars to stress the importance of applying economic theory to the interrelated problems of economic development and population, and his work was influential on public policy. Enke contributed greatly to the work in this field through his intellectual leadership, insightful and constructive criticism, and through his unusual ability to assess the policy importance of a particular question. Enke also contributed in many important ways to the articles presented here; he commented critically on earlier drafts of almost all. More importantly, he contributed his economic intuition, insight, and guidance to the field of population policy research of which these articles are a part. He never lost sight of the practical, policy uses, and implications of research; and the articles presented here hopefully reflect this view.

Since the purpose of this book is to provide analyses of both the causes and effects of demographic variables, the volume is divided into two parts. Part I deals with the economic consequences of rapid population growth, and Part II deals with the formulation of policies that affect population growth. The papers of Part I consider the problem of investigating the consequences of demographic change from the vantage point of macroeconomic-demographic models, and the papers of Part II take a microeconomic approach. A separate introduction precedes each of the two parts and contains a discussion of the articles in that part.

It is hoped that this volume will contribute to a better understanding of the interrelationships between economic development and demographic variables and that it will provide useful inputs into the public decision making process.

ACKNOWLEDGMENTS

Many people have contributed to this manuscript, and I would like to thank them for their efforts. The late Stephen Enke, who was manager of TEMPO's (General Electric's Center for Advanced Studies) Washington office, not only contributed to many of the articles but also originally conceived the idea of publishing a collection of articles dealing with the important problems of population and economic development and encouraged me to put together such a volume. John Turner of the University of Chicago and consultant to TEMPO provided valuable editorial advice and assistance by reviewing each of the articles, as well as the introductory sections. Richard Brown, the present manager of TEMPO's population studies group, provided much needed encouragement and advice and expertly resolved the many administrative problems associated with publication. Also, George Felman, Henry Cole, John Campbell, and John Palmisano of TEMPO provided helpful comments.

The program of research in population and economic development at General Electric TEMPO, Center for Advanced Studies, has been funded from its inception in 1968 by the U.S. Agency for International Development, Office of Population, whose support is gratefully acknowledged. However, the views expressed in these articles are the sole responsibility of the authors and are, of course, not attributable to the Agency for International Development.

I would like also to thank the Economic Journal for permission to reprint Stephen Enke's "Economic Consequences of Rapid Population Growth," and the Journal of Biosocial Science for permission to present an article by Stephen Enke and Bryan Hickman, "Offering Bonuses to Reduce Fertility," which appears here in revised form.

Further, I would like to acknowledge the many helpful comments of the late Stephen Enke to my chapter, as well as Anne Williams, Henry Cole, Ronald Hobson, George Felman, and John Turner. An earlier version of my paper was presented at the First Annual Meeting of the World Population Society, Washington, D.C., February 1974.

CONTENTS

Page

FOREWORD
by Mark Perlman   vi

PREFACE   viii

ACKNOWLEDGMENTS   xi

LIST OF TABLES   xvi

LIST OF FIGURES AND MAP   xx

PART I: THE ECONOMIC CONSEQUENCES
OF DEMOGRAPHIC CHANGE

Introduction and Summary to Part I   3

Chapter
1   ECONOMIC-DEMOGRAPHIC MODELING   9

Economic Consequences of Rapid Population Growth
Stephen Enke   11

Introduction   11
Distinguishing Population Size, Growth,
    and Fertility   12
Economic Development Through Reducing Fertility   15
International Consequences of Fertility Differences   21
    Comment   24

A Neoclassical Analysis of Economic-Demographic
Simulation Models
Michael C. Keeley   25

Introduction   25
The Neoclassical Framework   27
The Steady-State, Long-Run Effects of a
    Fertility Decline   29

Chapter	Page

Extensions of the Neoclassical Model 31
    Human Capital 31
    Capital Depreciation 31
    Alternative Savings Functions 32
    Technological Change 34
    Noninelastic Labor Supply 35
The Transitional Period 36
Summary and Conclusions 42
Notes 43

2 APPLICATIONS OF ECONOMIC-DEMOGRAPHIC
    SIMULATION MODELS 47

Economic Effects of Chilean Fertility Decline
Bruce H. Herrick 49

Introduction 49
Chilean Population and National Income 51
    Chilean Economic and Demographic Trends 51
    The Demographic Projections 56
    The Economic Projections of Output 60
Chilean Public Expenditures on Education and Health 63
    Education 63
    Health Care 75
Fertility, Human Capital Formation, and
    Economic Growth 78
Conclusions 83

Developed and Developing Countries: Closing the Gap
Douglas L. Maxwell and Richard Brown 85

Description of the Two Worlds Model 87
The Half Century Projections 93
Conclusions 101
Appendix 103
Notes 107

PART II: POLICIES TO AFFECT FERTILITY

Introduction and Summary to Part II 111
Note 116

3 DETERMINANTS OF FERTILITY IN DEVELOPING
   COUNTRIES   117

Review and Evaluation of the Literature
Anne D. Williams   119

   Introduction   119
   Theory of Fertility Determinants   120
      Utility Maximization   121
      Desired Family Size   124
      Control of Surviving Family Size   125
      Summary   126
   A Survey of the State of the Evidence   126
      Overview of Empirical Efforts to Date   126
      Income, Occupation, and Socioeconomic Status   129
      Education   132
      Female and Child Labor Force Activity
         and Wages   137
      Migration, Urbanization, and Industrialization   140
      Childhood Mortality   142
      Fecundity and Family Planning   145
      Marriage and Family Structure   147
      Attitudes, Roles, Son Preference, Tastes,
         and Institutions   151
   Conclusions   153
      State of Knowledge   153
      Unanswered Questions   155
      Possible Uses and Future Work   157

Fertility and Economic Development
Paul R. Gregory and John M. Campbell, Jr.   160

   Introduction   160
   Fertility and Economic Development: An Overview   164
   Population Pressures at Low Levels of Development   166
   An OLS Interaction Model of Fertility   166
   Modernization Turning Points: An Investigation
      of Elasticity Variability   171
   An Investigation of Elasticity Ranges   174
   Further Calculations--2SLS Results   175
   Policy Implications   177
   Notes   178

Chapter   Page

4   ECONOMIC-DEMOGRAPHIC POLICY ANALYSIS   189

Offering Bonuses to Reduce Fertility
Stephen Enke and Bryan D. Hickman   191

    Background   191
    Bonuses Versus Subsidies and Advertising   194
    Alternative Bonus Systems   197
    Difficulties in Practice   199
    Desirable Innovations   200
        Nonpregnancy Payments   200
        Commercial Distribution of Subsidized
            Contraceptives   201
        IUD Insertion Bonuses   202
        Bonuses for Vasectomies   203
        Bonus Eligibility and System Capacity   203
    Evaluating a System of Bonuses   204
    Summary   209

Child Spacing Strategies, Old Age Security, and
Population Growth
Donald J. O'Hara and Richard A. Brown   211

    Birth Limitation and Birth Spacing   211
    Desired Family Size, Mortality, and Population
        Growth   213
    Desired Family Size and Old Age Security   215
        Structural Characteristics of the Dynamic
            Programming Model   218
    Comparison of Results   225
    Interpretation and Policy Implications   226
    Notes   228

BIBLIOGRAPHY   230

ABOUT THE EDITOR AND CONTRIBUTORS   257

LIST OF TABLES

Table   Page

1.1   Effects of Declining Fertility on Output and per
Capita Income in "Developa"   18

1.2   Contrasting Attainment of Same Population in
Different Years: Unfavorable Economic
Consequences of Fast Population Growth
in "Developa"   20

1.3   Effects of Fertility on "Developa's" Ability to
Service Debts While Realizing a Stipulated Annual
Improvement in Income per Capita   23

1.4   Changes in the Dependency Rate for Assumed
Fertility Declines   41

2.1   Total Population of Chile   57

2.2   Crude Birth Rate (CBR) and Crude Death Rate (CDR)
per Thousand in the Chilean Population   57

2.3   Numbers of Youth and Old People per Hundred
Persons in the Population Aged 15-64 Under
Different Chilean Fertility Assumptions   59

2.4   Projected Chilean Labor Force Under Different
Fertility Assumptions   59

2.5   Chilean Labor Force to Population Ratios Under
Different Fertility Assumptions   59

2.6   Summary of Chilean Economic Projections, 1960-2000   61

2.7   Inputs to the Chilean Production Process   62

2.8   Year in Which Chilean GNP per Capita Reaches a
Given Level   63

2.9   Projected Chilean School-Age Population   65

2.10   Projected Chilean Enrollment Ratios and
Classroom Space   66

Table   Page

2.11   Projected Total Chilean Primary and Secondary
        School Enrollment and Teacher and Classroom
        Space Requirements   68

2.12   Projected Annual Chilean Primary and Secondary
        School New Teacher and New Classroom Space
        Requirements   68

2.13   Projected Annual Investment and Operating Costs
        of Chilean Primary and Secondary Schools   70

2.14   Parametric Coefficients Assumed for Projections
        Relating to University Education   70

2.15   University Enrollment and Teachers Required
        1960-2000   73

2.16   University Education: New Teacher Requirements,
        Training Costs, and System Operating Costs   74

2.17   Projected Extent of Coverage of Government-Provided
        Health Services   76

2.18   Projected Government Health Costs   77

2.19   Projected Numbers and Educational Attainment of
        the Chilean Labor Force, 1970-2000   81

2.20   Projected Chilean GNP and GNP per Capita with
        Labor Force Weighted by Educational
        Attainment, 1960-2000   82

2.21   Alternative Fertility Assumptions for Developing
        Countries   95

2.22   Alternative Savings Rate Assumptions for
        Developing Countries   96

2.23   Alternative Educational Investment Policies for
        Developing Countries   97

2.24   Different Official Assistance Assumptions for
        Developing Countries   99

Table		Page
2.25	Effects on Developing Countries of Restricting Foreign Private Investment	100
2.26	Third World Demographic Projection	104
2.27	First World Demographic Projection	105
2.28	Economic Projection	106
3.1	Children Ever Born to 1959 Sample of Ever-Married Women Aged 35-50 of Differing Incomes in Santiago	130
3.2	Relationship of Fertility to Female Education in San Juan Standard Metropolitan Statistical Area	134
3.3	Live Births to Currently Married Women in Cairo	134
3.4	Percentage of Latin American Legally or Consensually Married Women Ever Using Family Planning, by Education, 1963-64	136
3.5	Children Ever Born to Ever-Married Women in Thailand, by Labor Force Status, 1960	139
3.6	Children Ever Born to Ever-Married Women in Thailand, by Occupation, 1960	139
3.7	Child Deaths in Jordan and Israel by Number of Children Ever Born, 1961	144
3.8	Children Ever Born to Women in Bengal, India, by Family Type and Caste, 1960-61	150
3.9	Children Ever Born to Women in West Malaysia by Family Type and Age	150
3.10	OLS Interaction Model, Latin American Fertility, Combined Time-Series/Cross Sections (1950 and 1960)	170
3.11	Mean Elasticities and Modernization Turning Points (MTPs) for Latin American Fertility (CBR), OLS Results	172

Table   Page

3.12   Elasticity Ranges for Various UP Values   174

3.13   Mean Elasticities and MTPs, 2SLS, Latin American
            Fertility   176

4.1   Selected Demographic Consequences of Specified
            Family Planning Strategies at Various Levels
            of Life Expectancy   222

LIST OF FIGURES AND MAP

Figure   Page

1.1   A Steady-State Stable Equilibrium   28

1.2   Effect of a Decline in the Rate of Labor Force
       Growth   29

2.1   Annual Birth Rates, Death Rates, and Rates of
       Natural Population Increase in Chile, 1929-70   52

2.2   Observed and Projected Gross Reproduction Rate
       in Chile, 1960-69, Using CELADE-Based
       Fertility Assumption B   54

2.3   Gross Reproduction Rate in Chile Under Three
       Assumptions, 1960-2000   55

4.1   Bonuses, Advertising, and Subsidies   194

4.2   Family Size Required to Maintain Stated Intrinsic
       Growth Rates as Mortality Risks Decline   216

4.3   Population Growth Rates Under Different
       Strategies at Various Mortality Levels   221

Map

2.1   Two Worlds Country Division   88

I

THE ECONOMIC
CONSEQUENCES OF
DEMOGRAPHIC CHANGE

Most less developed countries (LDCs) are experiencing in the 1970s rapid population growth as a result of extraordinarily high fertility and a decline in mortality. The economies of the LDCs undoubtedly will be affected in many ways by this rapid population growth. Less obviously, the large differential in population growth rates between the developed and less developed countries may as well have important social, economic, and political implications for the developed countries. Thus, an understanding of the long-term implications of this demographic phenomena is of importance to planners and policy makers in both developed and developing nations.

The papers in this section represent evolving approaches to the problem of analyzing the economic implications of this historically unparalleled demographic occurrence. The models presented provide not only a framework for analyzing the economic effects of rapid population growth but also provide a general framework for investigating the interrelationships between demographic variables and economic variables.

Demographic variables have many important direct and indirect effects on various aspects of a nation's economy, such as the rate of economic growth, per capita income, the distribution of income, labor force participation and its age-sex composition, the rate of human capital formation, and the rate of saving. Policy makers should be cognizant of these effects when formulating and implementing development plans since ignoring demographic effects may render such plans meaningless and unusable. To cite a simple example, an educational plan that ignores the existing age distribution and its implications for future enrollments is not a useful policy tool and can lead to serious misallocations of resources. A problem common to all governments is the allocation of government-provided goods and services. Incorporating demographic variables into government planning should improve allocative efficiency greatly. Planners and policy makers concerned with formulating population policies should explore thoroughly the economic implications of the proposed demographic changes. Finally, since demographic variables have so many important economic effects, governments desiring to change various aspects of their economies may find that changing demographic variables is the most cost-effective way to accomplish that goal.

The primary purpose of this book is to provide a variety of tools and methodologies that will aid the policy maker, planner, or development economist in investigating the implications of various policies. The papers of Part I analyze the interrelationships between demographic and economic variables through macroeconomic-demographic modeling. Chapter 1 lays down the foundations of this approach, and Chapter 2 presents some applications. The models are computer-based simulation models, with the exception of the work by Michael Keeley, which is an analytical investigation of the economic framework on which the computer models are based.

Simulation models provide the researcher with a means of investigating the unknown behavior of a complex system by combining a set of interacting subsystems whose behavior is known. The simulation models of Part I should not be viewed as forecasting models since most of the relationships embedded in them are not empirically based and, more importantly, because the purpose of the models is to enable the investigator to analyze the interactions between various well-specified subsystems, especially economic-demographic interactions. Furthermore, these are not stochastic models. The results of the simulations are determined by the behavioral assumptions, both implicit and explicit, in the models as well as the initial conditions. Although the behavior of each submodel of these simulation models is fairly well understood, the strength of these models is their ability to analyze the interactions and interrelationships between the submodels, which is usually difficult to specify a priori. In addition, such models can be employed to make comparative projections. That is, the effects of a change in a particular variable can be evaluated by comparing the results to a base-run in which that variable is held constant, thus providing useful information on the effects of the variable in question even though neither run is a good representation (or likely prediction) of the future.

The interaction between demographic and economic variables is the focus of these models. However, the causality is assumed to run only one way--from the demographic sector to the economic sector--because of the type of policy questions that these models are designed to analyze. The models serve to highlight the importance of age-specific disaggregation of the population and are designed for investigating the economic implications of exogenously determined demographic trends, so the policy makers can evaluate the macroeconomic consequences of particular population policies. It is implicitly assumed that the connection between population policy and demographic trend is known. (The problems of formulating policies to meet specific demographic goals is considered in detail in Part II.)

The economics of the interrelationships between demographic variables and economic variables is a relatively new field with many unsolved conceptual problems and with far too few empiricial studies. In particular, the problem of analyzing, measuring, and even defining the externalities that presumably are associated with rapid population growth or with extreme population size are largely unsolved. Thus, a description of an "optimum" population policy that leads to maximum social welfare is beyond the scope of the analysis presented. Consequently, the models of Part I are not welfare models since they do not indicate which demographic trend maximizes social welfare nor do they suggest which level of population is optimal. An economic analysis of the social costs and benefits, which are presumably different from the private costs and benefits associated with various rates of population growth or population size, is currently lacking both on a theoretical basis and on an empirical level. In fact, only since 1970 have attempts been made to analyze systematically the private costs and benefits of children (which is extensively discussed by Anne Williams in Part II). Thus, the models do not indicate which population policy is "best"; rather they illustrate and contrast the effects of a particular population policy on such variables as the level of income per capita, the rate of growth of national income per capita, the size and rate of growth of the labor force, the rate of capital accumulation, the costs of an educational system, the savings rate, income per worker, and international trade. However, the welfare implications of the various changes in the above variables, associated with particular policies, are not specified by the models and must be evaluated by the planner.

The papers of Part I differ significantly in their approach, but they have in common the unifying economic framework of the basic neoclassical model of production. The neoclassical model assumes that output or GNP (gross national product) is determined by capital, here broadly defined to include human capital, labor, and the technology of the economy. Both factor markets and product markets are assumed to be in equilibrium at all times, and instantaneous adjustment to new market equilibriums is assumed. Since markets actually do not adjust instantaneously, the models are inadequate for short-term projections of economic fluctuations. However, in the long run, short-term adjustments are of much less importance. More important, changes in vital rates have important long-term effects on the economy, but have only limited short-term effects. Thus, these models are designed to analyze the long-term effects of demographic change by specifying how changes in demographic variables lead to changes in both the level and rate of change of capital and labor.

In Chapter 1, Stephen Enke outlines the essentials of a basic macroeconomic-demographic simulation model and presents some illustrative simulations of an idealized LDC. In particular, he contrasts the effects of sustained high fertility with those of declining fertility over a 30-year period. The primary finding is that GNP hardly is affected by the decline in fertility since capital rises

sufficiently to compensate for the decline in labor, partly because
the savings rate is assumed to depend negatively on population. Income per capita is thus higher than it otherwise would be since population is smaller with reduced fertility. The resulting increase in
income per capita is found to be insensitive to a variety of changes
in the basic parameters of the model.

The paper by Michael Keeley goes on to investigate these findings in detail using the analytical techniques of neoclassical growth
theory. He finds that the increase in income per capita is due to
changes in two distinct variables: the capital-labor ratio and the
fraction of dependents (that is, the fraction of the population not in
the labor force). In the short run, the smaller fraction of children
in the population that results from a decline in fertility must lead to
an increase in income per capita because output is unaffected until
the first cohort born under the regime of lower fertility enters the
labor force (usually 15 to 20 years after a fertility decline) and because population is smaller than it otherwise would be. However,
in the long run the dependency rate does not decline nearly as much
as in the short run because the increased fraction of old dependents
partially compensates for the decline in young dependents. Furthermore, Keeley points out that when the dependency rate is changing,
income per capita is a poor proxy for economic development. Society and individuals choose to have both young and old dependents,
and a change in per capita income caused solely by a change in the
dependency rate necessarily does not indicate a change in societal
welfare.

Keeley also demonstrates that the capital-labor ratio is higher
with reduced fertility than it otherwise would be, even if the fraction
saved does not depend on population and is constant, because of the
basic dynamics of the neoclassical system. Finally, the rate of
change of the capital-labor ratio when fertility changes is shown to
depend on the rate of capital depreciation, the responsiveness of
labor supply to the real wage, the responsiveness of savings to the
dependency rate, and the output elasticities of capital and labor in
production.

In Chapter 2, Bruce Herrick applies a model similar to that
previously outlined by Enke to the specific case of Chile. The model
is expanded to investigate the effects of changes in fertility on the
costs of government-provided social services such as education and
health; and, in addition, the effects of changes in education on output
and hence development are investigated. It is found that lower fertility enables the government to expand more rapidly the educational
system, even if the percentage of GNP spent on education is constant.
This is because the costs of providing a given level of educational
service decline with a decline in fertility. This result applies for all

social services that are disproportionately consumed by the young.
Finally, the increase in educational supply per child that is made
possible by lower fertility in turn has substantial independent effects
on national income and income per worker.

The last article in Chapter 2 by Douglas Maxwell and Richard
Brown is an analysis of the implications of the rapid population
growth in LDCs for both the LDCs themselves and the developed
countries. The one-sector neoclassical model considered in the
previous articles is expanded to include two separate but interacting
economies: the economy of the developed world (the First World)
taken as a whole and the economy of the less developed world (the
Third World). Perhaps the most important finding is that the widely
divergent rates of population growth (and labor force growth) between
the developed and less developed world (which, because of the very
young age structure, is likely to continue for some time even if fertility rates in the Third World decline) have important implications
for trade between the First and Third Worlds. The high ratio of
labor to capital in the Third World implies a high return to capital,
which increases with technical progress and rapid labor force growth.
Thus there is a large and increasing incentive for First World investors to invest in the Third World, which raises Third World incomes substantially higher than they would be without this investment.
Restricted foreign investment considerably reduces national income
and the rate of economic development. This model also indicates
that increases in human capital in the Third World will raise income
substantially and also increase the incentives for First World investment in the Third World. Fertility reduction in the Third World
does tend to reduce the gap between First and Third World income
per capita; but direct foreign aid has little independent effect on the
rate of development, partly because foreign aid and private investment are, to some degree, substitutes.

CHAPTER

1

ECONOMIC-
DEMOGRAPHIC
MODELING

ECONOMIC CONSEQUENCES
OF RAPID
POPULATION GROWTH
Stephen Enke

INTRODUCTION

"Population" was a major concern of the early classical economists. But subsequently it was forgotten by the profession for over
half a century. Today, when the consequences of population growth
are so especially important for the LDCs, barely a dozen economists
are writing articles on population issues.*

Described below are the principal conceptual findings of a
small group of economists that has been working together during the
past few years on various projects concerning interactions between
population growth and economic development.† None of their conclusions has hitherto appeared in an economic journal.[1] The time
has come to present to economists the more important conclusions
of this team research as described in various TEMPO publications.[2]

---

*Including J. J. Spengler, James E. Meade, Goran Ohlin,
Colin Clark, Henry Leibenstein, Ansley J. Coale, and the author.

†Most of the analyses presented here were done under contract
to the United States Agency for International Development. Colleagues have included Richard G. Zind, James P. Bennett, William E.
McFarland, Donald J. O'Hara, Ross D. Eckert, Arthur S. DeVany,
David N. Holmes, and Richard A. Brown. However, the author is
alone responsible for the views expressed here.

The author wishes to acknowledge the assistance of Richard A.
Brown of the TEMPO staff. He also has an obvious indebtedness to
present and former colleagues as listed in footnote (†) above.

These conclusions for LDCs relate to (1) distinctions among size, growth, and fertility of population; (2) the impact of fertility reduction on income per capita; and (3) the international consequences of fertility differentials among countries.*

DISTINGUISHING POPULATION SIZE, GROWTH, AND FERTILITY

It is necessary for economic analysts to distinguish among the economic incidence of population size, population growth, and population fertility.

Whether a country has a "large" or "small" absolute population usually should refer to the size of its total population (or labor force) relative to the availabilities of usable natural resources and/or produced domestic capital. This contrasts with population densities per square mile, which by themselves have little economic meaning. An economy with little capital per worker is likely to have a low level of consumption, and this situation will be worsened if "land" (natural resources) is also scarce. A population in this sense may be too large or small regardless of its rate of growth. In terms of available capital, Mauritius has a "large" population compared with that of Japan, for example.

Where an already "large" population is combined with rapid natural increase and high fertility, as in lands of ancient culture such as China and India, the demographic-economic situation is at its worst.

The economic danger of rapid population growth lies in the consequent inability of a country both to increase its stock of capital and to improve its state of art rapidly enough for its per capita income not to be less than it otherwise would be. If the rate of technological innovation cannot be forced and is not advanced by faster population growth, a rapid proportionate growth in population can cause an actual reduction in income per capita. Rapid population growth inhibits an increase in capital per worker, especially if associated with high crude birth rates that make for a very young age distribution. This is regardless of population densities. Although Brazil has a low population density in terms of "land," its population growth rate appears uneconomically high for adequate capital

_____

*TEMPO studies in population also have concerned the incidence of zero population growth in the United States, hardly attainable before 2040, on different industries and factor incomes. See S. Enke, Zero Population Growth (Santa Barbara: TEMPO, 1970).

accumulation; and more babies cannot usefully populate its "empty" lands.*

High fertility rates have the demographic effect of increasing the proportionate number of children.† A country with a crude birth rate of over 40/1000 a year is likely to have over 40 percent of its population under 15 years of age. Youngsters under 15 years of age are significant consumers but insignificant producers. Large families including many children, with consequently low incomes per family member, are comparatively poor contributors to domestic saving. Low savings per capita are associated with "young" populations and high fertility.‡

Public health measures have led to rather dramatic reductions in age specific death rates, especially since the 1930s, in poor and backward countries. The "killing" epidemics such as cholera have been far more successfully controlled than "crippling" diseases such as bilharzia. Continued high fertility rates have meanwhile led to natural population increases of 2 to 3 percent a year that double population every 35 to 23 years, respectively. Indeed, although often ignored, one of the characteristics most distinguishing backward from advanced countries is a high birth rate of over 35 per 1,000 a year (for example, Indonesia as contrasted with Japan).

---

*Many LDCs include large areas of unpeopled "empty" land that superficially seem to invite extra population for their development--as for instance the Amazon Basin of Brazil. Unfortunately for this easy analysis, high fertility means more babies born, not in the Amazon Basin, but where their mothers are in Sao Paulo, Rio, Recife, and such. Even assuming that high fertility eventually causes a migration of adult workers into the Amazon Basin, they would have very low productivity without accompanying capital. And it is no accident that capital does not flow into this area, bringing people with it as during the rubber boom days, but instead is profitably invested elsewhere. The "empty" land argument for high fertility proves invalid on analysis for most LDCs.

†Age distribution is far more sensitive to age-specific fertility rates than to age-specific mortality rates.

‡A very young age distribution, resulting from high fertility rates, ordinarily reduces the absolute value of domestic savings and investment. This is because there are disproportionately few adults of working age, so GNP is less than otherwise. This lower output effect is not fully offset by the fact that a population with disproportionately many children usually consumes less from a given GNP, even allowing in less developed countries for increasing expenditures on schooling.

Among countries as within countries, high fertility seems to cause relative poverty, besides often being a consequence of it.

If a nation's population is to increase naturally at $\underline{X}$ percent a year, it is better that this result from low rather than high crude birth and crude death rates. A 1 percent annual increase, for example, resulting from birth and death rates of 45 and 35 per 1,000, will be associated with more brutish living than if it were the outcome, respectively, of rates of 25 and 15 per 1,000 a year. In the latter case the ratio of children to work age adults will be lower, investment from domestic savings should be absolutely greater, and the income per equivalent consumer will be greater.*

In human terms, and perhaps far more important, low birth and death rates mean that there are fewer unwanted infants born too soon and fewer premature deaths. "Balanced" public health programs that include birth as well as death "control" could give each family a little more security. Perhaps the true essence of economic development is that it gives families and individuals more command over their lives.†

---

*The "equivalent consumer" concept accounts for the fact that relative consumption varies with age and sex. Thus children typically consume less private and public sector goods and services than do adult males of working age. Hence, the increase in output (or income) per head that ordinarily follows in an LDC from a reduction in fertility somewhat overstates the improvement in individual welfare, simply because there are now relatively fewer children and more adults. One solution is over time to divide GNP not by absolute population but by the estimated number of equivalent consumers. See S. Enke and R. G. Zind, "Effects of Fewer Births on Average Income," Journal of Biosocial Sciences 1 (January 1969): 41-55.

†It is sometimes erroneously supposed that, because income per capita can be increased arithmetically by having a smaller population, public health programs should concentrate more on preventing births and less on postponing deaths. However, families are more likely to save, invest and innovate, making and following plans for their own financial advancement, if uncertainties regarding deaths can be reduced. In circumstances of frequent, unpredictable, and premature deaths in a family, planning and executing courses of action are inhibited, except that of having more births to replace deaths.

ECONOMIC DEVELOPMENT THROUGH
REDUCING FERTILITY

The economic development of LDCs has many facets, but most of these, such as levels of education and health, availability of capital per worker and adequacy of infrastructure, tend to be associated with output and hence also income per capita. Thus higher ratios of GNP to population can usually serve as a surrogate for economic improvement. Moreover, although governments have concentrated customarily on accelerating the GNP growth numerator, an increasing number of LDCs are now also concerned with slowing the population growth denominator.

Rationally, if a government intends to spend $X over, say, ten years to increase output per head, it should estimate whether it could achieve a greater increase in this ratio through expenditures on birth control than on investments in physical capital. Certainly, where the marginal product of labor approaches zero, a reduction in births for, say, a decade must raise per capita income later. In this case, expenditures for contraception must be many times more effective per dollar in raising per capita income than expenditures for plant and equipment. *

Where labor has a very low marginal product relative to that of capital, which is reputedly the case in most backward as compared with most advanced countries, practically all economic-demographic models indicate that a gradual halving of fertility over several decades raises income per head substantially. The loss of labor force after 15 years is more than offset by the more immediate increase in per capita income and in aggregate saving. After 15 years there is less labor but more investment than otherwise, with more capital and output per worker, a lower underemployment rate, and fewer consumers to share in a GNP that has grown about as rapidly as it would have done with unchanged fertility.

---

*Where the marginal product of labor is zero, or when the analysis is for a ten-year period during which prevented babies do not reach 15 years to become lost workers, a reduction in births cannot reduce GNP and must raise income per head above what it otherwise would be. This is also because the cost of the contraceptives needed to prevent a birth is so much less than the discounted cost of the investment otherwise needed to provide a typical annual flow of goods and services to an extra person. Such a benefit/cost comparison is repugnant to some, but no less valid on that account. See also S. Enke, "Birth Control for Economic Development," Science, May 1969, pp. 798-802.

This has been shown in several analyses, both for an abstract country called Developa, and for Guatemala, Turkey, and most recently Chile.[3]

The main elements of the dynamic model used are

V/P,   gross domestic product per head, which by wiser public and/or private actions one hopes to see rising faster than it would otherwise;

B,   births, which depend on initial and changing age distributions and on projected age-specific fertility rates;

D,   deaths, which depend on projected age-specific mortalities, age distributions, and such;

P,   population, which is arithmetically last year's population plus B minus D;*

V,   gross domestic product, which is a function of employed labor force, domestic capital stock and state of technology;

K,   stock of capital, which increases according to aggregate domestic saving plus capital borrowings from abroad;†

S,   aggregate domestic saving, which is positively related to V and negatively to P;

E,   employed labor force, positively related to L and K, with E/L being monotonically related to K/E;

---

*International migration is here ignored. For countries with the worst population densities and growths, there is almost no in-migration and net out-migration is trivial in percentage terms. Emigration can seldom provide relief for population pressure either. A 1 percent emigration from India would mean 5 million people (net) moving permanently abroad each year. In itself this would constitute a major transportation job, greater than current air travel across the North Atlantic. More seriously perhaps, there are not enough countries willing and able to receive such a flow of people. The few small countries that do receive a considerable population growth from immigration--over 5 percent in Kuwait's case--are atypical. The migration that does affect economic development is the internal flow to city from countryside. These effects are now being incorporated into a two-sector economic-demographic model being developed at TEMPO.

† The basic model assumes no net international transfers of capital. It is programmed, however, to allow for any year-to-year exogenous capital movements that the analyst cares to assume. A modified program also provides for enough inflow of capital in each year to maintain a stipulated constant annual improvement in V/P.

$\underline{L}$,   available labor force, a function of population size and age
        distribution;

$\underline{T}$,   technology, with improvements in the state of art resulting in
        more $\underline{V}$ from a given $\underline{E}$ and $\underline{K}$.

In the models usually employed to date, $\underline{V}$ has been determined
by a modified Cobb-Douglas function, in which the output elasticities
of $\underline{E}$ and $\underline{K}$ have sometimes summed to less than unity to reflect
scarcity of natural resources. The influence of technology has been
compounded at a fixed annual rate and is incorporated in the aggregate production function as a shift factor. * Births and deaths have
influenced $\underline{V}$ indirectly through $\underline{L}$, $\underline{K}$, and hence $\underline{E}$, while affecting
$\underline{P}$ directly.†

The models have been used to examine contrasting fertility
projections upon projected $\underline{V}$ and $\underline{P}$, and hence $\underline{V}/\underline{P}$, over the next
35 years or so. Calculations are year by year. Results are usually
tabulated at five-year intervals.

In Table 1.1, for an abstract country named Developa a constant GRR (gross reproduction rate) of 3.025 is contrasted with the
case of a GRR that falls by arithmetic retrogression from 3.025 to
1.479 over 25 years. (The GRR is the number of live female births
a typical woman will have during her child-bearing years.) Subse-
quent $\underline{V}$ is hardly affected, the decline in fertility raising $\underline{K}$ enough
to compensate for the fall in $\underline{L}$. This increase in $\underline{K}$ results from a
"release" of consumption, part of which is additional saving, because
the number of children declines relatively. There is less unemploy-
ment and more output per worker because the K/E ratio is higher.
With similar $\underline{V}$, but a smaller-than-otherwise $\underline{P}$, $\underline{V}/\underline{P}$ is higher.‡

---

*This reflects an agnostic uncertainty as to whether technology
is especially associated with, say, increased capital stock, improved
worker education, or general level of welfare. In effect "technology"
here is the residual source of all increased output that cannot be attributed to capital or labor increments. The main impact of a high
rate of "technology" improvement in this model is to reduce the comparative importance of reducing fertility in raising projected $\underline{V}/\underline{P}$.

†In this formulation the demographic "side" of the model affects
the economic side, but not conversely. Conceptually it could be sup-
posed for instance that a rising $\underline{V}/\underline{P}$ after some lag would reduce age
specific fertilities. However, while this relation is often asserted,
it has still to be demonstrated.

‡The tables are for a case where technology improves 0.015 a
year compounded, the output elasticities of employment and capital
are 0.5 and 0.4, respectively, and aggregate domestic savings are
0.8$\underline{V}$ to 35\underline{P}$.

TABLE 1.1

Effects of Declining Fertility on Output and Per Capita Income in "Developa"

Item	1970	1985		2000	
		High Fertility	Low Fertility	High Fertility	Low Fertility
P, population (10^6)	10.0	15.9	14.4	25.7	18.8
V, output ($\$10^9$)	2.00	3.54	3.63	7.53	7.87
V/P, income per head ($)	200	223	251	293	419
L, available labor (10^6)	3.61	5.69	5.69	9.10	8.32
Unemployment rate (percent)	15	18	16	10	6
K, capital stock ($\$10^9$)	5.00	7.06	7.28	13.20	15.57
K/E, capital per worker ($)	1,626	1,509	1,521	1,637	1,984
S/V, savings from income (percent)	4.7	6.4	7.9	9.6	12.5
Earnings per worker ($)	325	378	378	459	501
Return on capital (percent)	16	20	20	23	20
Children/population (percent)	44	44	39	45	32
GRR, gross reproduction rate	3.025	3.025	2.092	3.025	1.479
Female life expectancy (years)	55.0	58.0	58.0	61.0	61.0

Source: These numerical results, employing the initial conditions of 1970 and the economic parameters listed in the text, were developed from the TEMPO demographic-economic model. See A. DeVany and S. Enke, Population Growth and Economic Development: Background and Guide (Santa Barbara: TEMPO, no. 119, 1968); and W. E. McFarland, Description of the Economic-Demographic Model (Santa Barbara: General Electric–TEMPO, no. 52, 1968).

Specifically, taking the case summarized in Table 1.1, V/P rises from $200 a year in 1970 to $419 with low fertility as against $293 with high fertility by the year 2000. After 30 years, with low fertility the capital stock is larger ($15.57 billion as against $13.20 billion), capital per worker is higher ($1,984 as against $1,637), and the unemployment rate is lower (6 percent as against 10 percent). The relative scarcity of labor has increased after 30 years, with annual earnings per full-time equivalent worker of $501 as against $459, while the return on capital is 3 percentile points lower than with high fertility. One basic reason for better economic performance is that by 2000 children are 32 percent of the population with low fertility as compared with 45 percent with unchanged high fertility.

The outcome of a higher-than-otherwise V/P with declining fertility has been shown to be most insensitive to labor and capital output elasticities, technology improvement rates, the savings equation, the employment of labor function, or the projected exogenous decline in mortality rates. For each single comparison of projected fertility differences, these assumptions, and of course the initial conditions of population size, age distribution, and capital stock, are always similar. In every case, if fertility is declining faster, V/P is nevertheless rising faster.[4]

A related point is that a lower fertility means slower population growth and hence more time for domestic capital to accumulate and the state of art to improve. This is shown in Table 1.2, based on the same case as Table 1.1, the difference being that Developa attains a population of 15.9 million in 1985 with unchanged fertility but only in 1990 with declining fertility. By waiting five more years for its population of 15.9 million, Developa can provide this size of population with a yearly V/P of $295 instead of $223, having a larger labor force (6.57 million as against 5.69 million) and a larger capital stock ($8.98 billion as against $7.06 billion). The argument is not that Developa should never have a much larger population. It is rather that population growth must be slow, regardless of "empty" lands waiting to be populated.

Dynamic models of this kind can also be used to sense the "return" from "investments" in contraception. This of course requires an assumption as to the annual cost per effective contraceptive user and the age distribution of these voluntary "acceptors." The "return" or gain can reasonably be defined as the gain in income per head times the population enjoying it. Over a period of 35 years this benefit-to-cost ratio ranges between 50 and 150 to 1.* But for any

---

*In the Table 1.1 case this benefit/cost ratio is 116 to 1 by 2000. The annual cost of practicing contraception is assumed to be $5 a year per user and effectiveness is supposed to be 0.8. The

historic period this arithmetic ratio must understate the return, especially for shorter periods, for even with no future costs there will always be future and generally increasing gains from past contraceptive expenditures.[5]

TABLE 1.2

Contrasting Attainment of Same Population in Different
Years: Unfavorable Economic Consequences of Fast
Population Growth in "Developa"

Item	1985 High Fertility	1990 Low Fertility
P, population (10^6)	15.9	15.9
V, output ($\$10^9$)	3.54	4.68
V/P, income per head ($)	223	295
L, available labor (10^6)	5.69	6.57
Unemployment rate (percent)	18	18
K, capital stock ($\$10^9$)	7.06	8.98
K/E, capital per worker ($)	1,509	1,543
S/V, savings from income (percent)	6.4	9.4
Earnings per worker ($)	378	402
Return on capital (percent)	20	21
Gross reproduction rate	3.025	1.817
Female life expectancy (years)	58.0	59.0

Source: A. DeVany and S. Enke, Population Growth and Economic Development: Background and Guide (Santa Barbara: TEMPO, no. 119, 1968); and W. E. McFarland, Description of the Economic-Demographic Model (Santa Barbara: General Electric-TEMPO, no. 52, 1968).

---

distribution of users by age is proportionate to the reduction in age-specific fertilities assumed for the lower fertility case in the comparison. Thus the benefit/cost ratios obtained from these dynamic economic-demographic models are very similar in magnitude to the benefit/cost ratios estimated in 1966 by far simpler and static means and published in S. Enke, "The Economic Aspects of Slowing Population Growth," Economic Journal 76 (1966): 44-56.

In these cases initial "size" of population is of minor importance. If natural resources are very scarce, so there are markedly diminishing returns to labor and capital taken together, it is true that reduced labor employment because of reduced fertility occasions a smaller loss in $\underline{V}$ attributable to $\underline{E}$. But by the same token the increase in $\underline{V}$ attributable to more $\underline{K}$ with fewer births is also smaller.

More important than size of population is the changing rate of its growth. An increasing growth rate, especially when due to a declining death rate, is economically disastrous. A decreasing population growth rate, because of declining fertility rates, is a major source of economic development.*

INTERNATIONAL CONSEQUENCES OF FERTILITY DIFFERENCES

High fertility rates tend to limit what LDCs can export and in addition make them less creditworthy as international borrowers.

International trade theory has always emphasized that what countries export and import depends largely on relative factor prices. Countries with high fertility rates have a comparative advantage in labor intensive products, because comparatively their labor's marginal productivity is low and their capital's marginal productivity is high. However, because high fertility countries have low per capita incomes, there are additional trade consequences.

High fertility, low income countries generally export primary agricultural commodities, except for those few and fortunate nations possessed of valuable mineral assets such as petroleum. Poverty makes for a consumption pattern of basic "necessaries," and hence a domestic production pattern of limited variety. Poor countries cannot afford the technological education and do not have the high

---

*Of course an LDC can instead raise its annual rate of per capita income improvement by faster innovating or saving. It is simple to calculate for any given case what these "trade-offs" are among fertility, savings, and innovating rate changes. See S. Enke and R. G. Zind, "Effects of Fewer Births on Average Income," Journal of Biosocial Sciences 1, no. 1 (January 1969): 41-55. But calculating arithmetical equivalences in terms of $\underline{V}/\underline{P}$ improvement does not create operational alternatives. Families do not save or innovate more because they increase their fertility. In fact a more plausible argument might be that the sort of families which practice birth control effectively are likely to be exceptional savers and innovators.

income market needed for products that are technically advanced, superior in performance, or which incorporate high styling. With less capital, the workers of these countries must compete for foreign exchange largely through muscle power, usually applied to exporting sugar, coffee, and other products of tropical agriculture. Such a worsening of the terms of trade between backward and advanced countries as may in fact have occurred* is probably as much due to continued fertility differentials among nations as to any other single cause. Those LDCs that are too much dependent on agricultural exports to finance adequate industrial product imports should usually blame their own excessive fertility.

The same high fertility rates that increase the "need" for assistance of LDCs also make them less creditworthy as borrowers and hence more dependent on grants. Aspirations for GNP increase are often several percentile points higher than is realistic because of the typically expected 3 percent annual growth in population. This in turn "requires" a larger yearly increment in capital stock. But the low ratio of work age population to children caused by high fertility reduces output and aggregate savings for investment. Unfortunately, the very inability to save that "requires" external borrowing also makes subsequent repayment difficult or impossible. Savings are, after all, the ultimate source of repayment.

These interactions can also be explored by the TEMPO economic-demographic model. A "required" annual improvement in per capita income can be stipulated. The computer can be programmed to assume an inflow or outflow of capital in each year depending on whether domestic savings are, respectively, insufficient or excessive to occasion precisely the stipulated improvement in per capita income. Ordinarily, if an LDC stipulates an unrealistic annual improvement, it will never be able to repay its borrowings with interest. Alternatively, an LDC with a lower fertility may be able to realize a higher annual improvement in per capita income, and eventually service all borrowings from abroad, than can an LDC with higher fertility.

Considering Developa again, Table 1.3 indicates some borrowing and repayment consequences of aspiring to alternative constant improvements in per capita income, contrasting again the two economic projections based on the same high and low fertility projections. Thus the highest sustainable annual improvement in per capita income is under 2.0 percent (actually 1.8 percent) with high

---

*It is by no means clear that the barter terms of trade have generally worsened for backward countries when unquantified improvements in industrial products exported from advanced countries are taken into account.

TABLE 1.3

Effects of Fertility on "Developa's" Ability to Service
Debts While Realizing a Stipulated Annual
Improvement in Income Per Capita

Stipulated Annual Improvement in GNP (per capita)	Future Year When Repayment of Principal Begins[b]		Future Year When Loans Are Completely Repaid		Debt Outstanding When Repayment Begins[c] (millions of dollars)	
	Fertility		Fertility		Fertility	
	High	Low	High	Low	High	Low
1.0	14	5	23	10	482	130
1.5	30	11	42	16	2,643	415
2.0	(a)	14	(a)	23	(a)	1,066
2.5	(a)	21	(a)	33	(a)	2,743

[a]Debt never repaid.

[b]Repayment begins in the year that domestic saving first becomes greater than is required to realize the stipulated annual improvement in per capita income.

[c]To be compared with initial year GNP of $2 billion.

Source: A. DeVany and S. Enke, Population Growth and Economic Development: Background and Guide (Santa Barbara: TEMPO, no. 119, 1968); and W. E. McFarland, Description of the Economic-Demographic Model (Santa Barbara: General Electric-TEMPO, no. 52, 1968); also, S. Enke, "High Fertility Impairs Credit Worthiness of Developing Nations" (New York: Gordon & Breach, 1971).

(unchanged) fertility and over 2.5 percent (actually 2.9 percent) with low fertility if external borrowings are ever to be repaid (including a 5 percent annual interest rate on the outstanding balance). Even at 1.5 percent yearly improvement, high fertility Developa does not commence repayment before 30 years, but a low fertility Developa can aspire to a 2.5 percent annual improvement and start repayment after 21 years. Alternatively, for a 1.5 percent sustained annual improvement in V/P, completed debt service takes 42 and 16 years, respectively, with high and low fertility, with a respective maximum outstanding debt of $2,643 and $415 million.*

The credit unworthiness associated with high fertility may give international lending agencies a powerful and more acceptable means of inducing certain LDCs to undertake vigorous birth control programs. It may be politically impossible for, say, the World Bank Group to make a loan for infrastructure conditional on the borrowing government's promoting contraception. But development assistance agencies when making loans are certainly entitled to consider all factors influencing a borrowing LDC's ability or inability to repay. It is, after all, a normal practice of borrowers to accept loan conditions. One problem throughout the 1950s and early 1960s was that international lending agencies were not prepared to do anything about perhaps the most important single cause of poverty in LDCs--excessive population growth.

Comment

Studies of political economy cannot logically fail to study people and hence populations. Economic development largely concerns the development of people, which means investments in education and health as well as in physical capital, both of which are encouraged when lower birth rates make labor more scarce relative to capital. One of the distinguishing and surely significant characteristics of the LDCs is their high fertility rates and their consequently high proportion of unproductive children. Reductions in fertility enable domestic capital to be accumulated more rapidly. Greater future savings of LDCs because of effective birth control programs should render them more creditworthy. The poverty induced by high fertility also affects commodity flows and terms of trade. The influences of population growth are so pervasive throughout all macroeconomic relations that they should surely become a major concern of the economics profession.

---

*Table 1.3 is based on the assumption that each year Developa borrows exactly enough from abroad to increase its domestic investment sufficiently to maintain the stipulated X percent annual improvement in V/P. Alternatively, if domestic saving is more than enough to maintain this X percent improvement, the excess domestic saving is used to repay international borrowings. The external liability for debt service includes a 5 percent interest charge on the current year's outstanding debt. See S. Enke, "High Fertility Impairs Credit Worthiness of Developing Nations," _Fetschrift_ in honor of Professor Edgar Hoover (New York: Gordon and Breach, 1971).

A NEOCLASSICAL ANALYSIS OF ECONOMIC-DEMOGRAPHIC SIMULATION MODELS

Michael C. Keeley

INTRODUCTION

There has been much academic interest and public policy concern about the effects of rapid population growth on both the level of income and the rate of economic growth. There is special interest in the consequences of rapid population growth for LDCs since many of these countries are experiencing high fertility rates and relatively low mortality rates. The articles in Part I of this volume deal with this important question using various approaches.

One approach to the problem is macroeconomic-demographic modeling in the framework pioneered by A. J. Coale and E. M. Hover (1958). The Enke-TEMPO models (1971, 1974) described in the first section of this chapter and a number of similar models by P. Demeny (1965), B. T. Walsh (1971), F. Denton and R. Spencer (1973), P. J. Lloyd (1968), G. Zaiden (1969), R. Barlow (1967), the Department of Commerce (LRPM models), and the International Labor Organization (BACHUE models), although differing in many ways, are all in the same vein.

Since the TEMPO models are central to the analysis of the articles in Part I of this book, they specifically are analyzed, although the analysis is generally applicable to a variety of macroeconomic-demographic simulation models of this type. The primary result of the TEMPO simulation analysis is that a reduction in fertility would result in higher income per capita than would otherwise occur if fertility rates remained unchanged, and as McFarland documents,[6] this result appears to be insensitive to a variety of parameter modifications. However, the theoretical and empirical assumptions, both implicit and explicit, needed to generate this important result are far from clear.

25

Although simulation analysis can be a powerful tool for analyzing the behavior of a complex system of interacting variables, it is important to understand analytically the behavior of as much of the model as possible. A priori specification and understanding of the subsectors of a simulation model greatly simplifies the interpretation of the results of the simulations and reduces the amount of sensitivity analysis needed to test the model.

The economic part of the TEMPO-I model closely parallels a standard one-sector neoclassical growth model, and it would seem that a better understanding of the workings and the policy implications of the TEMPO computer simulation models and other similar economic-demographic simulation models could be achieved by using the analytical techniques of neoclassical growth theory. By using analytical techniques (as opposed to simulation techniques), it is possible deductively to analyze the assumptions and mechanisms implicit in the computer models. Hopefully such a logical analysis contributes to a clear conceptualization of the limitations and strengths of such simulation analysis. In addition, by logically analyzing the various special assumptions implicit in the model, it is possible to better understand both the economic consequences of population growth and the policy implications of those consequences.

In the previous section Enke explained the almost "inevitable" negative relationship between fertility and income per capita by noting that "Primarily, a reduction in fertility alters a population's age distribution, so that the ratio of work-age to non-work-age population increases." In the short run (that is, before the first cohort born under the regime of lower fertility enters the labor force), income per capita must rise because the dependency rate must fall. However, this increase caused by the decline in young dependents may be negated by the eventual rise in the old age dependency rate that results from a fertility decline. In addition, the negative relationship between economic growth and population growth may depend crucially on the relationship between savings and dependency rates, as well as on technological change, capital depreciation, endogenous labor supply, and human capital. The remainder of this chapter analyzes the effects of the above factors on the steady-state equilibrium of the economy* and on the rate of transition to the new equilibrium steady-state path.

---

*Although economic theory suggests that fertility is affected by a variety of economic factors, this section, as do most of the computer simulation models discussed previously, takes a partial equilibrium approach that seeks to analyze the consequences of an exogenous fertility decline.

THE NEOCLASSICAL FRAMEWORK

The economic framework used here is the standard, one-sector neoclassical growth model formulated by Robert Solow (1956) and T. Swan (1956). It is assumed that a constant fraction of the aggregate output of an economy, which is determined by a two-factor (capital and labor) constant returns to scale production function, is either saved and reinvested for greater future production or is consumed. It is also assumed that the labor force grows at a constant, exogenously determined, exponential rate. These neoclassical assumptions may be summarized in the following equations.

Aggregate output per laborer may be written as

$$y = \frac{Y}{L} = \frac{F(K, L)}{L} = f(\frac{K}{L}) = f(k) \tag{1.1}$$

where $f(0) = 0$, $f'(k) > 0$ and $f''(k) < 0$ for $k > 0$. The variable y is output per laborer, Y is total gross output, K is capital, L is labor, and k is the capital-labor ratio. Savings, which equals investment, is given by

$$S = sY = I = \frac{dK}{dt} = \dot{K} \tag{1.2}$$

where S is total savings, s is the marginal propensity to save, I is total investment, and $\dot{K}$ is the rate of change of capital with respect to time (depreciation is assumed to be zero). The labor force grows at an exogenously determined, exponential rate n so

$$L(t) = L_0 e^{nt} \tag{1.3}$$

where L_0 is the initial stock of labor and n is the percentage rate of growth. Since the time patterns of capital and labor as well as the relationship between output and the inputs capital and labor are described by equations (1.1) through (1.3), the time path of output is implicit.

Equations (1.1) to (1.3) may be used to derive the basic dynamic equation of the neoclassical system.*

$$\dot{k} = sf(k) - nk \tag{1.4}$$

If f has the properties described in equation (1.1) and if n and s satisfy the inequality $0 < n/s < f'(0)$, then there exists a unique positive

---

*Since $\frac{\dot{k}}{k} = \frac{\dot{K}}{K} - \frac{\dot{L}}{L}$, $\frac{\dot{k}}{k} = \frac{sY}{K} - n$, thus $k - sf(k) - nk$.

steady-state value of $k = k_*$ such that $\overset{\cdot}{k} = 0$. Figure 1.1 shows the nk and sf(k) functions separately along with the steady-state value of k, which is k_*.

FIGURE 1.1

A Steady-State Stable Equilibrium

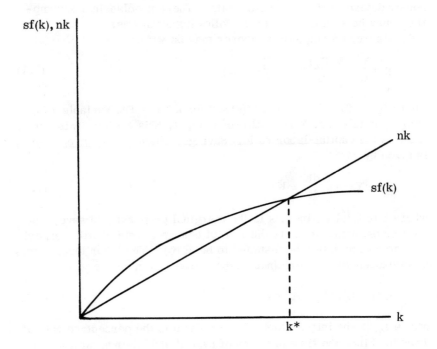

When the capital-labor ratio times the rate of population growth equals savings per laborer, there is no change in the capital-labor ratio ($\overset{\cdot}{k} = 0$); and when an economy reaches this point, it is in a steady-state, stable equilibrium, with output, capital, and labor all growing at the same rate n, the rate of growth of labor.

If the rate of labor force growth exogenously falls as is depicted in Figure 1.2, then the capital-labor ratio will rise until a new steady-state equilibrium is achieved. Since income per laborer y depends only on the capital-labor ratio, y will grow throughout the transitional period until the new k_* is achieved. Thus a reduction in the rate of labor force growth results in a once and for all increase in the level of income per laborer because of the increase in the capital-labor ratio. This effect is "once and for all" in the sense that once the economy reaches its new equilibrium, per worker income will have a zero rate of growth as it did at its old steady-state equilibrium.

FIGURE 1.2

Effect of a Decline in the Rate of Labor Force Growth

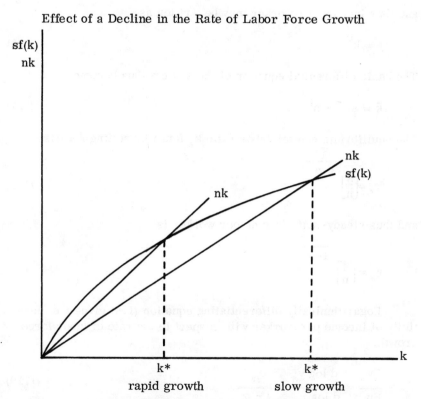

THE STEADY-STATE, LONG-RUN EFFECTS
OF A FERTILITY DECLINE

By comparing initial steady-state equilibriums with final steady-state equilibriums, the problem of choosing a time period that is encountered using the simulation approach is avoided* and an estimate of the permanent effects of a change in fertility may be obtained.

---

*A 30-year time period is typically used in the TEMPO simulations. However, there is always a danger in making policy prescriptions based on simulation runs that end after an arbitrary time period, since some unforeseen and undesirable effect caused by the policy may be just ahead.

To get specific results that indicate the relationship between fertility and income per worker, a specific production function, the Cobb-Douglas,* is used.

The Cobb-Douglas production function can be written

$$Y = K^{\alpha} L^{1-\alpha} \tag{1.5}$$

and thus income per worker may be written as

$$y = k^{\alpha} \tag{1.6}$$

The basic differential equation of the system thus becomes

$$\dot{k} = sk^{\alpha} - nk \tag{1.7}$$

The equilibrium capital-labor ratio k_* found by setting $\dot{k} = 0$ is

$$k_* = \left[\frac{s}{n}\right]^{\frac{1}{1-\alpha}} \tag{1.8}$$

and thus steady-state income per worker is

$$y_* = \left[\frac{s}{n}\right]^{\frac{\alpha}{1-\alpha}} \tag{1.9}$$

Logarithmically differentiating equation (1.9) gives the elasticity of income per worker with respect to the rate of labor force growth.

$$\frac{Ey_*}{En} = \frac{d \log y_*}{d \log n} = \frac{\alpha}{1 - \alpha} \tag{1.10}$$

where E denotes dln.

A typical value of the elasticity of income per worker with respect to the rate of labor force growth, found by setting $\alpha = 1/3$, is $-1/2$, which means that a 50 percent reduction in the rate of population growth (eventually leading to a 50 percent reduction in the rate of labor force growth) would lead to a 25 percent increase in steady-state income per worker.

---

*The Cobb-Douglas is chosen because it is used in the TEMPO models and because of its analytical simplicity.

However, this estimate is sensitive to the incorporation of human capital, technological change, endogenous labor supply, capital depreciation, and to the functional form of the savings function. The next discussion generalizes the model by incorporating these factors.

EXTENSIONS OF THE NEOCLASSICAL MODEL

Human Capital

Human capital may be incorporated into the production function by assuming it is another factor of production. Total savings are divided between investment in physical capital and human capital and the allocation between the two is determined by equating their marginal products. Assume a Cobb-Douglas production function

$$Y = K^a L^b H^c \qquad (1.11)$$

where $a + b + c = 1$ and H refers to human capital. Equating the marginal product of physical capital to the marginal product of human capital gives

$$\frac{dY}{dK} = \frac{aY}{K} = \frac{dY}{dH} = \frac{cY}{H} \qquad (1.12)$$

$$K = \frac{a}{c} H \qquad (1.13)$$

Thus human capital and physical capital are always used in fixed proportions. If $a = c$, then $K = H$, and Y may be rewritten as

$$Y = Z^{a+c} L^b \qquad (1.14)$$

where $Z = K = H$. Thus α in equation (1.10) could be interpreted as $a + c$, so a value of α approximately equal to two-thirds (assuming that $a = c = 1/3$), which is an approximate empirical finding[7] would not be unreasonable, implying that $Ey_*/En = -2$, which is a very substantial effect. Thus the elasticity of income per worker with respect to the rate of population growth is very sensitive to the incorporation of human capital (or more precisely to the interpretation of α).

Capital Depreciation

If instead of assuming that capital has infinite life, it is assumed that capital depreciates at a constant rate δ and that savings are a constant fraction of gross income, then by definition

$$\overset{\cdot}{K} = sY - \delta K \tag{1.15}$$

Thus the differential equation describing the rate of change of the2 capital-labor ratio becomes

$$\overset{\cdot}{k} = sf(k) - (\delta + n)k \tag{1.16}$$

Equation (1.16) shows that labor force growth is analytically equivalent in its effect on income per worker to capital depreciation. Lowering the rate of population growth is thus equivalent to lowering the rate of depreciation on the existing capital stock, and lowering either one increases the level of income per worker. Equation (1.16) implies that

$$y_* = \left[\frac{s}{\delta + n}\right]^{\frac{\alpha}{1-\alpha}} \tag{1.17}$$

Thus $Ey_*/En = \frac{-\alpha}{1-\alpha}\left[\frac{n}{\alpha+n}\right]$, which means that increasing the rate of capital depreciation decreases (in absolute value) the elasticity of y with respect to n.

Alternative Savings Functions

It is often argued, although usually with little empirical or theoretical support, that one of the major consequences of lowering fertility is that the resulting reduced dependency rate leads to an increased savings rate and, hence, more rapid development.

To investigate analytically such an effect, the simple savings function (S = sY) used in the neoclassical model may be modified to take into account the possible effects of dependency rates and income per capita on the fraction saved. A constant elasticity form* of the

_____

*The TEMPO savings function, S = aY - bP, may be rewritten as S/Y = a - b/(Y/P), which implies that the fraction saved rises with increases in per capita income to an asymptote of a. The basic equation for the rate of change of the capital-labor ratio using this savings function is $\overset{\cdot}{k} = af(k) - b(p/L) - nk$. Thus, for a large enough b, no steady state exists; otherwise two steady-state capital-labor ratios exist: one that is stable and one that is not. This illustrates the potential danger of simulation analysis when arbitrary functions are used without a priori analysis. Thus the effect of the TEMPO savings function on income per worker is sensitive to the selection of parameters.

savings function, suggested by N. Leff (1969), is used because of its analytical simplicity and because it has at least some empirical justification. [8] The functional form is

$$\frac{S}{Y} = a \left[\frac{Y}{P}\right]^{\epsilon_1} \left[\frac{P}{L}\right]^{-\epsilon_2} \tag{1.18}$$

where P is total population, ϵ_1 and ϵ_2 represent the elasticity of the fraction saved to income per capita Y/P and the ratio of population to labor force P/L, respectively. The elasticity ϵ_1 is taken generally to be nonnegative, and an increase in either the fraction of young dependents (prelabor force) or old dependents (postlabor force) is expected to reduce the fraction saved. However, as Allen Kelley (1973) points out, a decline in fertility leads to a decrease in young dependents and an eventual increase in the percentage of old age dependents in the population. Although the overall dependency rate usually falls (when the new stable age distribution is achieved), the net effect of the decline in overall dependency may be to decrease the fraction saved if the elderly dissave at a sufficiently greater rate than the young. However, using data from Leff's (1969) study, Kelley (1973) finds that for very low income countries the sign of ϵ_2 is likely to be positive, although the opposite may hold in high income countries.

   Equation (1.18) may be solved for total gross savings to determine gross investment.

$$S = a \left[\frac{Y}{L}\frac{L}{P}\right]^{\epsilon_1} \left[\frac{P}{L}\right]^{-\epsilon_2} \cdot Y = \dot{K} = I \tag{1.19}$$

Defining $\theta = P/L$, equation (1.19) may be rewritten as

$$S = ay^{\epsilon_1}\,\theta^{-(\epsilon_1+\epsilon_2)}\,\gamma \tag{1.20}$$

Thus the dynamic equation becomes

$$\dot{k} = af(k)^{(1+\epsilon_1)}\,\theta^{-(\epsilon_1+\epsilon_2)} - nk \tag{1.21}$$

Thus k_*, determined by setting $\dot{k} = 0$, is given by (assuming a C - D production function)

$$k_* = \left[\frac{a}{n}\,\theta^{-(\epsilon_1+\epsilon_2)}\right]^{\frac{1}{1-\alpha(1+\epsilon_1)}} \tag{1.22}$$

and thus the equilibrium value of income per worker is

$$y_* = \left[\frac{a}{n} \theta^{-(\epsilon_1 + \epsilon_2)} \right]^{\frac{\alpha}{1 - \alpha(1 + \epsilon_1)}} \tag{1.23}$$

Logarithmically differentiating equation (1.23) with respect to n gives the elasticity of y_* with respect to n:

$$\frac{Ey_*}{En} = \frac{d\log y_*}{d\log n} = \frac{\alpha}{1 - \alpha(1 + \epsilon_1)} \left[-(\epsilon_1 + \epsilon_2) \frac{d\log\theta}{d\log n} - 1 \right] \tag{1.24}$$

Since the elasticity of θ ($\theta = P/L$) with respect to n is greater than zero for a rapidly growing population with a relatively short life expectancy (which is the case in most LDCs), assuming $\alpha(1 + \epsilon_1) < 1$, implies that $EY_*/En < 0$ and $|Ey_*/En|$ is considerably larger the greater either ϵ_1 or ϵ_2.* However, since the fraction saved changes, consumption per worker would rise only if the economy's saving rate were less than the golden rule rate,[9] which is often the case in LDCs.

Technological Change

Since labor augmenting, capital augmenting, and neutral technological change are all equivalent when using the Cobb-Douglas production function,[10] labor augmenting technological change will be considered for ease of exposition. Define the stock of augmented labor, $\ell(t)$ at time t to be

$$\ell(t) = a(t) L(t) \text{ and assume that } \frac{\dot{a}}{a} = \gamma \tag{1.25}$$

Thus $\frac{\dot{\ell}}{\ell} = n + \gamma$, and defining $\tilde{k} = K/\ell$ and $\tilde{y} = Y/\ell$, the equation for $\dot{\tilde{k}}$ is given by

$$\dot{\tilde{k}} = sf(\tilde{k}) - (n + \gamma) \tilde{k} \tag{1.26}$$

---

*Note that if $\epsilon_1 = \epsilon_2 = 0$, then equation (1.23) simplifies to equation (1.9), which is derived using the assumption that $S = aY$. Note also that the dependency rate affects savings even if $\epsilon_2 = 0$.

Thus steady-state equilibrium is characterized by $\overset{\cdot}{\tilde{k}} = 0$. However,

$\dfrac{\overset{\cdot}{\tilde{k}}}{\tilde{k}} = \dfrac{\overset{\cdot}{k}}{a}$, so $\dfrac{\overset{\cdot}{k}}{k} = \dfrac{\overset{\cdot}{\tilde{k}}}{\tilde{k}} - \dfrac{\overset{\cdot}{a}}{a} = 0$, so $\dfrac{\overset{\cdot}{k}}{k} = \dfrac{\overset{\cdot}{a}}{a}$ in steady-state equilibrium.

The elasticity of income per augmented worker with respect to the rate of population growth is

$$\frac{E\tilde{y}_*}{En} = -\frac{\alpha}{1-\alpha}\left[\frac{n}{\gamma + n}\right] \tag{1.27}$$

but such an elasticity of income per (unadjusted) worker cannot be computed since income per (unadjusted) worker is growing at a constant rate because the capital-labor ratio k is growing at rate γ.

Noninelastic Labor Supply

The initial neoclassical model presented earlier assumes that the supply of labor is exogenous and perfectly inelastic, that is, all the labor force is employed regardless of the wage. In this section, labor supply is taken to be a function of the real wage, which is a function of the marginal product of labor. Thus

$$L(t) = p(w)\, A(t) \tag{1.28}$$

where $A(t) = A_0 e^{nt}$ is the population of adults at time t, w is the real wage, and p is the proportion of adults working. Differentiating with respect to time gives

$$\overset{\cdot}{L}(t) = \frac{dp}{dw}\frac{dw}{dk}\frac{dk}{dt}A + p\frac{dA}{dt} \tag{1.29}$$

$$\frac{\overset{\cdot}{L}}{L} = \frac{p'w'\overset{\cdot}{k}}{p} + n \tag{1.30}$$

where n is the percentage rate of growth of adults. Thus the differential equation of the system is

$$\overset{\cdot}{k} = \frac{sf(k) - nk}{1 + \dfrac{d\ln p}{d\ln w}\dfrac{d\ln w}{d\ln k}} \tag{1.31}$$

Assuming a Cobb-Douglas production function gives

$$\frac{d\ln w}{d\ln k} = \alpha \tag{1.32}$$

so assuming $\epsilon = \dfrac{Ep}{Ew} = \dfrac{d\ln p}{d\ln w} > 0$, gives

$$\dot{k} = \frac{sf(k) - nk}{1 + \alpha\epsilon} \qquad (1.33)$$

Equation (1.33) indicates that the value of ϵ does not affect the steady-state equilibrium value of k since setting $\dot{k} = 0$ gives

$$k_* = \left[\frac{s}{n} \right]^{\frac{1}{1-\alpha}} \qquad (1.34)$$

THE TRANSITIONAL PERIOD

Planners often are not interested only in the long-term, permanent effects of a given policy option, such as attempting to reduce the fertility of a population. Generally they are concerned with the immediate and medium-run effects of a particular policy. For example, how long does it take for a fertility reduction to affect an economy, and are short-run effects significantly different from the long-run effects?

When analyzing the effects of a decline in fertility throughout the transitional period from one steady state to another, the choice of a measure of (or proxy for) national welfare becomes important, especially when there are policy considerations. For example, in Enke's work, income per capita is the implicit policy target.[11] Income per capita automatically rises in the short run (15 to 20 years) when fertility falls, since population is less than it otherwise would have been and output is unaffected by the lower fertility until the first cohort born in the regime of reduced fertility enters the labor force. However, during this transitional period, income per adult or the real wage is unaffected.[12] Although expenditures by adults may have been shifted from children to other commodities, if parents did not reduce expenditures on children proportionally[13] then each child would have a higher income or consumption with lower fertility. An additional problem is that children have value to their parents, so the consumption of children is not just a cost but a benefit to their parents. Thus, to formulate population policy, a utility function that describes the social trade-off between market consumption per capita and the rate of population growth (which is of course related to the fertility of each family) would have to be brought into the analysis.[14] If children have no value to adults and if they have a positive cost, then adults are better off with no children and society's optimal birth rate would be zero. However, children do have value to their parents; and, in addition, both the level and rate of population growth may contain important elements of externality that call for government intervention. *

Policy questions aside, the relationship between income per capita and income per worker may be found by decomposing income per capita into income per worker times the ratio of workers to population:

$$\frac{Y}{P} = \frac{Y}{L} \cdot \frac{L}{P} = y \cdot \frac{1}{\theta} \tag{1.35}$$

To investigate the transitional period, the following conceptual experiment is performed. It is assumed that an economy has had constant fertility and mortality rates for a sufficiently long period of time that its age distribution has stabilized; all age groups are growing at the same percentage rate n. It is also assumed that labor force participation rates have been and are constant, so the labor force is also growing at the same rate n and the economy is in a steady-state equilibrium. It is now assumed that fertility rates fall exogenously and instantaneously. [15]

As equation (1.35) shows, to describe the time path of income per capita, it is only necessary to describe the time path of income per worker and the ratio of workers to the total population. Income per worker is completely determined by the capital-labor ratio in the absence of technological change. Income per "adjusted" worker is determined totally by the ratio of capital to adjusted labor, with labor augmenting technological change. The ratio of the labor force to total population depends in a complex way on a variety of economic and demographic factors, which makes it virtually impossible to describe analytically.

Thus the analysis proceeds by first describing the time path of income per worker y. Since y depends on the capital-labor ration and since when technological change is introduced, $\tilde{y}$ depends only on $\tilde{k}$, it is only necessary to describe the time path of $\tilde{k}$ to describe $\tilde{y}$.

The basic dynamic equation of the system describing $\tilde{k}$ is

$$\dot{\tilde{k}} = sf(\tilde{k}) - (n + \gamma + \delta) \tilde{k}, \tag{1.36}$$

---

*Children may be partially a public good in that "society" is concerned about their welfare over and above parental concern. More microeconomic investigation is called for on this issue to determine if society would be better off even though each parent individually might be made worse off by an imposed reduction of his/her fertility.

where $\tilde{k} = \dfrac{k}{a}$, the rate of capital depreciation is δ, and the rate of labor augmenting technological change is $\gamma = \dfrac{\dot{a}}{a}$. When an endogenous labor supply function, such as described previously, is introduced, equation (1.36) is modified to become

$$\dot{\tilde{k}} = \beta \, sf(k) - \beta \, (n + \gamma + \delta)\tilde{k} \qquad (1.37)$$

where $\beta = \dfrac{1}{1 + \alpha\epsilon} \leq 1$. The greater β, the greater the speed of adjustment, since for any set of parameters such that $\dot{k} > 0$, k is a maximum when $\beta = 1$ and $\epsilon = 0$. Thus, the more responsive the labor supply is to changes in the real wage, the longer the period of adjustment.

Since endogenous labor supply enters the analysis so simply, it is not explicitly included in the remainder of this section to simplify the exposition.

The differential equation (1.37) may be solved for $\tilde{k}(t)$ by substituting a specific production function, the Cobb-Douglas, for $f(k)$.[16] Initially at time zero it is assumed that $\tilde{k}(t)$ is in steady-state equilibrium and that instantaneously the rate of labor force growth falls from n_0 to n. Thus the initial value of $\tilde{k}$ is

$$\tilde{k}(0) = \left[\frac{s}{n_0 + \gamma + \delta} \right]^{\frac{1}{1-\alpha}} \qquad (1.38)$$

Substituting equation (1.38) into the solution of differential equation (1.36) yields*

---

*Differential equation (1.4) may be solved as follows: let $z = k^{1-\alpha}$, and note that $\dfrac{dz}{dt} = (1-\alpha)k^{-\alpha}\dfrac{dk}{dt}$, so equation (1.4) may be rewritten as $\dfrac{1}{1-\alpha}\dfrac{dz}{dt} + nz = s$. The general solution for a differential equation of form $\dfrac{dy}{dt} + ay = b$ is $y(t) = Ge^{-at} + b/a$, so $z(t) = Ge^{-(1-a)nt} + \dfrac{s}{n}$. Substituting k back in for z and specifying that $k(0) = \dfrac{s}{n_0}$ gives $k(t) = \left[\left(\dfrac{s}{n_0} - \dfrac{s}{n}\right) e^{-(1-\alpha)nt} + \dfrac{s}{n} \right]^{\frac{1}{1-\alpha}}$.

$$\tilde{k}(t) = \left\{ \left[\frac{\dfrac{s}{(n_o + \gamma + \delta)} - \dfrac{s}{n + \gamma + \delta}}{e^{(1-\alpha)(n+\gamma+\delta)t}} \right] + \frac{s}{n + \gamma + \delta} \right\}^{\frac{1}{1-\alpha}} \quad (1.39)$$

Equation (1.39) indicates that $\tilde{k}(t)$ reaches its new steady-state equilibrium value only after an infinite length of time.

To analyze the rate adjustment, define the exponential term in equation (1.39) as Z.

$$Z(t) = \left(\frac{s}{n_o + \gamma + \delta} - \frac{s}{n + \gamma + \delta} \right) e^{-(1-\alpha)(n+\gamma+\delta)t} \quad (1.40)$$

Thus

$$Z(t) = Z_o e^{-Bt} \text{ where } Z_o = \frac{s}{n_o + \gamma + \delta} - \frac{s}{n + \gamma + \delta} \quad (1.41)$$

and $B = (1 - \alpha)(n + \gamma + \delta)$. Note that when $t = 0$, $Z(t) = Z_o$ and that when $t = \infty$, $Z(t) = 0$, so the half-life of $Z(t)$, that is, the time when $Z(t_{\frac{1}{2}}) = \frac{1}{2}Z$ is given by*

$$t_{\frac{1}{2}} = \frac{(0.693)}{B} \quad (1.42)$$

Thus, the larger B, the smaller the half-life and the faster the rate of adjustment.

An increase in any of the parameters n, γ, δ, or $(1 - \alpha)$, tends to hasten the adjustment to the new equilibrium and thus leads to an earlier manifestation of the effects of a fertility decline. However, the elasticity of the steady-state value of income per adjusted laborer is given by

$$\frac{E\tilde{y}_*}{En} = - \left(\frac{\alpha}{1 - \alpha} \right) \left(\frac{n}{n + \gamma + \delta} \right)$$

---

*Note that when $Z(t_{\frac{1}{2}}) = \frac{1}{2}Z_o$, $k(t_{\frac{1}{2}}) = \left[\frac{1}{2} \left(\frac{s}{n_o} - \frac{s}{n} \right) \right]^{\frac{1}{1-\alpha}}$

Thus, an increase in either γ or δ, or a decrease in α lowers the elasticity of y_* with respect to n. Also, the smaller is n, the smaller is the elasticity of y_*, with respect to n. This means that, from a given percentage reduction in fertility, there would be a very small effect on income per adjusted worker. A small n also implies a longer half-life or a slower rate of adjustment. Finally, the more inelastic the supply of labor, the faster the adjustment process since increasing ϵ tends to reduce β. Thus the short-run effects of fertility on income per worker are less sensitive to parameter specification (although the model is still fairly sensitive) than either the rate of adjustment or the long-run effects since, if increasing a parameter increases the long-run elasticity, it also slows the rate of adjustment and vice versa.

The transitional path of the dependency rate is much more difficult to describe than the time path of y, although stable population techniques may be used to compare steady-state dependency rates. Initially θ, which is defined to be P/L, will fall in response to a fertility decline; and θ will reach a minimum when the first cohort born under the new lower fertility rates enters the labor force. At this point, θ will oscillate and finally will approach its new steady-state value, which is generally lower than the old steady-state value, if initially the population were growing rapidly and if life expectancies were relatively short compared with age at retirement.

Defining dependents somewhat arbitrarily as persons under 20 or over 60, the steady-state fraction of the total population in these two age groups is calculated for intrinsic rates of growth of 3, 2, 1.5, and 0 percent per year and life expectancies at birth of 40 and 65 years. Table 1.4 presents the percentage change in the fractions of dependents in stable populations in each category when the intrinsic rate of growth changes from 3 to 2 percent, from 3 to 1.5 percent, and from 3 to 0 percent. The percentage decline in the total number of dependents is considerably less than the decline in child-dependents, since the fraction of the population over 60 eventually rises substantially in response to a decline in fertility (which implies a decline in the intrinsic rate of growth). Thus, the decline in dependency rates accompanying a fall in fertility are much greater during the first several years following the fertility decline than the eventual decline since the ratio of the labor force to persons retired (or over 60) is not affected until the first cohort born under the regime of lower fertility enters the labor force. The results of Table 1.4 indicate that the permanent change in the dependency rate would be only about one half as much as the change in the child dependency rate because of the increase in the old age dependency rate. Thus, income per capita will increase appreciably during the short run due to the decreasing dependency rate holding the initial capital-labor ratio constant,* although income per capita will rise much less than this in the long run due to the eventual increase in old age dependents.† However, such an increase in income per capita due to a decline in child dependents is not in itself indicative of any improvement in societal or individual welfare. Rather, family monetary income is unchanged, and family size is smaller, which does not necessarily imply the family is any better off because there may be a reduction in family welfare due to the reduction in number of children, although it is possible that some individual family members are better off.

TABLE 1.4

Changes in the Dependency Rate for
Assumed Fertility Declines
(in percent)

Life Expectancy	Percentage Change in Population	Fertility Decline		
		3 to 1.5	3 to 1.5	3 to 0
40	Under 20	-12	-19	-39
	Over 60	+113	+165	+384
	Total	-7	-12	-21
65	Under 20	-18	-23	-46
	Over 60	+55	+91.1	+230
	Total	-8	-12	-18

Source: These numbers are derived from A. J. Coale and P. Demeny, Regional Model Life Tables and Stable Populations (Princeton: Princeton University Press, 1966), pp. 42, 62.

---

*The effect of the dependency rate on savings is not considered.
†Since a fertility decline causes a much greater change in the proportion of old persons in a population than other age groups, planners should take into account the changed demand for old age services as well as the changing demand for youth-oriented services, which would be occasioned by a fertility decline.

SUMMARY AND CONCLUSIONS

The increase in income per capita resulting from a decline in fertility, demonstrated under a variety of parameter assumptions in the simulation runs of the TEMPO models, is due to changes in two distinct variables. The decline in the rate of labor force growth leads to a greater capital-labor ratio than would have otherwise occurred (and hence greater income per worker) and the changing age structure generally leads to a lower fraction of dependents. The lower dependency rate increases income per capita (by definition) and increases income per laborer only if savings or other forms of capital accumulation are a function of the dependency rate.

A decline in fertility leads to a once-and-forever increase in the level of income per capita or per laborer, although the long-run, steady-state rate of economic growth per capita is unaffected by changes in fertility. Although the initial fall in the dependency rate that occurs immediately after a decline in fertility due to the decline in young dependents partially is offset by the eventual increase in old age dependents, the dependency rate usually does fall so there is a permanent increase in income per capita. Similarly, income per worker is permanently greater than it would otherwise be after a decline in the rate of population growth due to the greater capital-labor ratio.

The transition from an economy with high fertility and low income per capita to an economy with a low fertility and high income per capita is characterized by a declining dependency rate and an unaffected capital-labor ratio for the first 15 to 20 years following the fertility decline unless savings are a function of income per capita and/or the dependency rate. After this initial period there will be an increasing capital-labor ratio and a slightly increasing dependency rate. The rate of transition of the capital-labor ratio from one steady state to another following a decline in fertility depends on the rate of population growth, the rate of capital depreciation, the responsiveness of the labor supply to the real wage, the responsiveness of savings to the dependency rate, and the output elasticities of capital and labor in production. The magnitude of the change in income per worker in response to a decline in fertility also depends on these factors, although the effect of the dependency rate on income per capita depends only on the relationship between capital accumulation and dependency rates.

The results of the TEMPO models and the analysis in this section are not applicable directly to the welfare analysis of a fertility reduction, since no measures of the benefits or utility of children or of possible externalities are included in the analysis.

NOTES

Economic Consequences of
Rapid Population Growth
Stephen Enke

1. Instead they have appeared in such noneconomic journals
as Science, the Journal of Biosocial Sciences, and Policy Sciences.
2. See A. DeVany and S. Enke, Population Growth and Economic Development: Background and Guide, 1968; R. Eckert and
D. O'Hara, Manual for the Calculation of Government Expenditures
for Selected Social Services, 1968; S. Enke, Economic Benefits of
Slowing Population Growth, 1968; W. E. McFarland, Description of
the Economic-Demographic Model, 1968; and Sensitivity Analysis
of the Economic-Demographic Model, 1969; and W. E. McFarland
and D. O'Hara, Turkey: The Effects of Falling Fertility, 1969; and
Guatemala: The Effects of Declining Fertility, 1969 (Santa Barbara:
TEMPO, for all).
3. See B. Herrick and R. Moran, Declining Birth Rates in
Chile (Santa Barbara: TEMPO, 1971); and McFarland and O'Hara,
op. cit.
4. See McFarland, Sensitivity Analysis of the Economic-
Demographic Model, op. cit., for a detailed account of the sensitivity
analysis. However, some feeling for the insensitivity of the main
conclusion of the analysis, namely that a more rapid decline in fertility hardly affects V while significantly lowering P below what it
would otherwise be, can be gained from the following ratios given in
the cited document (which used slightly different parameters for its
production function.) In that case, by 2000, the "low fertility P" was
27 percent below the "high fertility P" in all the calculations, and
for the standard set of parameters, the ratio of "high fertility V" to
"low fertility V" was 1.005. If the rate of annual technological improvement was 2.5 percent instead of 1.5 percent, this ratio was
1.022. If the savings function were not $0.2V$ to $30P$ but rather
$0.07V$, this ratio was 1.036. If the respective output elasticities
of capital and labor were not 0.4 and 0.6 but rather 0.5 and 0.5,
this ratio was not 1.005 but 0.988. The results are also very insensitive to economies or diseconomies of scale: thus, if the output
elasticities sum not to unity but to 0.7 and 1.25, respectively, the
2000 ratios of V were not 1.005 but, respectively, 0.987 and 1.016.
Altogether, the interactions of the model seem to dampen the effect
of altering assumed parameters and initial conditions, a state of
affairs that strengthens the credibility of the conclusions.
5. See S. Enke and R. G. Zind, "Effects of Fewer Births on
Average Income," Journal of Biosocial Sciences 1, no. 1 (January

1969): 41-55. Also, S. Enke, in Macrosystems (New York: Holt Reinhart and Winston, 1971).

A Neoclassical Analysis of
Economic-Demographic
Simulation Models
Michael Keeley

6. McFarland, Description of the Economic-Demographic Model, op. cit.

7. See E. Denison, The Sources of Economic Growth in the U.S. and the Alternatives Before Us (New York: Committee for Economic Development, Library of Congress, 1962), for estimates of a, b, and c, using U.S. time series data.

8. N. S. Leff, "Dependency Rates and Savings Rates," American Economic Review 63, no. 4 (1969): 886-91, presents some empirical support for the effect of dependency rates on the fraction saved; K. L. Gupta, "Dependency Rates and Savings Rates: Comment," American Economic Review 61, no. 3, pt. 1 (June 1971): 469-71; and N. A. Adams, "Dependency Rates and Savings Rates: Comment," American Economic Review 61, no. 3, pt. 1 (June 1971): 472-75, present some criticisms of his work.

9. The golden rule savings rate is the savings rate that maximizes steady state consumption per worker; see E. S. Phelps, "Second Essay on Golden Rule of Accumulation," American Economic Review 55, no. 4 (September 1965): 793-814.

10. See R. G. D. Allen, Macro-Economic Theory (New York: St. Martin's Press, 1968), pp. 248-50.

11. This analysis follows closely that of E. Burmeister and A. Dobel, Mathematical Theories of Economic Growth (New York: Macmillan Co., 1970), pp. 36-38.

12. Income per adult would change during the first 15 to 20 years of the transitional period if female labor force participation rates were affected by the change in fertility or if the fraction saved depended on either the ratio of adults to children or on per capita income (see previous section).

13. The use of "equivalent consumers" partially corrects for the bias of using income per capita as a policy target. As S. Enke, "The Economic Consequences of Rapid Population Growth," Economic Journal 81, no. 4 (December 1971): 802, states,

> The "equivalent consumer" concept accounts for
> the fact that relative consumption varies with age
> and sex. Thus children typically consume less
> private and public sector goods and services than

do adult males of working age. Hence the increase
in output (or income) per head that ordinarily follows in an LDC from a reduction in fertility somewhat overstates the improvement in individual
welfare, simply because there are relatively fewer
children and more adults. One solution is to divide
GNP not by absolute population but by the estimated
number of equivalent consumers.

However, the equivalent consumer concept does not correct for the
loss of utility suffered by parents due to the fact that they have fewer
children.

14. See R. Brito, "Steady-State Paths in an Economy with
Endogenous Population Growth," Western Economic Journal 8, no. 4
(December 1970): 390-96.

15. This kind of experiment is not used in the TEMPO I simulation reported in Enke, "Economic Consequences of Population
Growth," op. cit., presumably because the simulations reported
were supposed to correspond to a "real world" situation. Generally
an LDC that has experienced a rapid mortality decline and no accompanying fertility decline will not have a stable population, nor will
its economy be in steady state equilibrium. This fact tends to am-
plify the demographic effects (through reducing the dependency ratio)
of a fertility decline since there are a disproportionate number of
children.

16. R. Sato, "Fiscal Policy in a Neoclassical Growth Model,"
Review of Economic Studies 30, no. 1 (February 1962): 16-23,
performs an analysis similar to the above on the response of the
capital-output ratio to changes in saving.

2

APPLICATIONS OF
ECONOMIC-DEMOGRAPHIC
SIMULATION MODELS

ECONOMIC EFFECTS
OF CHILEAN
FERTILITY DECLINE
Bruce H. Herrick

INTRODUCTION

This paper discusses the application of an economic-demographic projection model to pre-1970 Chile. Other papers in this volume discuss these models in detail, together with their implications for economic development in generalized situations. The present application to a single country illustrates both the possible usefulness and the inevitable difficulties with such models.

Projection models are not forecasting models. They usually summarize the most easily measurable aspects of the phenomena to be modeled and provide an answer to the elegantly simple question: "If a country's economic and demographic sectors continue to have the structure and parameters specified by the model, what future effects would be observed?" While the model's equations and parameter values should be "reasonable," projection models usually avoid questions about the "most likely" of these values, since the purpose of such models is not to forecast the future. Instead they give the analyst a tool to investigate the implications of his assumptions.

As described more fully both in other papers in this book and in the following, the demographic model used here has few surprises. Exogenously specified birth and death rates, specific by age and sex, were used to project future population size, rate of growth, and age-

The author acknowledges the collaboration of Ricardo Moran in doing the research and writing published earlier by General Electric-TEMPO under the title, "Declining Birth Rates in Chile: Their Effects on Output, Education, Health, and Housing." Financial support for that effort came from a contract with the Agency for International Development. Neither the agency nor the TEMPO organization is responsible, of course, for any of the views expressed here.

sex composition. Central to the economic model is an aggregate Cobb-Douglas production function. Labor inputs were calculated by the application of age and sex specific labor force participation rates. The capital stock in each period is the result of past saving, itself a function of per capita income. Output is also affected by exogenously specified disembodied technological change. The aggregate neo-classical nature of the production function implicitly rejects a "structuralist" view of the developing economy, in which sectoral relationships would be important while well articulated economic adjustment mechanisms (specifically, highly elastic demand supply, and factor substitution) would be absent.

The form of the model permits one to anticipate qualitatively some of its results: a priori, lower rates of population growth should result in higher per capita incomes, both because the number of dependents to share output would be relatively smaller and also because past per capita savings (and hence present capital stock per worker) would be relatively higher. The model's value lies in its ability to quantify these expected effects, taking into account the time period in which there is interest. How much? and how soon? are the targets of this inquiry.

The time pattern of social service expenditures in the areas of (formal) education and health also were calculated. Such calculations are potentially useful to economic planners. Their simplicity as linear functions of the age-eligible population, degree of coverage, and unit costs is noteworthy.

Finally, this investigation analyzes the effects of differential population growth rates on human capital formation. The assumption of a homogeneous labor force is discarded, and a labor force disaggregated by educational attainment is substituted in the model. Although conceptually straightforward, the computation requires assumptions about the probabilities of transition both from one educational status to the next and from different educational attainments into the labor force.

As noted above, the results describe a projection based on Chilean conditions before 1970. The effects of the subsequent changes in government and the associated reversals in policy would require an elaborate but separate work and are therefore not considered here. The model is sufficiently flexible that the goals for savings, investment, employment, and the social services of both the socialist government of Salvador Allende and the military one that followed it could be substituted for the parameter values originally used. The present work, then, deals with a poor country in the middle range of poverty having politically centrist social goals. Chile is also one in which human fertility has begun to decline without having reached the end of the so-called demographic transition.

CHILEAN POPULATION AND NATIONAL INCOME

Chilean Economic and Demographic Trends

Of primary importance to this study are growth of total national income and changes in birth and death rates. The rate of growth of real national income from 1940-62 was estimated at 3.5 percent per year.[1] Subsequent growth rates were higher; the period 1962-70 exhibited an annual growth rate of 4.1 percent.[2]

Movements of Chilean vital rates, together with the resultant natural rate of increase of the total population, are shown for the period 1929-70 in Figure 2.1. Death rates declined with only minor variations from the mid-1930s until the early 1950s. The economic stagnation accompanying unprecedented levels of inflation is usually blamed for the failure of the death rate to continue to fall in the mid-1950s. A renewal of the process of economic development in the mid-1960s, appearing unmistakably in the economic statistics of the period, is reflected in the renewed decline in the death rate.

Changes in the crude birth rate are no less interesting. The economic depression of the 1930s in Chile as in more highly industrialized countries was marked by a decline in fertility that was halted only by the economic revival spurred by preparations for World War II. The crude birth rate then remained approximately constant until the 1950s. The slight increase noted in the 1950s has been attributed by some observers to more complete birth registrations rather than to higher fertility per se.[3]

The birth rate increased from about 35 live births per thousand to about 37 in the early 1960s. Preliminary analysis seems to indicate that this increase in the birth rate was not explained by changes in the age composition alone. Instead, age specific fertility seems to have increased slightly. The degree to which this rise can be attributed simply to more complete birth registration is not known.

The most remarkable change in Chilean birth rates has been the sharp decline since 1962, noted above in Figure 2.1. The fall is all the more interesting because Chile's birth rate, while high compared with industrialized countries, is lower than most other Latin American countries. Only Argentina, Cuba, and Uruguay had lower birth rates than Chile during the early 1960s.

In 1965 Chile's National Health Service (SNS) began an officially sanctioned campaign against induced abortion. One element of the campaign was the provision of contraceptive materials and supplies through the countrywide network of SNS health posts. However, caution must be exercised in ascribing a cause and effect relationship to the SNS campaign and the observed drop in fertility. To date,

FIGURE 2.1

Annual Birth Rates, Death Rates, and Rates of
Natural Population Increase in Chile, 1929-70

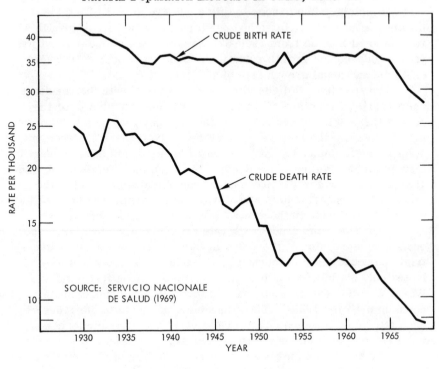

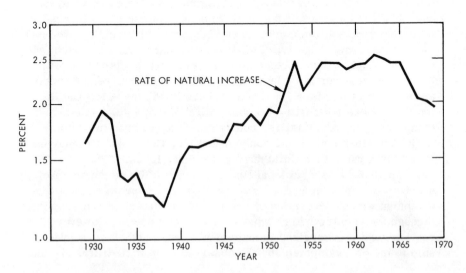

no nationwide study has been completed on the quantitative importance, if any, of the family planning element within the official campaign aimed at reducing induced abortion, although the matter has
been studied assiduously at the local level.[4] The declining birth rate
observed in the 1930s is evidence that fertility can fall without the
aid either of changes in contraceptive technology, such as the pill
and the intrauterine device, or of officially sponsored family planning campaigns. Individual decisions on the practice of contraception are made in the light of individual interests; and although official policy can be influential, it is not a necessary condition for declining fertility.

The Demographic Model

The demographic model projects future population size and
composition by subtracting deaths (disaggregated by age and sex)
and adding births to a base year (1960) population. Net international
migration was assumed to be zero. Age specific survival rates underlying the projection were adopted from the United Nations' Latin
American Demographic Center (CELADE).[5] Three assumptions
about future fertility were made. Comparing their implications is
of central importance to this work.

Future Fertility Assumption A

The first assumption postulates constant age-sex specific fertility rates at levels observed in 1960. The gross rate of reproduction was 2.5 in that year. The 1960 level represents an "historical"
or postwar level of fertility, whose economic and demographic effects serve as a benchmark for comparison with subsequent lower
levels. Although, as noted previously, a fertility decline has been
observed since 1963, the conditions posed by assumption A still appear important. Fertility declines are not necessarily permanent
or irreversible, as the U.S. experience following World War II
shows. Furthermore, for countries similar to Chile whose fertility
has not begun to fall, the projections of results from continued levels
of traditional fertility will have some interest.

Future Fertility Assumption B

The second assumption adopted the lowest of a set of CELADE
assumptions made in 1969. Interestingly, those assumptions nearly
were outdated instantly by the rapidity of the actual fertility decline.
The gross reproduction rates, both actual and projected, for the
1960s are shown in Figure 2.2.

FIGURE 2.2

Observed and Projected Gross Reproduction Rate in Chile,
1960-69, Using CELADE-Based Fertility Assumption B

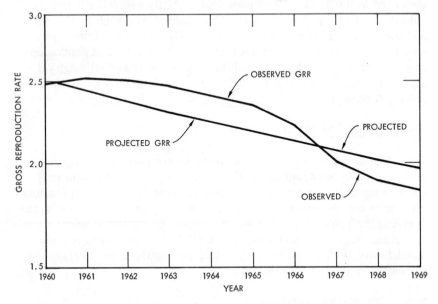

Future Fertility Assumption C

Assumption C reflects a more rapid fertility decline, one that
might effectively place a lower bound on future Chilean birth rates.
It extrapolates linearly the fall in fertility levels observed during
the 1960s into the future until a set of rates is reached that would be
consistent with an eventual equilibrium rate of zero population
growth and with an average family size of slightly more than two
children. Under assumption C, these birth rates are attained in
1985. Owing to Chile's initial age distribution and to demographic
momentum, fertility rates consistent with eventual stationary population would mean continued population increase until the fourth
decade of the twenty-first century.

Gross reproduction rates implied by assumption C are compared with those of assumptions A and B in Figure 2.3.

Thus, the three assumptions about future fertility change can
be summarized as follows:

A--high fertility at the traditional level, replicating that observed
   in 1960;
B--an official projection, denoted as a very rapid decline in fertility;

C--fertility rates consistent with a two-child family in a demographically stable population, an even more rapid fertility decline than
in B.

FIGURE 2.3

Gross Reproduction Rate in Chile Under Three
Assumptions, 1960-2000

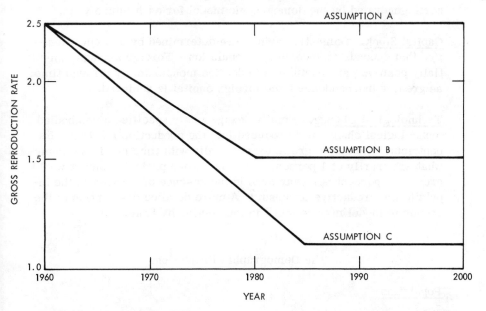

It is probable that projected changes under assumptions A and
C place upper and lower bounds on future fertility levels and, hence,
influence strongly the population sizes likely to be observed in Chile
during the remainder of this century.

The Economic Model

The economic model applies a Cobb-Douglas production function* to Chilean conditions. Output is generated by inputs of physical

_____

*The Cobb-Douglas production function used here is
$$Y = Ae^{rt} K^{\alpha} L^{\beta}$$

where α and β are the output elasticities of capital K and labor L,
respectively. The parameter A is a constant, and r is the rate of
technical progress.

capital and labor to the economic process together with the forces
implicit in technological change. Exponential weights are assigned
to the labor and capital inputs in the production function on the basis
of, and equal to, their estimated partial output elasticities. The
sum of these elasticities is equal to one, implying constant returns
to scale in the production process. [6]

Labor. The size of the labor input is calculated from the application
of constant age-sex specific participation rates to the population cohorts generated by the demographic model for each future year.

Capital Stock. Domestic savings are determined by a savings function that depends on income and population. Foreign savings, initially positive, are postulated to decline monotonically through time,
as greater independence from foreign capital is achieved.

Technological Change. Finally, exogenously specified disembodied
technological change is introduced into the production function. Its
contribution to output grows exponentially with time and is set somewhat arbitrarily at 1 percent per year. Thus projected output would
grow by 1 percent per year even in the absence of changes in the inputs to the productive process. [7] A more detailed description of the
economic model may be found in the section by Enke.

The Demographic Projections

Population

        The demographic model generates projections of the total popu-
lation disaggregated by sex and by five-year age cohorts. One of
the goals of this study is to illuminate the relationship between population size and total production. Aggregate GNP is not constant under varying population size, partly because the labor force depends
on lagged fertility levels. Thus, the demographic model provides
the frame of reference to make estimates regarding the labor force
by facilitating computation of the size and composition of the population.
        Starting from an initial population of 7.683 million in 1960 and
using the three different sets of fertility assumptions outlined previously together with a single set of assumptions concerning mortality throughout the projection period, the demographic model has been
used to project the population sizes shown in Table 2.1. The table
shows the increasing force of sustained declines in fertility; the projection based on traditional (1960) fertility yields a population 43

percent and 66 percent larger than those of projections B and C, respectively, by the end of the century. The crude birth rates and crude death rates that accompany these changes are shown in Table 2.2.

TABLE 2.1

Total Population of Chile
(thousands)

Year	Fertility Assumptions			Ratio of:	
	A	B	C	A/B	A/C
1960	7,683	7,683	7,683	1.00	1.00
1970	9,932	9,575	9,547	1.04	1.04
1980	13,112	11,591	11,295	1.13	1.16
1990	17,650	14,019	12,853	1.26	1.37
2000	23,983	16,803	14,465	1.43	1.66

Source: Bruce Herrick and Ricardo Moran, Declining Birth Rates in Chile: Their Effects on Output, Education, Health and Housing, 71 TMP-56 (Santa Barbara, Calif.: General Electric Company-TEMPO, 1972), p. 16, table 1.

TABLE 2.2

Crude Birth Rate (CBR) and Crude Death Rate (CDR)
per Thousand in the Chilean Population

	CBR Under Fertility Assumption			CDR Under Fertility Assumption		
Interval	A	B	C	A	B	C
1960	37	35	35	12	23	11
1970	37	28	27	10	9	9
1980	37	27	21	7	8	7
1990	36	25	19	6	7	7
2000	36	24	18	5	6	7

Source: Bruce Herrick and Ricardo Moran, Declining Birth Rates in Chile: Their Effects on Output, Education, Health and Housing, 71 TMP-56 (Santa Barbara, Calif.: General Electric Company-TEMPO, 1972), p. 16, table 2.

The calculations of dependency rates, shown in Table 2.3, are even more revealing. The higher proportion of youth in the population under continued high birth rates is apparent even though the Chilean birth rate at its traditional level is not as high as the rates exhibited by some other Latin American countries. Nevertheless, traditional Chilean fertility levels lead to increases in the proportion of the population less than 15 years of age: for each 100 people aged 15 to 64 in 1960 there are 71 children under 15; by the year 2000 the number increases to 78.

These movements contrast strikingly with the projections in which fertility falls. In projection B, the officially estimated fertility decline, the number of dependent youths falls from 71 per 100 to 50 per 100 by the year 2000, while the more extreme but nevertheless realizable two-child norm assumption C leads to a greater, more abrupt decline.

The lower relative numbers of dependent youths (those less than age 15) in the latter projections are offset only slightly by increases in the numbers of those 65 and older. Thus, for example, while the proportion of dependent youths in the two-child norm projection is falling from 71 (per 100 in the "working ages" of 15 to 64) to 37 by the year 2000, the numbers of old people rise from 8 to 10 per 100.

The potential impact of these changes in the age structure of the population is to increase income per capita, since the productive labor force is drawn almost exclusively from those aged 15 to 64.

Labor Force

The foregoing changes in the age composition of the population translate themselves fairly readily into changes in the labor force. Age-sex specific labor force participation rates are multiplied by the numbers in the work-age population to calculate labor force size.

The results of the labor force projections are shown in absolute numbers in Table 2.4. Ratios of the projected labor force to total population and the working age population appear in Table 2.5.

Absolute labor force size is not affected by fertility decline for 15 years, and even then the subsequent changes proceed only slowly. * Thirty years after the onset of falling birth rates, the labor force is

---

*A more refined model would include explicitly the greater female participation that accompanies lower fertility during the initial years. However, the effect of this change on overall labor force size is negligible for at least two decades under any fertility assumption used here.

TABLE 2.3

Numbers of Youth and Old People per Hundred Persons in the Population
Aged 15-64 Under Different Chilean Fertility Assumptions

	Assumption A			Assumption B			Assumption C		
Year	Total in Dependent Ages	Youth	Old People	Total in Dependent Ages	Youth	Old People	Total in Dependent Ages	Youth	Old People
1960	79	71	8	79	71	8	79	71	8
1970	81	73	8	74	66	8	74	66	8
1980	83	75	8	63	55	8	59	51	8
1990	86	78	8	61	52	9	50	41	9
2000	86	78	8	60	50	10	47	37	10

Source: Bruce Herrick and Ricardo Moran, Declining Birth Rates in Chile: Their Effects on Output, Education, Health and Housing, 71 TMP-56 (Santa Barbara, Calif.: General Electric Company-TEMPO, 1972), p. 16, table 3.

TABLE 2.4

Projected Chilean Labor Force Under Different
Fertility Assumptions
(in thousands)

	Fertility Assumption		
Year	A	B	C
1960	2,363	2,363	2,363
1970	3,077	3,077	3,077
1980	4,133	4,096	4,093
1990	5,550	5,119	5,068
2000	7,621	6,219	5,868

Source: Bruce Herrick and Ricardo Moran, Declining Birth Rates in Chile: Their Effects on Output, Education, Health and Housing, 71 TMP-56 (Santa Barbara, Calif.: General Electric Company-TEMPO, 1972), p. 18, table 5.

TABLE 2.5

Chilean Labor Force to Population Ratios
Under Different Fertility Assumptions
(in percent)

	Ratio to Entire Population Under Fertility Assumption			Ratio to Population Aged 15-64 Under Fertility Assumption		
Year	A	B	C	A	B	C
1960	30.7	30.7	30.7	55.1	55.1	55.1
1970	31.0	32.1	32.2	56.1	56.1	56.1
1980	31.5	35.3	36.2	57.5	57.7	57.7
1990	31.4	36.5	39.4	58.4	58.9	59.0
2000	31.8	37.0	40.6	59.1	59.4	59.8

Source: Bruce Herrick and Ricardo Moran, Declining Birth Rates in Chile: Their Effects on Output, Education, Health and Housing, 71 TMP-56 (Santa Barbara, Calif.: General Electric Company-TEMPO, 1972), p. 18, table 6.

less than 10 percent smaller under fertility assumption C than under traditional levels of reproduction.

When the focus changes from absolute to relative labor force size, however, the picture is altered as seen in Table 2.5. The ratio of the labor force to the overall population rises by a single percentage point in four decades under conditions of traditional fertility. But with the lower fertility assumptions, that increase is either 6 or nearly 10 percent. The projection associated with a two-child norm (assumption C) has 40.6 workers per 100, or one-third more by the century's end, compared with only 30.7 in 1960.

The impacts of these prospective changes on total GNP and on GNP per capita are explored subsequently. The degree of latitude given to the developing economy by these changes, otherwise made impossible by the youthful composition of the population, is one of the central mechanisms, if not the central mechanism, by which fertility decline produces its effects on income per capita.

The Economic Projections of Output

Superficially, it might appear that larger populations would be associated with larger total output, regardless of the relationship between population size and output per capita. But, as shown in Table 2.6, total Chilean GNP is almost completely unaffected by fertility until after 1990. The labor force after 30 years is only 10 percent lower under conditions of rapid fertility decline than it would be under historic fertility levels. As seen in Table 2.7, where the inputs to the production process are detailed, this relatively smaller labor force is almost completely offset by a higher capital stock, itself the result of the process of saving and investment.

The size of output is completely determined by the size of the labor force, capital stock inputs, and technology. As are labor force inputs, the stock of physical capital is influenced by population. It is assumed that at some (presumably low) level of GNP, aggregate savings are zero for a given population, with the absolute size of the GNP associated with zero savings increasing with population size. As GNP per capita exceeds this zero-savings level, savings increase.

During the initial decades of the projections, total GNP is notably insensitive to the differences among the three fertility assumptions, while population sizes corresponding to these assumptions increasingly diverge. Since savings flow from the excess of GNP over the zero-savings level in the model, higher fertility increases the zero-savings level of GNP and reduces resultant amounts of savings and capital formation. Thus, larger additions to the labor force are offset by smaller additions to the capital stock. The net results of these counteracting forces on GNP are shown in Table 2.7.

TABLE 2.6

Summary of Chilean Economic Projections, 1960–2000

| Economic Indicator | Year | Fertility Assumption | | | Ratios | |
		A	B	C	B/A	C/A
Total GNP (millions of 1960 escudos)*	1960	4,080	4,080	4,080	1.00	1.00
	1970	6,078	6,101	6,102	1.00	1.00
	1980	9,429	9,556	9,569	1.01	1.01
	1990	15,022	14,934	14,951	0.99	1.00
	2000	24,814	23,303	22,847	0.94	0.92
Average annual rate of growth of total GNP, 1960–2000 (percent)	--	4.6	4.5	4.4	--	--
GNP/capita (1960 escudos)*	1960	531	531	531	1.00	1.00
	1970	612	637	639	1.04	1.04
	1980	719	824	847	1.15	1.18
	1990	851	1,065	1,163	1.25	1.37
	2000	1,035	1,387	1,579	1.34	1.53
Average annual rate of growth of GNP/capita (percent)	1960	1.4	1.6	1.6	--	--
	1970	1.7	2.6	2.8	--	--
	1980	1.7	2.7	3.3	--	--
	1990	2.0	2.6	3.2	--	--
	2000	2.1	2.7	3.1	--	--
	1960–2000	1.7	2.4	2.8	--	--

*In 1960, the Chilean escudo was worth about one U.S. dollar. Specifically, E° 1.05 = $1.00.

Source: Bruce Herrick and Ricardo Moran, Declining Birth Rates in Chile: Their Effects on Output, Education, Health and Housing, 71 TMP-56 (Santa Barbara, Calif.: General Electric Company-TEMPO, 1972), p. 20, table 7.

TABLE 2.7

Inputs to the Chilean Production Process

Inputs	Year	Fertility Assumption			Ratios	
		A	B	C	B/A	C/A
Labor force						
(thousands)	1960	2,363	2,363	2,363	1.00	1.00
	1970	3,077	3,077	3,077	1.00	1.00
	1980	4,133	4,096	4,093	0.99	0.99
	1990	5,550	5,119	5,068	0.92	0.91
	2000	7,621	6,219	5,868	0.82	0.77
Capital stock						
(billions of						
1960 escudos)	1960	10.3	10.3	10.3	1.00	1.00
	1970	14.4	14.5	14.6	1.01	1.01
	1980	21.2	22.0	22.0	1.04	1.04
	1990	32.8	35.2	35.6	1.07	1.09
	2000	53.5	57.8	58.9	1.08	1.10

Note: In addition to labor and physical capital, technological progress is included in the aggregate production function and is assumed to proceed in these projections at a rate of 1 percent a year.

Source: Bruce Herrick and Ricardo Moran, Declining Birth Rates in Chile: Their Effects on Output, Education, Health and Housing, 71 TMP-56 (Santa Barbara, Calif.: General Electric Company-TEMPO, 1972), p. 21, table 8.

Turning to the evolution of GNP per capita, Table 2.6 lists the projection results for the three Chilean fertility assumptions. Even under historic fertility conditions, GNP per capita almost doubles over the 1960-2000 period. It nearly triples under the lowest fertility case. The model supplies answers to many other questions bearing on the projected Chilean economy. Table 2.8 shows, for instance, the years that per capita income reaches given levels under the three fertility assumptions. The table indicates that future contractions in the birth rate would be accompanied by a significantly faster rate of growth of per capita output and, hence, a reduction in the period required to attain given levels of this index of economic development. Chile's already moderate rate of population growth, in comparison with that of other developing countries, makes such a conclusion all the more striking. If the strength and growth of the so-called "rising expectations" are as great in Chile as they are commonly thought to be in other developing countries, the possibilities of reaching the indicated levels of GNP per capita a decade or more earlier in the lower fertility cases than in the high should be emphasized.

TABLE 2.8

Year in Which Chilean GNP per Capita
Reaches a Given Level

GNP/Capita	Fertility Assumption/Year		
(1960 escudos)	A	B	C
800	1986	1979	1978
1000	1998	1988	1985
1200	after 2000	1995	1991

Source: Bruce Herrick and Ricardo Moran, Declining Birth Rates in Chile: Their Effects on Output, Education, Health and Housing, 71 TMP-56 (Santa Barbara, Calif.: General Electric Company-TEMPO, 1972), p. 22, table 9.

CHILEAN PUBLIC EXPENDITURES
ON EDUCATION AND HEALTH

A projection model that provides information on population and GNP, as previously discussed, seems ideally suited as the basis for further insight into the size and growth of public expenditures. While our interest may center on education and health because of their immediate concern to the development process, the model is perfectly general. It can therefore be readily adapted to areas other than those explored in the current section. [8]

Education

Primary and Secondary Education

In general, expenditures on education are influenced by the numbers of children, the proportion of them in school, and the spending per student on current and capital items. Although this method can be readily disaggregated to any level of detail supported by available data, the long period of time under consideration led to an aggregated approach. As will be seen, a similar set of considerations was used to make expenditure projections for health under the different fertility assumptions.

Among social expenditures, education is affected most dramatically by changes in human fertility. The previous discussion showed that changes in fertility affect the absolute and relative numbers of young people more quickly and more strongly than other groups in the population. Educational expenditures are made primarily for the young. By contrast, expenditures both in health and in housing are not so highly age specific and hence are more insensitive to changes in the size of the most youthful cohorts in the population.

Current expenditures for education include the average expenditure per teacher in the system, an amount comprised not only of salaries but also of noncapital items of supplies and equipment. In general, however, remunerations absorb nearly the whole current budget.

Two main items are included as capital expenditures: construction costs of schools and the costs of providing university training for prospective teachers. This treatment of teacher training recognizes the cash flows associated with it. It thus differs from other approaches (for example, Bowles in 1969) that consider teachers as rented from the economy, their training costs being completely reflected in their salaries as rental payments.

The changes in spending necessitated by the three fertility assumptions are each related to the different numbers of school age population present. Table 2.9 shows the numbers in the primary school ages, here taken as 7 to 14, the secondary school ages, 15 to 18, and the university ages, 18 to 24.

The table points up the pressures on the system by the end of the century. Even if fertility continues to fall as in assumption B, there will be 800,000 more children in the primary school ages in the year 2000 than in 1970; and well over a million more than there were in 1960. The table also shows what would have happened if fertility had not declined during the 1960s: children of primary school age would more than double by century's end over their present level. That number, 4.8 million, would represent more than three times the number eligible for education in 1960. An even more dramatic comparison would include six-year-olds and possibly even five-year-olds among those eligible for primary education. By contrast, fertility levels consistent with the two-child family (assumption C) would result in a number of primary school age children largely constant in absolute terms between now and the year 2000.

The secondary school age and university age groups are less quickly affected by changes in fertility occurring after 1960. The lag of 15 years, in the case of potential secondary students, and 18 years for would-be university entrants, results in both groups remaining unchanged by fertility decline until after 1975. However, once the lags are overcome, both groups are affected almost as strongly as the primary age group.

TABLE 2.9

Projected Chilean School-Age Population

Number of Students and Average Annual Growth	Year	Fertility Assumption		
		A	B	C
Primary school age (7-14)				
(thousands)	1960	1,439	1,439	1,439
	1970	1,937	1,902	1,900
	1980	2,523	2,001	1,944
	1990	3,484	2,262	1,874
	2000	4,772	2,704	1,879
Secondary school age (15-18)				
(thousands)	1960	590	590	590
	1970	812	812	812
	1980	1,054	976	971
	1990	1,424	1,034	966
	2000	1,376	1,217	909
University age (18-24)				
(thousands)	1960	916	916	916
	1970	1,220	1,219	1,219
	1980	1,659	1,641	1,639
	1990	2,160	1,735	1,692
	2000	2,988	1,954	1,640
Average annual growth rates, 1960-2000 (percent)				
Primary school age	--	2.97	1.59	0.68
Secondary school age	--	2.14	1.82	1.09
University age	--	3.00	1.91	1.47

Source: Bruce Herrick and Ricardo Moran, Declining Birth Rates in Chile: Their Effects on Output, Education, Health and Housing, 71 TMP-56 (Santa Barbara, Calif.: General Electric Company-TEMPO, 1972), p. 24, table 10.

Enrollment ratios and per-student expenditures represent society's goals and norms, whether of the Chilean society or any other. Interviews with officials directly connected to education together with study of the formal educational planning documents, where they exist, are the most helpful sources for the model builder. Enrollment ratios and space requirements, historical and projected, appear in Table 2.10. Other norms could be tested readily by the projection model.

TABLE 2.10

Projected Chilean Enrollment Ratios
and Classroom Space

Year	Enrollment Ratios		Space per Student (meters^2)	
	Primary	Secondary	Primary	Secondary
1960	0.79	0.26	1.5	2.5
1970	0.95	0.35	1.5	2.5
1980	0.95	0.50	2.0	3.3
1990	0.95	0.60	2.0	3.3
2000	0.95	0.60	2.0	3.3

Sources: Space per student data is based on Ernesto Schiefelbein, El sistema educacional chileno (Santiago: Ministerio de Educacion Publica, Superintendencia de Educacion, 1970), and interviews with education planning officials. Other data are from Bruce Herrick and Ricardo Moran, Declining Birth Rates in Chile: Their Effects on Output, Education, Health and Housing, 71 TMP-56 (Santa Barbara, Calif.: General Electric Company-TEMPO, 1972), p. 26, table 11.

Other parameters necessary for the successful operation of the model included the following:

student-teacher ratio: 1970, 1:37; projected, 1:35;
teacher attrition rate: 3 percent per year;
depreciation rate on physical plant: 4 percent per year;
costs of training a new teacher: E^O 2700 (in 1960 escudos); and
costs of new plant: E^O 98 per square meter (in 1960 escudos).

The operating costs (current costs) of the school system, as
noted above, consisted almost completely of salaries. Three options
were considered for treatment of future increases in pay:

1. Constant real salaries--this approach was discarded since
income per capita and, more significantly, income per worker,
rises in each projection over time. Thus, constant salaries, even
in real terms, would imply that the relative wage to teachers declined. This appeared to be an unrealistic assumption.

2. Increasing salaries; constant wage differentials--raising
expenditure per teacher by the percentage that GNP rises in the
various projections would maintain current wage differentials, what-
ever their size.

3. Increasing salaries and increasing wage differentials--
this option recognizes the possibility that increases in relative pay
might be necessary to attract the increased number of teachers required in some of the projections and in some periods in the future.
Such an approach assumes a labor market initially in equilibrium
but requiring a higher pay differential for educators if shifts are to
occur toward education in the composition of the labor force.

The second option was adopted, since the model represented
by the third seemed less applicable to Chile than the job vacancy
model of the second. It implies that employment in education was
(and continues to be) limited not by lack of labor but by demand conditions.

The projected results deriving from the assumptions on, and
educational goals of, the Chilean primary and secondary school system are contained in Tables 2.11 through 2.13. By century's end,
primary enrollment (Table 2.11) in the event of a continuing fertility
decline will be slightly more than half that which would occur for a
constant 1960 fertility rate. The difference for secondary enrollment is somewhat less because of the greater lag in impact.

The primary enrollments necessary between the 1970s and
2000 if the educational goals outlined are to be met proved further
cause for reflection. Even if fertility were to decline at the officially projected rate embodied in assumption B, more than three-
quarters of a million additional children would be in primary school
in the year 2000 if the postulated enrollment ratios were maintained.
Teaching capacity and classroom space would require expansion by
more than one-half their 1970 levels. By contrast, virtually no expansion would be necessary in the event of the accelerated fertility
decline of assumption C. The number of students would fall slightly,
while the number of teachers and classroom floor space would rise
slightly because of higher educational standards.

TABLE 2.11

Projected Total Chilean Primary and Secondary School Enrollment
and Teacher and Classroom Space Requirements

Item	Year	Primary Education Under Fertility Assumption			Secondary Education Under Fertility Assumption		
		A	B	C	A	B	C
Enrollment (thousands)	1960	1,137	1,137	1,137	153	153	153
	1970	1,840	1,807	1,805	284	284	284
	1980	2,396	1,901	1,847	527	488	485
	1990	3,310	2,149	1,780	854	620	580
	2000	4,534	2,569	1,785	1,186	730	545
Teachers required (thousands)	1960	28.4	28.4	28.4	3.8	3.8	3.8
	1970	49.7	48.8	48.7	7.7	7.7	7.7
	1980	69.5	55.1	53.5	15.3	14.2	14.1
	1990	96.0	62.3	51.6	24.8	18.0	16.8
	2000	131.5	74.5	51.8	34.4	21.2	15.8
Classroom space required (thousands of square meters)	1960	1,705	1,705	1,705	383	383	383
	1970	2,760	2,711	2,707	710	710	710
	1980	4,793	3,803	3,693	1,740	1,611	1,602
	1990	6,620	4,298	3,561	2,820	2,048	1,913
	2000	9,068	5,138	3,569	3,913	2,410	1,800

Source: Bruce Herrick and Ricardo Moran, Declining Birth Rates in Chile: Their Effects on Output, Education, Health and Housing, 71 TMP-56 (Santa Barbara, Calif.: General Electric Company-TEMPO, 1972), p. 28, table 12.

TABLE 2.12

Projected Annual Chilean Primary and Secondary School
New Teacher and New Classroom Space Requirements

Item	Year	Primary Education Under Fertility Assumption			Secondary Education Under Fertility Assumption		
		A	B	C	A	B	C
New teachers required (thousands)	1970	3.6	3.4	3.3	0.6	0.6	0.6
	1980	4.1	2.1	1.9	1.2	1.0	0.9
	1990	5.4	2.6	1.2	1.7	0.9	0.7
	2000	7.2	3.2	1.7	1.9	1.0	0.3
New classroom space required (thousands of square meters)	1970	203.0	191.4	190.4	59.6	59.6	59.6
	1980	397.8	247.0	227.6	171.6	144.0	142.0
	1990	426.4	214.6	113.2	215.0	121.8	98.6
	2000	570.6	264.8	149.2	251.0	129.0	53.8

Source: Bruce Herrick and Ricardo Moran, Declining Birth Rates in Chile: Their Effects on Output, Education, Health and Housing, 71 TMP-56 (Santa Barbara, Calif.: General Electric Company-TEMPO, 1972), p. 30, table 13.

Although the expansion of secondary enrollments during the 1960s was remarkable, even under the lowest official fertility assumption, B, enrollment would continue to accelerate during the 1970s. Given the goals for secondary enrollment ratios shown in Table 2.10, by the year 2000 almost 450,000 more secondary students would be enrolled than in 1970. Such an increase would require growth of the secondary system to more than two and one-half times its size in 1970 to serve adequately what seems likely to be sustained social demand.

Table 2.12 projects the numbers of new teachers and the amounts of floor space required for expansions in enrollment for the first year of each decade from 1970 through 2000. The table shows that by the year 2000 the numbers of new primary teachers required annually under fertility assumption A would be more than four times those of assumption C. At the secondary level, educational planners would have to face in the highest fertility case a teacher training program about six times the magnitude of that required by the lowest fertility projection. Similarly, annual requirements for additional classroom space would be nearly four times as great for primary education under assumption A as they would be for assumption C, and nearly five times as great for secondary education.

The foregoing comments on projections for training new teachers and adding new classroom space apply equally to the projections of investment costs given in Table 2.13 for teacher training and for classroom construction. The system operating costs (current costs) of Table 2.13, which disregard (definitionally) the substantial investment expenditures implied by the projections, provide a less dramatic comparison among fertility assumptions than do the teacher training costs. But in absolute terms they rise considerably. For the last projected year, 2000, the necessary primary level total investment and operating expenditures of 479 million escudos in the lowest fertility assumption can be compared with those of 1,016 million escudos for the highest. Similar relative magnitudes obtain for secondary level system expenditures. Although the educational system grew swiftly and steadily during the latter half of the 1960s, the continuation of that expansion at the rates made necessary by these projections will clearly intensify pressures on already strained public budgets.

Although the results of the projections reviewed in the preceding paragraphs are highly aggregated, include some coefficients that are constant over time, or at best grow at constant rates and disregard many details of concern to planners, they do deal with the most important features of the system. At the same time, the analytical scheme underlying these projections provides the skeleton for future, more detailed models of the system.

TABLE 2.13

Projected Annual Investment and Operating Costs of
Chilean Primary and Secondary Schools
(millions of 1960 escudos)

Item	Year	Primary Education Under Fertility Assumption			Secondary Education Under Fertility Assumption		
		A	B	C	A	B	C
Investment for training new teachers	1970	9.6	9.0	9.0	1.7	1.7	1.7
	1980	11.0	5.7	5.0	3.2	2.6	2.5
	1990	14.5	6.9	3.2	4.6	2.5	1.9
	2000	19.4	8.6	4.6	5.2	2.6	0.9
Investment costs for new classroom space	1970	19.8	18.6	18.6	5.8	5.8	5.8
	1980	38.8	24.2	22.2	16.8	14.0	13.8
	1990	41.6	21.0	11.0	21.0	11.8	9.6
	2000	55.8	25.8	14.6	24.6	12.6	5.2
System operating costs	1970	211.8	210.4	210.2	31.6	31.6	31.6
	1980	358.6	302.6	297.4	73.4	71.4	71.4
	1990	570.6	410.6	360.8	142.0	115.4	111.2
	2000	941.4	625.0	460.2	245.4	176.6	145.4
Total investment and operating costs	1970	241.2	238.0	237.8	39.1	39.1	39.1
	1980	408.4	332.5	324.6	93.4	88.0	87.7
	1990	626.7	438.5	375.0	167.6	129.7	122.7
	2000	1,016.6	659.4	479.4	275.2	191.8	151.5

Source: Bruce Herrick and Ricardo Moran, Declining Birth Rates in Chile: Their Effects on Output, Education, Health and Housing, 71 TMP-56 (Santa Barbara, Calif.: General Electric Company-TEMPO, 1972), p. 31, table 14.

TABLE 2.14

Parametric Coefficients Assumed for Projections
Relating to University Education

Year	Enrollment Ratio	Teacher-Student Ratio	Annual Attrition Rate (percent)	Teacher Training Unit Costs (E^o of 1960)	Annual Operating Cost per Teacher Under Fertility Assumption (E^o of 1960)		
					A	B	C
1960	0.03	0.12	3.0	4,590	8,425	8,425	8,425
1970	0.06	0.10	3.0	4,590	9,640	9,660	9,660
1980	0.10	0.08	3.0	4,590	11,135	11,325	11,350
1990	0.18	0.06	3.0	4,590	13,210	14,115	14,275
2000	0.30	0.05	3.0	4,590	15,890	18,095	18,810

Source: Bruce Herrick and Ricardo Moran, Declining Birth Rates in Chile: Their Effects on Output, Education, Health and Housing, 71 TMP-56 (Santa Barbara, Calif.: General Electric Company-TEMPO, 1972), p. 35, table 15.

Although the projections consider qualitative improvements in the student-teacher ratio, in the classroom space per student, and in teachers' (and others') salaries, equally important qualitative improvements have been proposed for the system. Higher rates of retention of skilled employees, an orientation of education toward more meaningful general education on the one hand and more immediately useful vocational training on the other, a better way of evaluating educational progress, and a greater emphasis on in-service training all fall within this context. Merely naming these improvements makes clear the difficulty of their inclusion as quantitative parametric changes in the present mode. But it is equally clear that higher quality education is likely to be more expensive education. Therefore, failing to account for these improvements explicitly in the projections means, in turn, that the projections understate differences in the economic implications of the different fertility levels.

University Education

University education in the development process frequently is regarded as qualitatively different from primary and secondary education. It is viewed as having a special role in the formation of high-level manpower required to introduce and manage the changes that accompany economic development. But although projections can and do use different sources as bases for the model's parameters, the basic projection method is the same as that already outlined. Enrollment ratios, teacher-student ratios, attrition rates, and training costs, must all be estimated (Table 2. 14). [9] Once again, educational planners interested in the details of the process would be led to disaggregate to a far greater extent than has been done here. The method, however, is perfectly general.

The spectrum of influential views on university enrollment appears extremely wide and lacks any clearly distinguishable modal points. One extreme of this spectrum holds that Chilean universities should be abolished in their present form or, at least, that their enrollment should be rendered highly selective and, correspondingly, drastically reduced. The other extreme may be capsuled by its well-known slogan: "universidad para todos" (university for everyone). The ratios used here represent a compromise position, somewhere between those poles. Owing to the wide variations in student-teacher ratios among schools, any estimate of that ratio used for projection implies something not only about the educationally desirable ratio but also about the composition of enrollments among schools. The same remark applies to teacher training costs.

Although this additional potential source of variation exists in the absolute orders of magnitude of the projected input requirements and their total cost, it does not interfere with the validity of the main thrust of the projection exercises if it is assumed that the career composition of university students at any point in time is essentially independent of the fertility regimes, past or present. Under this assumption it can be asserted that the relative differences in input requirements to meet future demands for university education associated with each fertility assumption are uniquely attributable to the differences among these fertility assumptions.

The foregoing point, although made in the context of the educational sector, is equally relevant to all other social services treated in this book. It may be stated more generally as follows: the greater the degree of heterogeneity and compositional instability of the service (for example, medical care, housing) to be rendered, the less reliable are projected absolute magnitudes (and corresponding absolute differences) associated with each fertility assumption. Since proportional differences among these magnitudes are less sensitive to compositional changes that may occur independently in the interim, correspondingly greater importance should be attached to proportional differences in assessing the impact of differential fertility regimes on the relative future demands for the service in question.

The assumptions and methods used in projecting current expenditures at the lower educational sectors apply equally to university education projections, that is: (1) wage and salary payments exhaust the sector's operating budget, (2) the composition of the educational work force remains stable over time, (3) relative wages among the various personnel categories are constant from period to period, and (4) wage rates increase over time in proportion to GNP per worker.

Projected tertiary enrollment and the corresponding number of teachers required for the first year of each decade from 1960 to 2000 are shown in Table 2.15.

University enrollment, and consequently the number of teachers required, remains unaffected by the changing fertility assumptions until 1980 because of the lag between the introduction of alternative fertility assumptions in 1960 and the movement of corresponding cohorts into university-eligible ages. Indeed, the differences in each of these variables under the three regimes is still relatively small in 1990. It is not until century's end that they become substantial. Specifically, year 2000 enrollment and teachers required under assumption A, traditional fertility, turn out to be 82 percent greater than under assumption C, the two-child family.

Table 2.16 shows the number of new teachers who must be trained during selected years to meet requirements imposed by projected enrollments. These figures were obtained, as in the cases of lower education, from aggregating the number of new teachers required to replace those who drop out of the system with the number of additional teachers needed to meet growing enrollment. The estimated training costs and the costs of operating the higher educational establishment for the same years are also shown in this table.

TABLE 12.15

University Enrollment and Teachers Required 1960-2000
(in thousands)

	Fertility Assumption		
Year	A	B	C
Enrollment			
1960	27.5	27.5	27.5
1970	73.2	73.2	73.2
1980	165.9	164.1	163.9
1990	388.8	312.2	304.6
2000	896.0	586.2	492.0
Teachers required			
1960	3.3	3.3	3.3
1970	7.3	7.3	7.3
1980	13.3	13.1	13.1
1990	23.3	18.7	18.3
2000	44.8	29.3	24.6

Source: Bruce Herrick and Ricardo Moran, Declining Birth Rates in Chile: Their Effects on Output, Education, Health and Housing, 71 TMP-56 (Santa Barbara, Calif.: General Electric Company-TEMPO, 1972), p. 39, table 16.

Although the differences among the alternative assumptions in the number of new teachers required and the cost of training them are large by the last period considered, the differences in operating costs are comparatively much smaller. Teacher requirements and teacher training show a threefold difference between assumptions A and C, although the corresponding system operation costs differ by only 43 percent because of the more rapidly rising salaries of university personnel under assumption C.

The substantially greater magnitude of operating costs in relation to teacher training cause the relative divergence in total costs between, say, assumptions A and C to be dominated by operating costs, and thus, for the last period, total costs of A exceed those of C by less than 50 percent despite the 300 percent difference in training costs.

TABLE 2.16

University Education: New Teacher Requirements,
Training Costs, and System Operating Costs

| Year | Fertility Assumption | | |
	A	B	C
New teachers required (thousands)			
1970	0.6	0.6	0.6
1980	0.9	0.9	0.9
1990	1.6	0.9	0.8
2000	3.3	1.8	1.1
Teacher training costs*			
1970	2.8	2.8	2.8
1980	4.1	4.0	4.0
1990	7.1	4.0	3.7
2000	15.3	8.2	5.1
System operation costs*			
1970	56.0	56.0	56.0
1980	120.6	121.9	122.0
1990	247.0	222.1	220.2
2000	570.7	439.6	397.2
Total training and operation costs*			
1970	58.8	58.8	58.8
1980	124.7	125.9	126.0
1990	254.1	226.1	223.9
2000	586.0	447.8	402.3

Note: * = Millions of 1960 escudos.

Source: Bruce Herrick and Ricardo Moran, Declining Birth Rates in Chile: Their Effects on Output, Education, Health and Housing, 71 TMP-56 (Santa Barbara, Calif.: General Electric Company-TEMPO, 1972), p. 40, table 17.

Health Care

Demands for health care are affected less dramatically by fertility changes than are demands for education. Fertility declines affect the youngest first, altering their relative and absolute numbers in the population; and these declines are quickly translated into changes in demand for education. Demands for health care are much more evenly spread out, covering all age groups in a population.

As with education, the main expenditure items in the health sector, both now and in the future, can be specified. Requirements for medical personnel, from the highly skilled to the considerably less skilled, are well known or can be readily determined. In addition, two basic types of physical facilities can be distinguished: hospital beds and consulting rooms. These categories of medical personnel and physical facilities do not cover all requirements for the provision of health services; also necessary are administrators, inspectors, and clerical and janitorial personnel, on the one hand, and all the physical instruments of the great metropolitan research hospitals, on the other. The categories, however, do allow quantification of ratios of availability of health services to the user population.

Available Chilean data allowed seven groups of health workers to be individually recognized.* The numbers of each in 1968 were known; values were assigned to their training costs, salaries, attrition rates, and average rates of growth in numbers.[10] In addition, for the hospital beds and examination rooms, construction and operating costs were combined with data on goals for improvements in the ratios between these facilities and the population they serve.

The final important variable to be considered in this investigation of the impact of different fertility conditions on public expenditures for health care is the extent of coverage of the public health system. Survey data of the Ministry of Public Health showed in 1970 that about 73 percent of the population was covered by some sort of public health service, of which SNS was the most prominent. The degree of SNS coverage did not reflect with any degree of accuracy the size of the population receiving health care in the country. Among those not covered by the SNS, some used private health services; others used SNS facilities simply because no private care was available, because the individuals were medical indigents, or both. This was particularly common outside large metropolitan centers. Finally, some who are entitled to SNS services did not use them but

_____

*Physicians, dentists, pharmacists, nurses, midwives, medical technicians, and nurses' auxiliaries.

obtained private health care. These partially offsetting factors tend
to weaken the accuracy of SNS coverage as an index of effective
populationwide coverage.

The historical trend has been one of expanding government-
provided health services, although even if this process continues,
it is unlikely to encompass the entire population in foreseeable future. Some people will continue to buy private health care. Rural
areas, especially in the far north and far south, may remain medi-
cally isolated. However, future extension of coverage seems inevitable. An estimate of its future extent and the numbers of people
covered under the three fertility assumptions appears in Table 2.17.

TABLE 2.17

Projected Extent of Coverage of Government-Provided
Health Services

Year	Extent of Coverage (percent)	Millions of People Covered, Under Fertility Assumption		
		A	B	C
1960	73	5.61	5.61	5.61
1970	73	7.25	6.99	6.97
1980	76	9.97	8.81	8.58
1990	80	14.12	11.22	10.28
2000	85	20.39	14.28	12.30

Source: Bruce Herrick and Ricardo Moran, Declining Birth
Rates in Chile: Their Effects on Output, Education, Health and
Housing, 71 TMP-56 (Santa Barbara, Calif.: General Electric
Company-TEMPO, 1972), p. 49, table 24.

Table 2.18 shows the impact of these numbers on public spending in terms of aggregate operating and capital expenditures. These
expenditures reflect the assumptions that the government pays for
varying amounts of current expenditures, as shown by the data in
Table 2.17, and pays for all expenses and capital costs involved in
human capital formation and in construction of physical facilities.

With traditional (1960) fertility levels, a fivefold increase in
government expenditures between 1970 and 2000 would have to occur
if the postulated medical standards were to be maintained and improved. Even under fertility assumption C, the least demanding
from the standpoint of the provision of health care, more than a
threefold increase would be required.

TABLE 2.18

Projected Government Health Costs
(millions of 1960 escudos)

Year	Fertility Assumption		
	A	B	C
Operating expenditures			
1970	138.0	134.8	134.8
1980	225.0	205.6	202.0
1990	389.0	329.6	308.8
2000	705.8	557.6	498.2
Capital expenditures			
1970	31.4	27.8	27.6
1980	26.6	55.6	32.8
1990	68.8	46.4	37.6
2000	103.0	59.2	45.2
Total expenditures			
1970	169.4	162.6	162.4
1980	271.6	241.2	234.8
1990	457.8	376.0	346.4
2000	809.0	616.8	543.4

Source: Bruce Herrick and Ricardo Moran, Declining Birth
Rates in Chile: Their Effects on Output, Education, Health and
Housing, 71 TMP-56 (Santa Barbara, Calif.: General Electric
Company-TEMPO, 1972), p. 49, table 25.

The projections made here are highly aggregated, tend toward
an artificially stable growth rate, and deliberately exclude many details. No doubt Chilean health experts, particularly those profes-
sionally involved in providing health service to Chile's expanding
population, could develop a more detailed and realistic analytical
framework for assessing the impact of diverse fertility schedules
in the years to come. Although the scope of the present study pre-
cluded such refinements, the author feels confident that such an exercise, in addition to being valuable for national resource allocation, would reinforce the basic conclusions of this section.
    In summary, the faster the population grows, the higher are
the costs that society must sustain (and the greater, accordingly,
is the diversion from other ends) to finance the expansion and operation of an adequate public health system. The validity of this

conclusion is strengthened by the assumptions used, since these
tend to minimize the cost differentials associated with varying fertility levels.

FERTILITY, HUMAN CAPITAL FORMATION,
AND ECONOMIC GROWTH

Fertility has changing effects on educational attainment of
workers and, in turn, on their productivity. Decreased fertility
lowers the number of young people in the population. For any given
educational budget, the resulting reduction in enrollments allows
either more years of school attendance for each student, higher
quality (more costly) education, or both. In any case, lower fertility provides the opportunity to upgrade stocks of human capital,
both in total and on a per capita basis.

Within this frame of reference, the model's initial assumption of a homogeneous labor force is modified by weighting labor inputs differentially according to their respective educational attainment. Although it is easy to assert that more education and higher
productivity raises incomes, the magnitude of these effects under
different fertility assumptions can be derived only through the application of an integrated conceptual and computational model.

Changing fertility eventually affects the size of the labor force.
With the two-factor neoclassical production function used to this
point in the study, the smaller labor force that eventually would result from lower fertility implies (ceteris paribus) correspondingly
lower levels of output.

Previously it was discussed how greater savings out of higher
per capita income could offset the effect of the smaller labor force
for a fairly extended period. It considered the effect in terms of
absolute numbers in a homogeneous population. Thus, that discussion dealt only with physical capital formation. In fact, the possibility exists that when population is smaller and per capita product
higher, the economy also may be able to produce more human capital. If more human capital is formed, the greater productivity of
workers could more than offset their smaller numbers. Then, even
in the restrictive case in which physical capital formation did not
rise, output would be higher. If, in addition, savings and resultant
investment increased, the combined effects of lower fertility, smaller population, higher per capita output, greater human capital formation, and higher labor force productivity would be reinforced by relatively greater amounts of physical capital.

To explore these effects, four levels of educational attainment
are posited. Weights representing the elasticity of output with

respect to the input of labor of each level are attached to them. The weights, β_i, represent the percentage by which output changes when the labor force in a given educational category grows by 1 percent.

Consider the disaggregated production function

$$Y = Z(1 + T)^t K^\alpha L_1^{\beta_1} L_2^{\beta_2} L_3^{\beta_3} L_4^{\beta_4}$$

where Y = national income,

Z = a constant,

T = average annual rate of (disembodied) technological change,

t = number of years elapsed since the base year,

K = physical capital stock,

L_i = number of workers in the ith group,

α = output elasticity with respect to physical capital inputs, and

β_i = output elasticity with respect to the labor input of the ith group.

Constant returns to scale are assumed, that is,

$$\alpha + \sum_i \beta_i = 1$$

and the marginal product of factors is assumed equal to their prices. The estimation of β_i then follows from

$$\frac{\partial Y}{\partial L_i} = W_i = \frac{\beta_i Y}{L_i}$$

where W_i = wage rate for L_i; and thus

$$\beta_i = \frac{W_i L_i}{Y}$$

In this study, human capital formation is assumed to occur exclusively as a result of formal education. Although inclusion of the effects of on-the-job training in the model would have been desirable, no life cycle earnings data existed.

Weighting the labor force involves some considerations that should be made clear. If the weights are constant over time, this implies that the relative elasticities of output with respect to labor inputs in the various educational categories are themselves constant. Alternatively, an initial set of weights using observed relative wage differentials among the educational classes and a final set reflecting the narrower wage structure (and presumed underlying productivity differentials) observed in the industrialized countries can be postulated.

The computer model can then be programmed to interpolate between these two sets of weights as time passes. Because of the limited time available for exploring the education-weighted model, only the constant-weights case is treated. The β_i weights used are derived from the expression already noted above, and are as shown.

Education	Weights
None	$\beta_1 = 0.03$
Primary (1-8)	$\beta_2 = 0.23$
Secondary (9-12)	$\beta_3 = 0.11$
University	$\beta_4 = \underline{0.13}$
Total labor force	0.50

An educational budget proportion is derived as a simple percentage of GNP from United Nations Educational, Social, and Cultural Organization data for Chile and other Latin American countries. Budgeted amounts are allocated among the various classes of education in two stages by the computational model. First, the existing educational plant--square feet of school rooms net of depreciation; teachers net of attrition--is operated to determine current spending.

The second stage involves investing in new educational capacity in terms of both teachers and buildings. Here a variety of alternatives is open. As a preliminary treatment of the allocation problem for new investment expenditures, the model expands the various levels of the system (primary, secondary, and university) by equal proportional amounts to the extent allowed by educational budgets.

The amount of expansion desired, in turn, depends on the age-eligible population, taken from the basic population projections, and on transition matrices describing the passage of students through the three educational levels. These transition matrices allow the calculation of potential educational "demand" in each year.[11] Students pass through the system according to the matrices, following essentially a Markov chain process at each year of age and each calendar year. Students continuing at the same level as the previous year or passing on to a higher level are the potential demanders for education. Dropouts and graduates pass into the nonstudent population and become eligible for labor force participation. Thus, the model tallies the numbers in the population by age, sex, and educational attainment for each calendar year and disaggregates student and nonstudent populations on the basis of budget capabilities to provide education. The resultant numbers in the labor force, disaggregated according to the same variables, also are calculated. The projected numbers in the labor force for 1970-2000, by educational attainment, appear in Table 2.19.

TABLE 2.19

Projected Numbers and Educational Attainment
of the Chilean Labor Force, 1970-2000
(in thousands)

Education	Year	Fertility Assumption		
		A	B	C
None	1970	330	330	330
	1980	255	255	255
	1990	170	170	170
	2000	85	85	85
Elementary (grades 1-8)	1970	1,940	1,940	1,940
	1980	2,605	2,590	2,590
	1990	3,465	3,185	3,150
	2000	4,740	3,635	3,530
Secondary (grades 9-12)	1970	600	600	600
	1980	840	840	840
	1990	1,130	1,150	1,150
	2000	1,510	1,560	1,555
University	1970	100	100	100
	1980	160	160	160
	1990	230	240	240
	2000	320	365	375
Total labor force	1970	2,970	2,970	2,970
	1980	3,865	3,855	3,850
	1990	4,995	4,750	4,725
	2000	6,655	5,695	5,540

Source: Bruce Herrick and Ricardo Moran, Declining Birth
Rates in Chile: Their Effects on Output, Education, Health and
Housing, 71 TMP-56 (Santa Barbara, Calif.: General Electric
Company-TEMPO, 1972), p. 68, table 35.

The economic impact of the education-weighted labor force on
GNP and on GNP per capita is reflected in Table 2.20. The GNP of
the smaller labor force associated with lower fertility is almost exactly offset by the productivity increases attributable to greater educational attainment. As a result of the essential invariance of total
output among the three fertility assumptions in any given year, GNP
per capita rises rapidly, more rapidly in fact than under the assumption

of a homogeneous labor force, as indicated by the comparisons of projected average annual growth in the table.

TABLE 2.20

Projected Chilean GNP and GNP per Capita with Labor
Force Weighted by Educational Attainment, 1960-2000

Output/Growth	Year	Fertility Assumption			Ratios	
		A	B	C	B/A	C/A
GNP (millions						
of 1960 escudos)	1960	4,080	4,080	4,080	1.00	1.00
	1970	6,695	6,710	6,710	1.00	1.00
	1980	10,770	10,885	10,900	1.01	1.01
	1990	17,250	17,550	17,610	1.02	1.02
	2000	27,775	27,905	28,010	1.00	1.01
GNP per capita						
(1960 escudos)	1960	530	530	530	1.00	1.00
	1970	675	700	705	1.04	1.04
	1980	820	940	965	1.14	1.18
	1990	980	1,250	1,370	1.28	1.40
	2000	1,160	1,660	1,935	1.43	1.67
Average annual growth rates, 1960-2000 (percent) Weighted labor force model						
GNP	--	4.91	4.93	4.94	--	--
GNP per capita	--	1.97	2.39	3.28	--	--
Unweighted labor force model						
GNP	--	4.61	4.45	4.40	--	--
GNP per capita	--	1.68	2.43	2.76	--	--

Source: Bruce Herrick and Ricardo Moran, Declining Birth Rates in Chile: Their Effects on Output, Education, Health and Housing, 71 TMP-56 (Santa Barbara, Calif.: General Electric Company-TEMPO, 1972), p. 69, table 36.

The feedback mechanism that leads from lower fertility through higher incomes to higher investment in human capital is clearly a complex one. The methods used in the calculation described above suggest readily a series of extensions that educational and economic planning offices would do well to consider seriously.

Transition matrices, rather than remaining constant over time, could be altered to reflect plausible improvements in entrance, promotion, and retention rates. A variety of budget proportions could be tested. [12] Varying the rates of growth of the different parts of the educational system according to impressions (or empirical studies) of their cost effectiveness would lend an additional element of realism to the study. Allowing wage differentials to vary over time would have similar effects. Consideration of private as well as public expenditures on education would reveal a more complete picture of economywide human capital formation.

Further investigation of the complex economic and demographic interrelationships suggested by the foregoing considerations could prove to be exceptionally fruitful in obtaining a better understanding of any country's potential for human development and economic growth.

CONCLUSIONS

The application to Chile of a projection model that measures the effects of declining fertility on a number of economic variables has been reviewed. Linked demographic and economic models allow quantitative estimation of income per capita and expenditures on a variety of social services under various fertility conditions.

The model goes well beyond earlier and simpler formulations in which the numerator and denominator of the income per capita quotient are projected independently. The linkages between exogenously specified demographic changes and their effects on total output, as influenced by changes in labor supply and capital stock, are the most notable and useful features of the present model. In addition, the penultimate section disaggregated the labor force by educational attainment and productivity to ascertain the effects of lower fertility and as a consequence more rapid human capital formation on productivity and GNP.

The results are highly aggregated, however. As noted, sectoral planners would be quick to increase the level of detail. Although one could say that the overall results of the effects of lower fertility would not be altered by such disaggregation, only the experience of individual countries with their own particular circumstances would demonstrate the matter convincingly.

In a general vein, one could ask whether the form of the projection model somehow predetermines its results. In particular,
are the economic gains shown under lower fertility conditions crucially dependent on the specification of the model? The question
cannot be answered exhaustively here, but the following observations
may be useful. The model has focused on output, its dependence on
inputs, and their relation in turn to demographic change.

Labor force inputs are unequivocally higher with high fertility,
and lower with low, unless participation rates change drastically or
unless individuals' expenditures of effort are demographically influenced. The link between female participation and fertility is not
explored extensively here, but it should be noted that overall participation rates vary only slightly under widely varying conditions of
development. Higher female participation rates during adulthood
are offset by lower rates among the young (schooling) and old (retirement) of both sexes.

Capital formation is linked in the model to per capita incomes.
Private savings are postulated to be determined by an essentially
Keynesian function, and public savings are assumed similarly to be
determined by per capita income. In the model's final extension,
human capital formation is stimulated by the same force.

It is through demographic influences on inputs that output is
affected by fertility variations. Only in this sense can it be said
that the specification of the model "determined" the results that
have been quantified above.

Policy implications are clear. Lower fertility permits a society to engage in consumption and the provision of public services
at levels that would otherwise be unattainable. Failure to grasp this
point would delay tragically the achievement of many of the most
deeply held aspirations of the development process.

DEVELOPED AND DEVELOPING COUNTRIES: CLOSING THE GAP

Douglas L. Maxwell
Richard Brown

The world is experiencing increasing tensions between developing and developed countries. Since World War II, the per capita GNP in the developing world has grown at a lower percentage rate than in the developed world. This section examines the prospects for the future and possible strategies for increasing economic growth in the developing countries, both absolutely and relative to the more developed countries.

Effective methods for inducing growth in developing countries are not now being applied widely. Even during the 20 years of official development assistance, which totaled close to $100 billion, the gap in per capita incomes has grown almost 2 percent annually. There are several explanations for this. First, the population growth rate of the developing countries (Third World) has accelerated from 1 percent before World War I to over 2 1/2 percent today. Better nutrition and certain public health measures such as malaria eradication have contributed to a rise in the life expectancy in the Third World from about 40 years in 1955 to about 53 years today. Also fertility rates rose slightly. Second, as the number of surviving children has risen dramatically, the percentage of the population of labor force age has dropped. Third, the process of economic development is slow, complicated, and involves high levels of internal investment in both physical and human capital.

The work for this paper was completed in part under a contract from the Office of Population of the U.S. Agency for International Development. The authors wish to express their appreciation for the assistance of others, most especially Stephen Enke, who originally conceived this project. Neither USAID nor General Electric necessarily subscribes to these analyses and conclusions.

In 1972 the Third World had an average population growth rate of 2.7 percent and a GNP per capita of $289. The First World (non-Communist developed countries), in contrast, had a population growth rate of 1 percent and a GNP per capita of $3,989. Approximately 20 percent of the world's population, or 650 million people, reside in the First World; and about one-half the world's population, or 1,800 million, live in the Third World. If current population growth rates were maintained, the First World's share of total world population would fall to 15 percent by the year 2000 and the Third World's share would rise to almost 60 percent.

Economic growth in the Third World during the period 1955-72 has been significant--on the order of 4 percent per year in real GNP. But since the population growth rate has averaged 2.5 percent per year, economic growth has had a smaller impact on per capita income.

The impetus of this section is the development debate that started when development assistance began after World War II. The strategies for promoting development have been discussed at length elsewhere, for example by Lester Pearson;[13] but the particular thrust of this effort is to analyze, through the use of a simulation model, the development trade-offs of the following strategies to achieve sustained long-term growth in Third World output per capita: increased official assistance, increased internal savings, increased educational investment, and decreased fertility.

A two-sector economic-demographic simulation model is used to examine the prospects of developing countries for per capita economic growth both absolutely and relative to the developed countries. Each of the two worlds has an economic-demographic model somewhat similar to that described in Enke's contribution to Chapter 1. As in that model, output depends on capital, labor (here including human capital), and technical progress. These factors enter into standard Cobb-Douglas production functions. The employed labor force depends on the size and age-sex composition of the population. The aggregate saving depends on the saving rates and GNPs in the two worlds. An important innovation is the inclusion of an educational submodel, which calculates current enrollments and school costs and also the educational attainment embodied in the labor force. The Cobb-Douglas production function treats this attainment as a contribution to the productivity of the labor force. Other additions include interactions between the two regions in the form of migration, foreign investment in the developing world in response to the relative scarcity of capital, and official assistance. This investment and official assistance is counterbalanced by interest earned on foreign-owned capital in the developing world plus a flow of real resources in the form of net exports from the developed to the developing world. The data were obtained from standard sources including the United Nations, International Labor Office, and the U.S. Agency for International Development.

The model is applied to only two sets of countries. The non-Communist developing countries (or Third World) constitute one world and the non-Communist developed countries (or First World) constitute the other. The omitted countries include not only the Communist (Second World) countries but also some middle-income and oil-producing countries. An implicit assumption is that over a 50-year period, the migration, net investment, and net exports (exports less imports) between the omitted countries and included countries will be small. Of course, there may be a large trade and investment flow, but no large net flow. For details see Map 2.1.

A 50-year projection is made from 1972-2022. Variables such as total capital stock and existing educational attainment in the labor force are obtained partially from the calibration of the model over a 1955-72 historical period. Accelerated fertility reduction, increased domestic savings, increased education, and increased official assistance are compared as methods of raising per capita incomes in the Third World over the projection period.

The simulation runs show that a fertility reduction has a large impact on Third World per capita incomes. In a projection with constant fertility, Third World per capita income reaches $1,057 by 2022, whereas a 50 percent fertility decline results in a per capita income of $1,365 (starting from $289 in 1972). Other runs indicate that increased official assistance has a surprisingly low impact on economic growth, although it does add to the Third World income in the year received. This occurs because only a portion of official assistance is invested and because this new official investment replaces some of the private investment.

The following describes the mathematical model used and its application to a 50-year projection. Additional projections show the effects of alternative policies, and a conclusion discusses the policy implications.

DESCRIPTION OF THE TWO WORLDS MODEL

The Two Worlds Model is a two-region economic-demographic simulation model with the First World as one region and the Third World as the other region. The factors of production are capital, labor, and the educational attainment of labor. The demographic submodel is described first, then the educational submodel, and finally the economic submodel.

Demographic Submodel

The demographic submodel influences but is not influenced by the rest of the model. The population is divided into one-year cohorts

MAP 2.1

Two Worlds Country Division

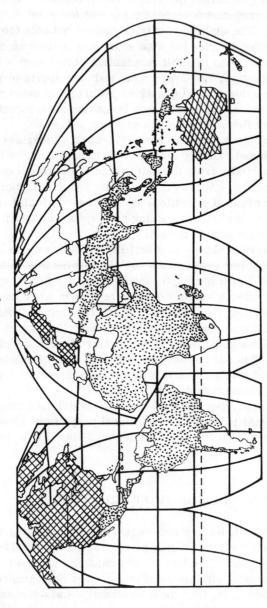

▨ First World or developed countries: Australia, Canada, Japan, New Zealand, Puerto Rico, United States, and non-Communist Europe, excluding Greece, Portugal, and Spain.

⣿ Third World or developing countries: the Americas, Africa, and Asia, except those listed elsewhere.

☐ Omitted countries: (1) Communist countries; (2) oil-exporting countries: Kuwait, Libya, Qatar, Saudi Arabia, United Arab Emirates, and Venezuela; (3) middle-income countries: Argentina, Cyprus, Greece, Hong Kong, Malta, Namibia (Southwest Africa), Portugal, Singapore, South Africa, Spain, Trinidad, and Tobago.

and categorized both by sex and by residence in the First or Third World. (As a slight simplification, all persons of age 65 or more in the same sex-region category are counted together.)

Each year the size of each cohort is calculated from the corresponding cohort of the previous year by the use of survival rates, with the youngest cohort depending on births. Births are determined by applying age specific fertility rates to the female population of child-bearing age. The size of each cohort is modified slightly by migration from the Third to the First World, but the migration is so slight that the First and Third World demographic submodels are largely independent of each other. The labor force is determined by applying age- and sex-specific labor force participation rates to the relevant populations.

Educational Submodel

The educational submodel uses exogenous enrollment rates applied to the school age population to calculate the enrollment in each grade. The enrollment rates vary by region and time. As with physical capital, the human capital resulting from school attendance is valued at cost. Educational costs increase with grade level. The most important inputs into the schooling process are the student's time and the teacher's time. The student's time becomes more valuable as he progresses through the school system, being taught by teachers with higher qualifications and sharing the teacher with fewer students (lower student-teacher ratio) at higher grades. The amount spent on a cohort is added to the cumulative educational value-added of that cohort. This educational value-added is retained by the cohort as it passes through its years of labor force participation. The overall educational value-added is calculated for the labor force and used to adjust the productivity of labor in the economic submodel. The educational value-added is the only form of human capital in the model.

Economic Submodel

The Cobb–Douglas production function for each world is

$$GDP = A(1 + q)^t K^u L^v E^w \qquad (2.1)$$

where GDP is gross domestic product, A is a constant, q is the rate of technical progress, K is physical capital, L is labor, and E is the total stock of education embodied in the labor force.* The capital

---

*The capital, labor, and educational attainment from the previous year are used in calculating this year's production. The

stock is augmented each year by the savings generated during the
year. The saving in each world is calculated by applying the saving
rate for that world to the gross product of that world. *

Interactions Between the Two Worlds

Each year there are flows of migration, official assistance,
investment, interest, and trade between the worlds. The least significant is the migration flow. The total size of net migration to the
First World is calculated as a percent of the First World population,
but the age and sex structure is determined by applying age- and sex-
specific rates to the Third World population.

The economic interactions involve a distinction between gross
domestic product, GDP, and gross national product, GNP. The capital stock in the Third World is partly owned by First World investors.
(Since no distinction is made between debt and equity, the phrase
"owned by" should be interpreted as including "mortgaged to.") The
earnings on this capital are included in First World GNP and Third
World GDP. Algebraically,

$$GNP1 = GDP1 + EARN$$
$$GNP3 = GDP3 - EARN$$

$$(2.2)$$

where EARN is the net return to First World owned capital located
in the Third World. (Any Third World owned capital in the First
World is netted out.)

The official assistance is calculated as a percent of First
World GNP. A certain fraction of this is assumed added to the
Third World capital stock. Algebraically,

$$OA = a \cdot GNP1$$
$$K3_t = K3_{t-1} + c \cdot OA + PI$$

$$(2.3)$$

---

production function is identically equal to GDP $= A(1 + q)^t K^u L^{v-w} E^w$
where $E = E/L$ is the average educational attainment of the work
force.

*The Third World initially has a lower savings rate than the
First World. The model assumes that this is a result of the attempt
to consume nearer First World levels than income warrants. If
relative incomes rise, the savings rate of the Third World would approach the First World savings rate. In the runs presented here,
this effect was so small that practically no change occurred in the
savings rate of the developing world.

where OA is official assistance, K3 is the Third World capital stock, PI is net private investment (both from the First World and the Third World), a and c are appropriate fractions, and t is a time subscript.

Private investment in the Third World by First World investors occurs because capital earns a higher return in the Third World than in the First World. The marginal product of capital in each world can be calculated from the production function. Algebraically,

$$MPK = \frac{u \cdot GDP}{K} = \frac{u \cdot A \, (1+q)^t K^u L^v E^w}{K} \qquad (2.4)$$

or, with constant returns to scale,

$$MPK = A(1+q)^t \, (L/K)^v \, (E/K)^w \qquad (2.5)$$

The abundance of labor in the Third World and the high average level of education in the First World partially offset each other. The capital-labor ratio dominates, however, producing a higher marginal product of capital in the Third World. Initially, the marginal product of capital in the Third World exceeds that of the First World by a certain factor. Algebraically,

$$MPK3 = MPK1 \, (1 + RISK) \qquad (2.6)$$

where RISK may include both elements of risk and predictable elements such as high taxes. Each year, First World investors invest enough to drive down the Third World return to capital to the First World level plus the risk factor. In this manner the foreign private investment FPI of the Third World is determined,* so equation (2.6) is satisfied with the following algebraic results:

---

*The computation of the proportion of new investment proceeds as follows: the new labor force L and the education attainment E are projected. The only remaining unknown in calculating MPK is the size of the capital stock. The total two-world capital formation ΔK is known from the savings rates and official assistance. As a first approximation,

$$\Delta K3_t = \Delta K_t \left(\frac{\Delta K3_{t-1}}{\Delta K_{t-1}} \right), \quad \Delta K1_t = \Delta K_t - \Delta K3_t$$

MPK3 and MPK1 are then calculated. If MPK3 > MPK1 (1 + RISK), then $\Delta K3_t$ is lowered, and so on. The value of $\Delta K3_t$ and $\Delta K1_t$ is

$$K1_t = K1_{t-1} + S1_t - FPI$$
$$K3_t = K3_{t-1} + S3_t + FPI + c \cdot OA \tag{2.7}$$

where S is the amount saved from GNP and $c \cdot OA$ is the fraction of official assistance that is invested. [S3 and FPI constitute the PI of equation 2.3.]

The foreign private investment and official assistance constitute a flow of resources to the developing world. This is partly offset by interest on the accumulated claims. For the private sector, this is calculated as follows:

$$PCLAIMS_t = PCLAIMS_{t-1} + FPI_t$$
$$PINT_t \quad = r_p \cdot PCLAIMS_{t-1} \tag{2.8}$$

where PCLAIMS is the net stock of accumulated private claims by First World investors, PINT is the amount of private interest, and r_p is the private interest rate.

The official assistance is treated similarly, although a much lower interest rate is used. (If grants are involved there is no accumulation of claims or repayment of interest.) Algebraically,

$$OCLAIMS_t = OCLAIMS_{t-1} + OL_t$$
$$OINT_t \quad = r_o \cdot OCLAIMS_{t-1} \tag{2.9}$$

where OL_t is the nongrant portion of official assistance and r_o is the low official interest rate.

The model does not project gross exports and imports between the two worlds, but only net exports (exports less imports) from the First to the Third World. It is assumed that the net exports equal the excess of official assistance and investment over the return interest payments. * Thus there is a transfer of real resources to the Third World.

---

found by successive approximation. The foreign private investment FPI is then calculated.

$$FPI = \Delta K3 - S3 - c \cdot OA$$

where S3 is Third World saving from GNP3 and $c \cdot OA$ is capital formation due to official assistance.

*If the repayments grow faster than new assistance and investment, then the First World might reach a position as a mature creditor where income from previous investments abroad exceeds new net

X = FPI + OA - PINT - OINT

where X is net exports. (The algebra allows X to be negative--but that does not happen within the 50-year projection period.) It is assumed that the Third World as a whole would neither accumulate nor draw down reserves over the projection period.

THE HALF CENTURY PROJECTIONS

Accelerated fertility reduction, increased domestic savings, and increased education are compared as methods for raising Third World per capita incomes. Official assistance is viewed as a method by which developed countries can assist in raising Third World income. The effects of restrictions on private investment by the First World in the Third World are explored. A standard, plausible, projection for the period 1972-2022 is made, simulating the effects of alternative policies. (For standard run assumptions and results, see the appendix to this section.) These simulations also reveal important long-term trends that are relatively insensitive to a wide range of assumptions.

The Standard Demographic-Economic Projection

Assuming a continued rise in life expectancies in the developing world from about 50 in 1972 to 60 years in 2022, it was found that a 23 percent drop in the total fertility rate is needed just to keep the population growth rate from rising. When this drop in fertility is spread evenly over the period, the population growth rate of the developing countries stays at a high 2.7 percent per year. In the standard run, it was assumed that the total fertility rate declines 23 percent in the Third World and remains constant in the First World. The GNP per capita (in 1972 dollars) of the developing countries under the standard assumption grew from $287 to $1,181, a relatively rapid growth rate of 2.86 percent a year.

The labor force growth rates of the two worlds diverge sharply in the projection period. During the period 1955-72 the First World labor force grew at 1.9 percent a year, while the Third World labor force grew at a slightly more rapid 2.0 percent. However, in the standard projection, the First World labor force grows at only 0.8

---

foreign investment (including official assistance as a low-interest investment). At that point, the Third World would start making net exports to the First World.

percent a year, while the Third World labor force grows at 2.8 percent a year--a 2 percentage point difference.

A large amount of First World private investment in the Third World is induced by the fast growth of the Third World labor force relative to the First World. New investment is assumed to occur whenever the productivity of capital in the Third World, adjusted for risk, rises above that of capital in the First World. The relatively rapid growth of the labor force in the developing countries over the next 50 years thus draws in a large amount of private foreign investment.

Over the 50-year projection period, the GNP per capita grows at a higher annual rate in the Third World (2.86 percent) than in the First World (2.51 percent). However, the 2022 Third World GNP per capita of $1,181 falls short of the 1955 First World level of $2,103. (Although comparisons of different regions 67 years apart are treacherous, the authors have tried to correct all figures to 1972 dollars.)

The period 1955-72 was a period of slow growth for the Third World relative to the First World. In 1955, the GNP per capita of the First World was 10.3 times that of the Third World. By 1972, that ratio had risen to 13.8, indicating relatively slower growth in the developing world. However, most of the gap in growth rates occurred at the beginning of the period.

All the projections that have been made indicate a further slight decline in Third World per capita GNP relative to that of the First World, but then a turnabout should occur with continued relative growth for the rest of the projection. In the standard projection, the ratio reaches a peak of 14.4 in 1981 and then improves to 11.7 by the end of the projection in 2022. Thus the relative per capita GNP of the developing world ends up higher at the end of the projection than in 1972, although not back to the levels of 1955. Of course, the absolute level of GNP per capita rises each year in the developing countries.

Accelerated Fertility Decline

For the Third World, accelerated fertility decline has a substantial impact on income per capita growth. Each drop of 1 percent in the developing country total fertility rate over the 50-year projection causes approximately a 0.5 percent rise in Third World GNP per capita in 2022, a 0.66 percent fall in the child dependency ratio in 2022, and a 0.5 percent rise in the proportion of the population in the labor force in 2022 (see Table 2.21).

TABLE 2.21

Alternative Fertility Assumptions for Developing Countries

| | 50-Year Drop in Total Fertility Rate[a] | | | |
	0 percent	23 percent[b]	35 percent	50 percent
Final year GNP per capita	$1,059	$1,181	$1,256	$1,365
Final year child dependency ratio	90.0	73.4	64.5	53.2
Final year proportion of population in labor force	30.2	33.1	35.0	37.6
Ratio of First World to Third World GNP per capita	12.9	11.7	11.0	10.1

[a]These runs differ only in the fertility rate assumptions. The reduction in rate is evenly spread over the projection period.

[b]Standard run; for assumptions, see the appendix to this chapter.

Source: Computer output supplied by authors.

Increased Domestic Savings

Increasing the domestic savings rate in the developing world has a positive effect on Third World GNP per capita growth. The standard assumption is a nearly constant savings rate of 8.6 percent of Third World GNP. The domestic net savings rate must almost triple to cause the same increase in per capita GNP as a decline in the final total fertility from 23 percent to 50 percent. However, the consumption per capita is even lower than the standard run. Part of the increased savings displace private investment from the First World. This reduces the benefits of increased saving (see Table 2.22).

Increased Education

Increased education offers another alternative for increasing per capita income growth. To achieve the same effect on growth of

income per capita as a fertility reduction of 50 percent, school enrollment rates would have to rise more than in the standard run. The
average schooling of the labor force rises to about eight years of
school in the standard run, but the average must rise to about nine
years to achieve a per capita income of $1,370 in 2022. In the final
year of the projection, educational expenditures would be not 3.7 but
4.5 percent of GNP. This additional 0.8 percent of Third World GNP
is not nearly as large as the required 13.8 percent for increased
domestic savings. To a large extent, this is due to the fact that education is complementary to foreign private investment whereas domestic investment in physical capital is competitive.

TABLE 2.22

Alternative Savings Rate Assumptions
for Developing Countries

Final Net Savings Rate[a] (percent)	Final GNP per Capita (dollars)	Assumed 50-Year Drop in Total Fertility (percent)	Final Third World Consumption per Capita (dollars)
8.6[b]	1,181	23	987
14.6	1,257	23	955
22.4	1,359	23	914
8.8[c]	1,365	50	1,137

[a]Third World net savings rate for the initial year is 8.6 percent. The rate rises uniformly over the projection period. (The
First World net savings rate is a constant 14.5 percent.)

[b]Standard run.

[c]This is the 50 percent fertility decline presented in Table
2.21. The savings rate changes very slightly here and in the standard run as explained in the footnote on page 90.

Source: Computer output supplied by authors.

The model assumes that the curriculum will be designed to
teach needed skills and that students will be directed into the programs with the highest economic returns. In some developing countries, the rate of return to lower levels of education is over 30 percent, but the rate of return to higher education is less than 5 percent.

Clearly, in such cases enrollment should be expanded at the lower levels. (At the end of the standard projection, the return is a uniform 24 percent.)

Higher enrollment rates and a more rapid fertility decline are mutually reinforcing. In Anne Williams' "The Determinants of Fertility in Developing Countries," which appears in Chapter 3, evidence is cited that education, especially of females, reduces fertility rates. Such an effect is not included in the model; but this means that a more rapid fertility decline is easier to achieve with more ambitious enrollment increases, provided females are included. An additional projection with both the higher enrollment rates and the 50 percent fertility decline shows that the percent of GNP spent on education is no higher than in the standard run. This is a result of both the higher GNP and the lower ratio of school children to work force in this projection. The combination of rapid fertility decline and higher enrollment rates results in a Third World per capita GNP $400 higher than in the standard run. Since the higher enrollment rates facilitate fertility reductions and fertility reductions cut the cost of education, this combination is especially powerful (see Table 2.23).

TABLE 2.23

Alternative Educational Investment Policies
for Developing Countries

Final Educational Expenditures as a Percent of GNP[a]	Final GNP per Capita (dollars)	Assumed 50-Year Drop in Total Fertility (percent)	Ratio of First World to Third World GNP per Capita
3.7	1,181	23	11.7
4.5[b]	1,370	23	10.0
3.0	1,365	50	10.1
3.7[b]	1,581	50	8.7

[a]The allocation of GNP for the initial year is 2.62 percent.

[b]Represents a set of enrollment rate targets where Third World enrollment rates rise three-quarters of the way toward 1955 First World rates. Under standard assumptions, the rise was one-half.

Source: Computer output supplied by authors.

Rising Official Assistance

Official assistance increases per capita GNP in the Third World, but the improvement is largest when the assistance augments education rather than physical capital. The hope for the past 25 years has been that development assistance, largely for physical capital, would play an important role in accelerating the growth of developing countries' GNP. To date the results are not dramatic.

To study the effects of official assistance directed toward physical capital, the standard projection (which assumes that the current 0.3 percent of First World GNP is allocated to official assistance) is contrasted with a rise in official assistance to the UNCTAD goal* of 1 percent of First World GNP. Both projections assume that 40 percent of official assistance augments the Third World capital stock--in the authors' judgment this is a high estimate considering that the fungibility of resources makes it easy to use outside aid to free domestic funds for other uses. Increased official assistance has only a moderate effect on final Third World GNP per capita--less than a 1 percent improvement after 50 years. The effects on final consumption per capita are greater, since by assumption 60 percent of official assistance is consumed. Under these assumptions, official assistance must rise to 22 percent of First World GNP to have the same effect on developing countries' GNP per capita as a 50 percent fertility decline! To achieve the same effect on consumption per capita as a 50 percent fertility decline, official assistance must rise to 8.8 percent of First World GNP.

There are several reasons for the relative ineffectiveness of official assistance. First, the model assumes only 40 percent of official assistance augments Third World capital stock, since even if official assistance is given for a particular investment project, it may end up freeing domestic funds that would otherwise be spent on that project. Second, increased official assistance has a larger relative impact in 1972 when the total First World GNP is about five times the size of Third World GNP.† By 2022, First World GNP is only 37 percent larger than Third World GNP. Thus official assistance declines in importance as a percentage of Third World GNP.

---

*United Nations Committee on Trade and Development (UNCTAD) adopted this goal in 1968. Only official assistance (no private investment) is counted here.

†Official assistance can have a substantial effect on consumption per capita in the short run. A rise to the UNCTAD goal by 1980 adds $8 to 1982 Third World GNP per capita, which is higher than the $3 additional for rapid fertility decline projection.

Third, these projections assume that official assistance increases physical investment rather than education. Since this investment is competitive with foreign private investment, less help is available from that source.

Increased official assistance has a much bigger impact on Third World GNP if the increase goes into appropriate education rather than the physical capital stock. An increase in official assistance to 1.9 percent of First World GNP is necessary to have the same impact on GNP per capita as a 50 percent fertility decline. This greater gain from education stems in part from its role in attracting foreign private investment, since human capital is a complementary factor. Even though official assistance takes a smaller percent of First World GNP to achieve the same impact through education, 1.9 percent is nearly double the UNCTAD goal and is rising at the end of the projection (see Table 2.24).

TABLE 2.24

Different Official Assistance Assumptions
for Developing Countries

Final Official Assistance as a Percent of First World GNP	Final GNP per Capita (dollars)	Assumed 50-Year Fertility Drop (percent)	Final Consumption per Capita (dollars)	Type of Official Assistance
0.3[a]	1,181	23	987	loan[b]
1.0	1,195	23	1,002	grant
8.8	1,300	23	1,137	grant
0.3	1,365	50	1,137	loan[b]
22.0	1,365	23	1,366	grant
1.9[c]	1,365	23	1,159	grant

Note: Forty percent of official assistance augments Third World capital stock unless otherwise noted.

[a]Standard run.

[b]The interest rates are so low that the loan is almost equivalent to a grant.

[c]Forty percent of official assistance is assumed to augment Third World educational expenditures.

Source: Computer output supplied by authors.

Third World Restrictions on
Foreign Private Investment

The policy of restricting private investment from the First
World is considered here because some developing countries do limit
the amount of foreign investment to the extent of avoiding investments
that are mutually beneficial to the Third World country and the First
World investor. Such restrictions affect the trade-offs between the
various strategies for development. Although this policy increases
the fraction of physical capital that is locally owned, it lowers the
amount of capital with which local workers (with their human capital)
can work. Over the next 50 years, a restriction of private investment from the First World to the present percentage of Third World
GNP would lower GNP per capita in 2022 more than 12 percent relative to the standard projection. The smaller amount of capital per
laborer is responsible for this (see Table 2.25).

TABLE 2.25

Effects on Developing Countries of Restricting
Foreign Private Investment

Final Foreign Private Investment as Percent of Third World GNP[a]	Final GNP per Capita (dollars)	Assumed 50-Year Drop in Total Fertility (percent)	Ratio of First World to Third World GNP per Capita
5.4[b]	1,181	23	11.7
1.5	1,035	23	13.8

[a]In both projections, the First World initially makes net private investments in the Third World equal to 1.5 percent of Third
World GNP. In the second projection, this investment is restricted
to 1.5 percent throughout the projection.

[b]Standard run.

Source: Computer output supplied by authors.

It does not follow, of course, that artificial stimulation of investment or uncritical acceptance of all investment proposals would
be beneficial. However, a government following a policy of limiting
mutually beneficial projects would find development trade-offs

different from those presented here. In particular, those policies
that increase physical capital per worker (higher savings, lower
fertility rate, and obtaining official assistance) would increase in
attractiveness, but increasing the educational level of the labor force
no longer would help induce more foreign private investment.

CONCLUSIONS

An economic-demographic model is used to compare various
methods of raising Third World per capita incomes. The model is
in the tradition of Coale-Hoover and Enke but includes investment in
human capital and foreign private investment in the Third World.

To produce a 1 percent increase in per capita incomes to
$1,193 over the 2022 standard value of $1,181, one of the following
must be done: achieve a 2 percentage point additional drop in the
fertility rate (25 percent drop instead of 23)--about 0.12 fewer children per couple; increase school expenditures by 0.06 percent of
GNP (from 3.7 percent); increase the savings rate from 8.6 to 9.6
percent of GNP; or increase official assistance to 0.9 percent of
First World GNP from the present 0.3 percent. The equivalences
would be somewhat different if they were measured from a different
base (for example, a run with a different fertility assumption), or if
the criterion were different (for example, consumption per capita
instead of GNP per capita). The first three are alternatives from
which developing countries can choose. Official assistance can be
offered only by the First World.

If it costs $40 or less to prevent a birth,* then the fertility rate
drop involves the smallest costs; increases in school budgets are
next smallest. Of course, it is assumed that school budget increases
would be spent productively. It also should be noted that education of
females is important to reducing fertility.

Official assistance can be an important aid in raising consumption levels in the short run but is of less value in raising Third World
GNP over the longer term.

Increased saving rates are much more costly as a way of increasing GNP per capita. Consumption per capita actually will be

---

*Monetary incentives to reducing fertility may involve negli-
gible resource costs and might even improve the distribution of income. However, there are possible problems with irreversible
methods of fertility control or with payments that exceed the value
of net external costs (costs less benefits) to society. These external
costs are hard to measure.

lower over the 50 years than with standard savings rates. Any increased consumption could only occur after 2022.

One beneficial policy to the Third World is the provision of a reasonable climate for private investment from the First World. Some costs are associated with such a policy, since fraud must be detected and prevented and Third World negotiators must be knowledgeable enough to ask for reasonable terms. It is not necessary that every sector of the economy be open to foreign investment as long as enough is open to free domestic savings for those sectors closed to the outside. It is likely that controlling shares in some enterprises must be available to attract much foreign investment, but a portion of the investment might be obtained in the form of noncontrolling equity or debt.

Official assistance can only be offered by the First World. In the short run, official assistance is one of the fastest methods of raising consumption per capita in the Third World. For example, a rise to 0.6 percent (from 0.3 percent) of First World GNP devoted to official assistance raises 1982 Third World consumption by 1 percent. This underscores the need for official assistance now while Third World consumption is at its lowest level of the 50-year projection period. As the aggregate GNP of the Third World increases relative to the First World, official assistance becomes less powerful. By 2022, foreign aid is of negligible importance in raising Third World GNP per capita.

In conclusion, the best policy for the Third World seems to be a mutually reinforcing combination of increasing school enrollments, especially female ones, and directly promoting fertility reduction. Allowing foreign investment with appropriate safeguards is also important for maximum growth. The First World should view official assistance as an important way of increasing consumption levels now, although it is not an efficient means of promoting long-term economic development.

APPENDIX: STANDARD RUN ASSUMPTIONS AND RESULTS

Demographic Assumptions

	1972	2022
Life expectancy		
First World	71.1	74.2
Survival rate schedule[14]	west	west
Third World	49.8	60.2
Survival rate schedule[15]	east	west
Total fertility rate		
First World	2.43	2.43
Third World	6.60	5.05
Migration (Third to First)		
Percent of First World population	0.05	0.05

(These assumptions generate a Third World population growth
rate of an approximately constant 2.7 percent a year.)

Economic Assumptions

Cobb-Douglas function parameters
    Elasticity of capital = 0.35
    Elasticity of labor   = 0.65
    Elasticity of average education = 0.40
    Annual technological change   = 1.0 percent
Prices in constant purchasing power equivalents of 1972 U.S. dollars
Initial capital output ratio
    First World = 2.5
    Third World = 2.3
Net savings rate (initial)
    First World = 14.5 percent of GNP
    Third World = 8.6 percent of GNP
Capital flows
    Private net foreign investment (First to Third)--rises from 1.5
        percent of Third World GNP to 5.4 percent of Third World
        GNP based on higher returns to capital in the Third World.
    Official assistance--a constant 0.3 percent of First World GNP
        over the period.
Education enrollment rates
    First World rates rise--the largest increase being college level
        rates, which double
    Third World rates rise one-half the way to First World 1955 levels
Labor force participation rates remain constant over the projection
    period.

TABLE 2.26

Third World Demographic Projection

	1972	1977	1982	1992	2002	2022
Population						
Total (in millions)	1,805	2,055	2,339	3,055	4,005	6,818
Aged 0–14	773	879	997	1,299	1,702	2,783
Aged 15–64	973	1,105	1,259	1,643	2,157	3,792
Aged 65+	59	71	83	113	146	243
Population growth rates (in percent)						
Crude birth rate	4.42	4.34	4.30	4.22	4.02	3.64
Crude death rate	1.74	1.68	1.64	1.52	1.30	0.93
Natural increase	2.68	2.66	2.66	2.70	2.71	2.71
Migration rate	-0.02	-0.02	-0.02	-0.01	-0.01	-0.01
Population growth rate	2.66	2.64	2.64	2.69	2.70	2.70
Population parameters						
Total fertility rate	6.60	6.42	6.27	5.97	5.66	5.04
Life expectancy	49.50	50.30	51.30	53.30	55.50	60.20
Dependents (in percent)						
Child dependency ratio	79.4	79.5	79.2	79.1	78.5	73.4
Old age dependency ratio	6.1	6.3	6.7	6.9	6.8	6.5
Total dependency ratio	85.5	85.8	85.9	86.0	85.3	79.9
School age (6–14)						
Percent of population	22.8	23.1	23.2	23.0	23.1	22.5
Percent of population aged 15–64	42.3	43.0	43.2	42.8	42.6	40.5
Labor force						
Total (in millions)	581	659	750	980	1,289	2,263
Percent of population	32.2	32.1	32.1	32.1	32.2	33.2

TABLE 2.27

First World Demographic Projection

	1972	1977	1982	1992	2002	2022
Population						
Total (in millions)	640	669	701	762	821	943
Aged 0-14	163	163	172	185	190	214
Aged 15-64	405	424	443	477	521	582
Aged 65+	72	80	86	100	110	147
Population growth rates (in percent)						
Crude birth rate	1.81	1.80	1.78	1.74	1.70	1.63
Crude death rate	0.95	0.95	0.94	0.95	1.05	1.08
Natural increase	0.86	0.85	0.84	0.79	0.65	0.55
Migration rate	0.05	0.05	0.05	0.05	0.05	0.05
Population growth rate	0.91	0.90	0.89	0.84	0.70	0.60
Population parameters						
Total fertility	2.44	2.44	2.44	2.44	2.44	2.44
Life expectancy	71.00	71.30	71.60	72.30	72.90	74.20
Dependents (in percent)						
Child dependency ratio	40.1	38.9	38.8	38.8	36.5	36.8
Old age dependency ratio	17.8	19.1	19.4	20.8	21.0	25.2
Total dependency ratio	57.9	58.0	58.2	59.6	57.5	62.0
School age (6-14)						
Percent of population	14.8	14.5	14.2	14.5	13.7	13.5
Percent of population aged 15-64	23.4	22.8	22.4	23.9	21.5	21.8
Labor force						
Total (in millions)	324	341	358	389	425	481
Percent of population	50.6	50.9	51.1	51.0	51.7	51.0

TABLE 2.28

Economic Projection

	1972	1977	1982	1992	2002	2022
Gross product						
First World (in billions of dollars)	2,553	3,094	3,742	5,290	7,336	12,472
Third World (in billions of dollars)	521	663	867	1,514	2,653	8,051
GNP per capita						
First World (in dollars)	3,989	4,622	5,340	6,942	8,938	13,759
Third World (in dollars)	289	323	371	496	662	1,181
Ratio of First World to Third World	13.8	14.3	14.4	14.0	13.5	11.7
Educational attainment						
First World (index)	45.4	49.3	53.0	59.5	65.4	75.5
Third World (index)	9.1	9.9	11.0	13.6	16.5	23.0
Annual increase in capital stock						
First World (in billions of dollars)	361	419	495	664	871	1,289
Third World (in billions of dollars)	56	89	125	236	424	1,289
Foreign sector (in billions of dollars)						
Net exports (First to Third)	4.6	16.2	20.2	29.2	46.1	94.0
Net interest (Third to First)						
Official	1.4	- 1.8	2.2	3.3	4.8	9.0
Private	5.6	13.5	24.6	59.2	113.7	367.9
Net investment (First to Third)						
Official assistance	5.5	6.5	7.6	10.4	14.4	23.9
Private investment	6.1	25.0	39.3	81.2	150.3	446.9

NOTES

Economic Effects of Chilean Fertility Decline
Bruce H. Herrick

1. Instituto de Economia y Planificacion, La economia de
Chile en el periodo 1950-1963 (Santiago: Univ. de Chile, 1963).
2. United Nations, Yearbook of National Accounts Statistics
(New York: United Nations, 1973), Vol. 1.
3. The apparent sharp jump in the birth rate in 1953 is a statistical artifact. For details, see Bruce Herrick and Ricardo Moran,
Declining Birth Rates in Chile: Their Effects on Output, Education,
Health and Housing, 71 TMP-56 (Santa Barbara, Calif.: General
Electric Company-TEMPO, 1972).
4. Jose Pugo et al., "Efectos de la aplicacion y difusion de
sistemas de control de natalidad en el area hospitalaria norte de
Santiago de Chile y en mujeres tratadas en la clinica obstetrica de
la Universidad de Chile," Revista chilena de obstetricia y ginecologia
32 (1967): 220-27; Anibal Faundes, German Rodriguez-Galant, and
Onofre Avendano, "The San Gregorio Experimental Family Planning
Program: Changes Observed in Fertility and Abortion Rates,"
Demography 5, no. 2 (1969): 836-46; and Benjamin Viel and S.
Lucero, "Analysis of Three Years' Experience with IUDs Among
Women in the Western Area of the City of Santiago," American
Journal of Obstetrics and Gynecology 106 (March 1970): 765-75.
5. The CELADE projections (Julio Morales, Chile: Nuevas
proyecciones de poblacion por sexo y grupos de edades, 1960-2000
[Santiago: CELADE, 1969], series A, no. 99) evolved from earlier
CELADE estimates (Leonel Alvarez, Proyeccion de la poblacion de
Chile por sexo y grupos de edad, 1960-2000 [Santiago: CELADE,
1966], series A, no. 84). These projections, in turn, were given
official status by the (Chilean) Corporacion de Fomento de la Pro-
duccion (CORFO) (1970).
6. Some empirical support for such weights in Chile appears
in Arnold Harberger and Marcelo Selowsky, "Key Factors in the
Economic Growth of Chile," Cornell University Conference on the
Next Decade of Latin American Development, April 1966. Further
details about the weights chosen and the basis for their selection appear in Herrick and Moran, op. cit., Appendix A.
7. Some empirical evidence on the speed of technological
change appears in J. R. Behrman, "Sectoral Elasticities of Substitution Between Capital and Labor in a Developing Economy: Time
Series Analysis in the Case of Postwar Chile," Econometrica 40,
no. 2 (March 1972): 311-26.

8. An earlier version of this paper devoted attention to housing as well. For that subsection, see Herrick and Moran, op. cit., pp. 51-64, and Appendix C.

9. Ibid. Details concerning the sources of these estimates and some of the interesting problems that accompanied them appear in that book.

10. Ibid.

11. The matrices for Chile were derived from the 1960 census and from single-year transition matrices for 1967-70 provided by the Planning office of the Ministry of Education. See R. Stone, Demographic Accounting and Model-Building (Paris: OECD, 1971) for a more general treatment.

12. In one sensitivity test reported in Herrick and Moran, op. cit., pp. 70-71, results proved insensitive to changes of 10 percent in the proportion of the budget allocated to education.

Developed and Developing Countries:
Closing the Gap
Douglas L. Maxwell and Richard Brown

13. Lester B. Pearson, Partners in Development (New York: Praeger Publishers, 1969).

14. From Ansley J. Coale and Paul Demeny, Regional Model Life Tables and Stable Populations (Princeton: Princeton University Press, 1966).

15. Ibid.

Currently, governments representing 81 percent of the population of the developing world, although still a minority of LDC governments, have declared their population growth rates to be excessive.[1] However, to affect population growth rates, a knowledge of the determinants of demographic variables is needed. In particular, government planners and policy makers concerned with the formulation and implementation of public policies intended to affect demographic variables need both a conceptual framework describing the causal structure and reliable empirical estimates of the determinants of fertility.

Government planners may wish to influence demographic variables because demographic variables have so many social and economic effects. Whether the planner is interested in changing income distribution, savings and investment, income per worker or per capita, labor supply, educational supply and costs, international capital flows, migration, or such, one policy approach is to affect fertility. On the other hand, even if a government has no explicit population policy and has no desire to alter demographic variables, it should be aware of the fact that many social and economic policies do have important demographic impacts. For example, changes in education, income distribution, demand for female labor, or infant mortality can have significant effects on fertility.

Policies designed to reduce the rate of population growth usually concentrate on ways to change fertility because increasing mortality is neither politically feasible nor socially desirable. However, some LDCs implicitly could be choosing eventual high mortality since continued high fertility and accompanying rapid population growth, with decreasing income per capita, implies that mortality will rise. Although large increases in migration from the developing countries to the developed countries is another potential alternative, the current political outlook seems to preclude any such change.

Accordingly, the papers presented in Part II present a variety of methodologies that have important implications for the design and implementation of effective population policies intended to change fertility. Not all the papers present specific policy programs, in part because current knowledge regarding the determinants of fertility is too limited; but they do present a variety of frameworks that are useful to policy makers and, in addition, suggest just what sorts of new knowledge and research are needed.

The first step in attempting to formulate a policy that will affect fertility is to specify the causal structure of the determinants of
fertility. Theories of the determinants of fertility and population
change date back to Malthus, who speculated that an increase in income would be accompanied by an increase of population due to lower
mortality and higher fertility, so income per capita would remain
unchanged. Currently, at least among some policy makers, there is
an "epidemic" theory of high fertility, which postulates that high
fertility is as a contagious disease that can be "cured" by the appropriate therapeutic intervention, in this case contraceptives. This
belief may stem in part from the apparent success of public health
measures as a means of reducing mortality. Although there is probably some truth in these ideas, both theories are too narrow to explain differences in fertility between societies or individuals, or
changes in fertility over time. Cultural, religious, and sociological
variables also have been stressed by some authors as determinants
of fertility, but it is only recently that a unifying, systematic theoretical framework of the determinants of fertility has become available.
This framework is an economic framework that stresses that fertility
is determined by relative costs, both monetary and nonmonetary;
opportunities, both market and nonmarket; and preferences or tastes.
Thus the fertility of a given set of parents is the outcome of a constrained choice that maximizes their self-interest. Although the
economic theory of the demand for and supply of children is far from
complete, and far too little is known empirically, it is the best (and
only) existing theoretical framework that allows the analyst to consider systematically the effects of social, economic, and cultural
variables on fertility.

Children are a commodity that differ in many ways from market
goods: they are produced and consumed in the home, their welfare
or consumption affects the utility of their parents, and they are the
result of a joint production process that produces both births (conceptions) and sexual pleasure. However, an economic framework
that utilizes the household production model, provides a systematic
framework where these very differences are emphasized. The major
theoretical advantage of this approach is that decisions regarding the
numbers and quality (or consumption) of children can be analyzed
systematically in a framework that emphasizes the fact that children
are produced, investments in children are made, and their services
are consumed in the home. Thus, the costs of children (both in
terms of the cost of quantity and the cost of quality) are affected by
the technology and costs of household production, which in turn are
affected by a variety of socioeconomic variables. The demand for
children also may depend on the structure of household production,
since especially in LDCs children's time is a very important input

into the production of household commodities, as well as commodities that will be sold or traded in the market.

Finally, even though the production and consumption of children and the services they provide are a complex and imperfectly understood process, economic analysis can be used to investigate how various government policies are likely to affect fertility and hence the rate of population growth. The number of children a family or society has is determined by the underlying supply and demand for children, and any policy intended to affect fertility must either affect the supply of or demand for children by making it in the parents' self-interest to alter their fertility.

Most policies directed at fertility reduction seek to increase the costs of children or of births. For example, since conceptions and sexual pleasure are produced jointly, costly contraception acts as a subsidy to conception. Thus by reducing the costs (monetary or information costs) of contraception through government-subsidized family planning programs, the subsidy to conceive is reduced and the number of conceptions declines. Similarly, direct payments for not conceiving or for being sterilized raise the costs of conceiving and so tend to lower fertility. However, the effectiveness of all policies designed to increase the costs of births depends crucially on how responsive fertility is to changes in cost, that is, the price elasticity of demand for births. Good estimates of the price elasticity of demand of births are not available, although the limited evidence available suggests that demand is not exceedingly responsive to changes in price. If correct, these estimates imply that small contraceptive subsidies or small bonus payments for nonpregnancy are unlikely to have large independent effects on fertility.

Policies that seek to reduce fertility by changing the demand (instead of the cost of children) are usually much more difficult to implement. For example, changing the distribution of income would change the demand for child services for those whose incomes were affected by the change. However, assessing how aggregate fertility would change is difficult without knowing the details of the distributional policy, as well as knowing much more about the effects of income on quantity, quality, and costs of children. However, it is unlikely that a government would promote such a far-reaching policy with implications for economic growth, political stability, and social welfare, solely on the basis of altering fertility. Similarly, policies designed to limit the usefulness or enjoyment parents receive from their children are likely to be politically unpopular. Finally, very little if anything is known about the determinants of preferences and values or how to change them.

Chapter 3 begins with a paper by Anne Williams that summarizes the state of the theory and the empirical evidence regarding the determinants of fertility. In many ways this is the key paper of Part II since any policy, whether it be designed to reduce demand or increase supply, should take into account what is known about the determinants of fertility. Her paper provides a general framework for evaluating the theoretical effects of any policy designed to reduce fertility. In addition, she summarizes the empirical evidence regarding the determinants of fertility, which is relevant to evaluating the likely effects of any given policy.

One of the most important points of her paper is that fertility is determined by a variety of interacting socioeconomic variables. Thus, theories that stress only one factor as the "cause" of high fertility are too narrow and restrictive and can lead to unwarranted policy prescriptions. She also stresses that the number of children a family has is, in large part, the result of constrained choice (fertility is 40 to 60 percent below the biological maximum in virtually all LDCs). Parents are acting in their own self-interest in having large families (although not necessarily in society's interest); and until the social and economic incentives to have large families are changed, the substantial reductions in fertility that are necessary to check the current rapid rates of population growth will not occur. Her paper also points out the lack of high quality reliable data and empirical research regarding the determinants of fertility in LDCs. More research of both a theoretical and, especially, empirical nature is needed if planners are to formulate and implement consistent and effective policies to reduce fertility.

The second paper in Chapter 3, by John Campbell and Paul Gregory, is an investigation, within an economic framework, of the effects of economic development on fertility. An important innovation of this paper is an interaction model of development, proxied by urbanization, and the determinants of fertility. That is, it is postulated that the various socioeconomic variables that determine fertility have different effects, both in terms of magnitude and sign, depending on the level of development. For example, female labor force participation may be positively related to fertility at very low levels of development when labor force activity is in home-based "cottage" industries, where working is not incompatible with child-bearing; but at high levels of development, where female labor force activity is away from the home, it may be negatively related to fertility. Similarly, at very low levels of development, increases in income can lead to larger increases in quantity of children than quality, and hence higher fertility; but at high levels of development the quality elasticity can dominate the quantity elasticity, leading to a drop in fertility (perhaps because the price of quantity relative to quality changes during the course of development). Empirically, they find that at low levels of development the effect income has on fertility is positive, and that most of the price effects that tend to reduce fertility do not have significant impacts until at least moderate levels of modernization are obtained.

Thus, an important policy implication is that economic development, in itself, does not lead necessarily or automatically to lower fertility, especially in very poor countries. If such countries do desire slower rates of population growth and lower fertility, then specific population policies need to be adopted.

The final chapter of the book is concerned with the analysis of specific population policies intended to reduce fertility. The first paper by Enke and Bryan Hickman considers the design and implementation of a system of bonuses intended to reduce fertility. They point out that if the social value of a birth prevented exceeds the private value, then a case can be made for government to subsidize lower fertility. Payments to low fertility couples (or equivalently, taxes on high fertility couples), are an efficient means for government to internalize the positive externalities associated with additional births. Since the payments are transfer payments, the only resource costs of such a system are the costs of administration. Currently, virtually all countries offer implicit bonuses for families to have large families through tax incentives, incentives to marry, the provision of unpriced social services to children, and special social services for large families. Even if there are no externalities associated with additional children, a bonus scheme outlined by the authors could be used to offset present subsidies to having children through the provision of unpriced social services, so on a net basis there would be no transfers from the childless or those with small families to those with large families. Alternatively, if the social costs of children exceed the private costs, such a system should go further, so on net there would be transfers from larger to smaller families. Providing that administrative costs are not too high, with large enough payments, such bonuses could reduce fertility to any desired level, although the determination of the socially optimal level depends on a careful formulation and measurement of the externalities associated with additional children.

The second paper by Richard Brown and Donald O'Hara presents an analysis of the relationship between old age security and family size, and the spacing strategy necessary to provide it. By recognizing the fact that childbearing is essentially a sequential process (that is, parents may postpone their decisions on completed family size so they may take into account the increased information that becomes available in the future), they demonstrate that old age security is consistent with relatively small family size. The essence of their argument is that if parents have access to effective, reversible contraceptives, then they can postpone births and have additional births depending on the realized mortality of their existing children.

Using a programming technique known as dynamic programming, they compare the population growth rates that would occur under a variety of spacing strategies and mortality levels, assuming that old age security is ensured. Contrary to previous studies, which neglected sequential decision making, they find that old age security is compatible with very low fertility and population growth rates.

This finding has two important policy implications. First, governments in LDCs can promote family planning without the fear that old age security will be jeopardized as long as effective reversible contraception is available. And second, since old age security can be achieved with small families, parents in LDCs that have effective, reversible contraception are not having large families only to ensure themselves of old age security. There must be other important motives. Thus, population policies that seek to provide alternative means of old age security probably will have only small effects on fertility.

The fertility of a nation or a family is influenced by an assortment of complex and interacting social and economic factors. Generally, parents choose to have the family size that best satisfies their own perceived individual self-interest, subject to a variety of constraints. This complex decision process is only beginning to be understood; and if governments desire to modify the behavior of parents regarding fertility, then more theoretical and empirical research is needed. Hopefully, the papers presented in Part II represent a step forward in this direction. Although the papers cover a wide range of topics, they present new ideas and empirical findings that have important bearing on the formulation and implementation of public policies to affect fertility.

NOTE

1. W. P. Mauldin, D. Choucri, F. W. Notestein, and M. S. Teitelbaum, "A Report on Bucharest," Studies in Family Planning 5, no. 12 (1974): 357-96.

DETERMINANTS OF FERTILITY IN DEVELOPING COUNTRIES

REVIEW AND EVALUATION
OF THE LITERATURE
Anne D. Williams

INTRODUCTION

This paper reviews and evaluates available literature on the determinants of fertility in developing countries. This paper may serve to guide future work by showing where evidence is deficient, by providing a framework for policy makers who wish to affect fertility, and by going beyond existing models and considering particular aspects of the population question in detail.

The first discussion is a formulation of a theory of the determinants of fertility. It approaches the question from the point of view of the individual household, which chooses its fertility behavior from the alternatives available in a given environment. The characteristics of the environment and their relation to economic development are discussed extensively.

The comments of the late Stephen Enke, and Bryan Hickman, James Johnston, Michael Keeley, Douglas Maxwell, William McFarland, and John Turner at General Electric-TEMPO were most helpful during the preparation of this paper. In addition, Sylvia Forman of the University of Massachusetts, Donald O'Hara of the University of Rochester, Margaret Reid and T. W. Schultz of the University of Chicago, and Boone Turchi of the University of North Carolina kindly reviewed the paper and made many useful suggestions. An earlier version of this paper, entitled, "Effects of Economic Development on Fertility: Review and Evaluation of the Literature," was published as a TEMPO Report GE74TMP-32 in July 1974. The U.S. Agency for International Development provided research support.

The principal determinants of fertility are isolated and examined next, with the evidence on each factor summarized. Much of the literature on fertility has come from studies in the United States and other industrial countries. Although this body of literature is an important frame of reference and a source of provocative questions, the present paper concentrates on studies of developing areas, where factors not relevant for consideration in richer nations may be important.

Finally, the findings and limitations of investigations of fertility to date are summarized. The use of the analysis for different policy questions is discussed. There is a brief discussion of how the theory and evidence might be incorporated into particular models.

THEORY OF FERTILITY DETERMINANTS

This section reviews the theory of the determination of fertility drawing heavily on the work of G. Becker, R. Freedman, R. A. Easterlin, R. J. Willis, and T. P. Schultz.[1] The theory is set in terms of a utility-maximization framework, in the sense that fertility is assumed to be the outcome of a set of rational decisions that weigh both costs and benefits (not only of births but also of control of births). The costs and benefits to be discussed include both monetary and (sometimes more importantly) nonmonetary ones, such as forgone time, pleasures, and displeasures of children, and the costs and benefits of conforming to perceived social norms. The assumption of rationality simply rules out inconsistent behavior or choices that could be improved, given a set of preferences and constraints.* Thus, those families that reach the biological maximum of fertility need not be irrational; they have not, however, reached the point where the marginal costs outweigh the marginal benefits of an additional birth. The utility maximization framework, though most familiar to economists, is also consistent with the theories of

---

*In fact, if prediction rather than explanation is the goal of the researcher, the assumption of rationality need not be necessary. [See G. Becker, "Irrational Behavior and Economic Theory," Journal of Political Economy 70, no. 1 (February 1962): 1-13. Rationality is also not a necessary assumption as long as units that make suboptimal decisions fail to survive, such as overpopulated tribes that succumb to a famine. In this case, as well as in the case of rationality, in the long run the only units observable will be those successful in the given environment.

other social scientists. Traditionally, researchers such as sociologists and anthropologists have stressed nonmonetary factors and
factors affecting preferences, whereas economists have emphasized
measurable monetary costs and benefits and have assumed preferences were fixed. Fields such as the analysis of fertility offer a
common ground where both emphases can be brought together within
the same framework.

In outlining fertility theory for the purposes of this paper, some
restrictions are imposed on its scope. First, only fertility is analyzed, although a full model of family behavior would treat fertility
as only one of several simultaneously determined phenomena. For
example, the labor force activity of women is an important determinant of fertility, but one for which the causation goes both ways.
Fertility also affects the supply by women of their time to the market.
Furthermore, although the analysis may point to labor force participation as a critical factor influencing fertility decisions, policy prescriptions must be preceded by an analysis of the other important
determinants of labor force behavior and possible means of influencing it during the course of development. Second, this paper stresses
the determinants of completed family fertility. The analysis can be
extended to look at optimal patterns of spacing, and even at dynamic
decision making at different points in the life cycle contingent on previous outcomes. Spacing decisions, however, have relatively little
impact on population growth rates in the developing nations of the
world, compared with decisions on family size. They are thus re-
ferred to only fleetingly in the work below. Third, the characteristics of a family's children, here to be denoted by the rather unsatisfactory shorthand term "quality," are treated as a secondary dimen-
sion of fertility decisions. This limitation is dictated by the state of
knowledge, both theoretical and empirical, about the determinants of
parental investments in child quality, such as education, nutrition,
and health.

The theory of utility maximization is sketched out in its bare
essentials in the following paragraphs. Then it is applied to household fertility behavior. A handy, though partly artificial, separation
can be made between decisions on desired family size and decisions
about the means of control used to achieve that size, where desired
family size differs from natural fertility.

Utility Maximization

The theory focuses on the individual couple as the primary
decision-making unit. (The influence of others, such as in-laws, can
easily be incorporated into the framework where they are important

culturally.) The couple is seen as maximizing utility in a situation where their wealth, the relative prices they face, the technological environment, and their preferences are given. These four elements are treated in turn although it is possible that in empirical work their separate influences may not be distinguishable.[2]

Wealth

As long as goods are scarce and have positive prices, higher wealth (or income, the flow from wealth) permits higher possible consumption. This applies not only to material sources of satisfaction but also to children as a source of satisfaction. Except for inferior goods, people consume more as wealth rises. This, of course, is a "pure" wealth effect in the sense that it is assumed that relative prices, tastes, and technology are held constant. That the observed correlation of fertility with income is usually negative need not imply that children are inferior when it is realized that income changes are almost invariably accompanied by changes in other parameters faced by parents. Furthermore, it is possible that people choose less of one commodity to purchase a better quality commodity yielding the same type of satisfactions. For instance, the value of the total stock of a commodity, say automobiles, can rise, though the actual number of automobiles can fall. Similarly, total investments in children may rise when the number falls.*

Relative Prices

Relative prices determine how much one good costs in terms of forgone consumption of other satisfaction-yielding goods. The more expensive a good, the greater is the inducement to seek substitute sources of satisfactions (assuming constant income, preferences, and technology). For many goods, the simplifying assumption can be made that the money price of the good represents the forgone consumption in the sense that the money could have been spent on something else. In discussing children, however, it is imperative to recognize that there are both money and nonmoney costs of children. Children can be considered a commodity yielding satisfactions (comparable, say, with travel, boating, or dining as

---

*Parents appear to treat children equally, and common environments in the home tend to affect all children in the family equally. Thus a rise in wealth is more likely to lead to an increase in quality at the expense of quantity for children than for other goods, where both high and low quality items can be simultaneously consumed.

opposed to tickets, boats, and food). Such a commodity cannot be purchased in the marketplace strictly with money. Rather it must be produced by the consumer, using both time and market goods as inputs. Thus the price of such a commodity is not only the money outlay for the market goods but also the implicit outlay in terms of time. Had that time been spent at work, the added income could have been used to purchase more goods. The wage rate gives a measure of the value of each hour spent in "home production" as opposed to "market production" at work for pay. Even if working for pay is not the relevant alternative to spending time on children, there are other competing uses for the scarce resource of time. Time spent on children means time forgone on other activities such as travel. To the extent that it is possible to substitute among different inputs (time of one spouse versus time of the other spouse versus purchased goods), parents try to find the least costly way to bear and rear a certain number of children.

Technology

Technological improvements enable the family to achieve more satisfaction with the same income. Improvements may lower the prices of market goods so that a given income will purchase more. Or technological change may take place within the household so that the same commodities can be produced with fewer inputs. For example, increased control of family size may be achieved through the use of new, cheap contraceptives, or by education leading to more efficient use of older less reliable family planning methods.

Preferences

Preferences determine the utility that families obtain from a certain combination of goods. The strategy of many economists has been to explain as much variation as possible with wealth, relative prices, and technology, on the grounds that there is no systematic theory of taste formation. Others have tried to explain changes in tastes that lead to changes in consumption, particularly when it is felt that nontaste variables do not account for important behavioral differences.[3] The value that people place on a given commodity may depend on the levels of consumption of that commodity by others in society, because people may be concerned not only with their absolute level of well-being but also with their well-being compared with others in society. Thus the rising levels of income brought by economic development may be accompanied by systematic changes in the value attached to different types of consumption, according to whether a good is seen to help one maintain or improve relative status.

The framework of utility maximization has several specific implications when it is applied to fertility in the context of a developing economy. The following discussion gives a "bare bones" outline of factors affecting desired family size and the control problems associated with reaching that family size. The discussion is couched in terms of the general utility maximization framework, but it also tries to relate the theoretical concepts to the empirical variables actually used in work on fertility.

Desired Family Size

The pure effect of rising income associated with development is to increase desired family size as long as children are not inferior goods. This effect, however, is offset by other changes that tend to reduce desired family size. Chief among these are changes in relative prices. Children become relatively more costly and also yield relatively fewer benefits due to a wide variety of changes that accompany development. With the general movement away from labor-intensive agriculture, there are fewer opportunities for children to contribute to family income by joining in farm production. Urbanization is accompanied not only by fewer productive opportunities for children but also by sanctions against child labor and pressure for compulsory education. Food and housing for children are more costly in urban areas. Furthermore, the time of the mother is more valuable, causing a higher implicit cost of children. Although women may work more in traditional rural settings (on family farms or in cottage crafts), these forms of labor force activity can be carried on along with childrearing activities. Urban modern work, however, involves a more rigid schedule of time away from home and is associated with the breakup of the joint family, which formerly provided childcare. Even if women do not work in the city, higher educational levels open up new nontraditional activities, which challenge the exclusive use of women's time for childrearing. Institutional changes with development, such as the provision of social insurance, also reduce the value of children as future providers of income for the parents' old age.

Rising education of parents can be seen as a technological change that improves their efficiency at home as well as on the job. This increased efficiency is especially manifest in the ability to raise high quality children with investments in health and cognitive skills and the concentration of these investments on a smaller number of children.

Finally, both individual preferences and cultural norms change in the process of economic development. Exposure to nontraditional ideas as development proceeds can reduce fatalism and encourage new opportunities not associated with children. The proliferation of consumer goods and the increasing possibility of social mobility induce parents to shift away from children to raise their own standard of living. The rising status of women gives them more voice in societies where women were previously subservient to the wishes of their husbands. Patterns of marriage and family that encourage large families, such as early permanent marriage, joint families, and polygamy, are succeeded by nuclear families, and perhaps, a greater prevalence of impermanent consensual unions. Inheritance patterns such as primogeniture or subdivision among all children also change during development and affect desired family size.

Control of Surviving Family Size

Economic development has two opposing effects on parents' ability to control their family size. First, improvements in health with rising development lead to higher natural fertility. With improved nutrition and the elimination of certain diseases (for example, malaria, venereal disease) and the abandonment of breastfeeding, the capacity to conceive and bear children rises. And after children are born, improved public health brings stunning improvements in survival. Second, economic progress brings with it greater control, not only of deficient but also of excess fertility. Improved methods of fertility control spread with education, development of communications, and provision of health services. Falling desired family size means that more parents face the control problem of excess fertility rather than deficient fertility.

The variation among families in how much control is exerted over surviving family size can, as desired family size, be related to wealth, relative prices, technology, and taste variables. Rising income is associated with less waste due to fetal and childhood mortality, and with a longer, more fecund reproductive period for the women. Rising income promotes more use of contraception. Parents are willing to spend more resources to reduce uncertainty and prevent the arrival of extra children, who would require larger expenditures, or to try to space their children more to their liking.

Price is one important variable influencing the adoption of contraception. The development of medical services (family planning clinics, maternal and child health, as well as general medical services) reduces the cost of obtaining information about contraception. Furthermore they are associated with reduced price of contraception, in terms of both money and in terms of the time expended to get to a clinic.

Technological change affects both excess and deficient fertility. To control excess fertility, new contraceptives are adopted that are more efficient and thus easier to use than the traditional methods of withdrawal or mechanical devices. Furthermore, rising levels of education equip individuals to seek out and better use the methods available to them, in effect an improvement in the efficiency of the parents. With respect to deficient fertility due to fetal or child loss, medical technology and more knowledge of good care in raising children means that fewer conceptions are needed to achieve any given surviving family size. Changes in price and technology of family size control also have secondary effects on desired surviving family size itself, as well as the number of births the family must have to achieve it. For example, when survival is cheaper, the cost per survivor is lower; and parents may wish to have a larger completed family size, ceteris paribus.

Changes in preferences that affect the control of family size are concentrated primarily in changes in attitudes associated with modernization. Higher education, the weakening of religious or traditional sanctions concerning the use of contraception and abortion, and the use of modern medical services leads to more methods of controlling family size.

Summary

Modernization affects not only parents' desired family size but also their ability to achieve it. Rising opportunities for women, higher investments in children, reduced value of children's production, changes in institutions and culture, and the preferences of parents all lead to a reduction in desired family size. The difference between the biological maximum and desired family size widens because of this decreasing desired family size and because of elimination of maternal and child wastage, so excess fertility and even actual fertility may rise initially. The spread of modern birth control, however, enables a reduction of fertility so that persons are closer to achieving their lower family size goals.

A SURVEY OF THE STATE OF THE EVIDENCE

Overview of Empirical Efforts to Date

The empirical work on the determinants of fertility has not been able to investigate all the influences on fertility hypothesized above. In particular, the separate channels in which a variable affects fertility usually have not been identified. For example, the extended family is thought to stimulate fertility by providing resources for earlier marriage, by assuring reliable childcare for working mothers, and by maintaining traditional values through the dominance of elders. Yet the empirical work only correlates family structure with fertility without testing the strength of the different causal mechanisms. Thus, this empirical part of the paper focuses on the broad topics that have been the subject of investigation, such as family structure, education, and labor force activity. Where particular channels of influence have been tested, the results are discussed. Untested hypotheses are noted.

The studies reviewed here range widely in complexity. Some are the simplest cross tabulations or correlations of fertility with one other variable. Others take into account the different effects of several variables with multidimensional tabulations, partial correlations, or multivariate regression analyses. The most complex are the studies that simultaneously explain fertility with other important endogenous variables such as female labor force behavior and marriage rates. These simultaneous systems are crucial where several variables affect each other by different causal paths, such as labor force activity and fertility. An attempt to analyze only one variable can lead to serious biases because the feedbacks from it are not properly taken into account.

Although the simplest studies are useful in pointing out areas for future research, they shed little light on causal mechanisms and thus give little information on how to change fertility. Further, if other variables are not held constant, the results may not represent the true relationship. Where two variables tend to vary together, such as income and education, it is impossible to assess the importance of one without taking the other into account. Sometimes definitional links between the variables produce spurious correlations. The simple correlation between fertility and per capita income is negative partly because population is the denominator of per capita income.

It is particularly important in discussing demographic phenomena to hold age constant. For instance, family income tends to rise through the reproductive years as workers acquire experience and skills and are promoted to higher paying jobs. It is also during these years that the parents are building their families. A naive tabulation of family income and number of children, without controls for age, can show a positive relationship simply because younger families have not yet completed childbearing and also have not yet attained their highest possible income.

It is also important when comparing different age groups to separate life cycle effects from cohort effects. If groups differed only because they were observed at different stages of the life cycle, these combined observations then would give a complete picture of fertility behavior. In reality, however, the picture is distorted because of factors that differ for each cohort. Parents who started their families during the depression of the 1930s or during World War II may have had different responses from those of young couples today. Although some of the causes of differences between cohorts such as education or income can be specified, many inevitably are left out.

Limiting fertility studies to women beyond the childbearing ages eliminates some of the life cycle effects, but not the cohort effects. Such studies may be of limited relevance for planners interested in the fertility of young adults in the process of building their families. Holding constant (standardizing for) age or marriage duration enables the examination of these younger groups. Standardization, although it tends to obscure cohort effects or changes in the spacing of children, often is preferred to age specific fertility measures because it yields a single comprehensive measure of fertility.

Apart from questions of statistical techniques the quality of the data used in fertility studies is critical to the evaluation of their conclusions. Some surveys are designed specifically to acquire information on fertility from individuals. These studies usually obtain information about the number of live births (children ever born). Other studies rely on information already tabulated in censuses or, less frequently, in registration of vital events. These often are forced to rely on fertility indicators such as the child-woman ratio (the ratio of children age zero to four to women of reproductive age). The child-woman ratio includes the effects of childhood mortality and of errors in enumeration and age reporting. It must be interpreted cautiously to draw any conclusions about fertility.

Most of the studies discussed below deal with actual fertility. Many give information on ideal or desired family size, and a few of the studies focus exclusively on this variable. Some of these results are discussed, but interpreting such attitudinal variables as desired or ideal family size is very difficult. Often the context of the question is not clear. The respondent could be referring to a vague ideal; what is ideal for the respondent, or what the respondent would like if cost were no object. Because many couples do not wish to reject existing children, they will not admit to a desired family size containing less than their own number of living children. Although studies in the United States have done much to refine these attitudinal measures, their meaning across various developing countries, or even within one country, as asked by different interviewers, is not well defined.

The unit of analysis ranges from the individual household, to aggregates for geographical or other groups within a country, to aggregates for different countries. Most of the work deals with cross-country studies of one of these units at a given point in time. These cross-country studies are undoubtedly the least reliable. Not only does the quality of the data vary in nonrandom ways across countries at different levels of development, but also definitions are not uniform. Adjustments to make comparable different definitions of female labor force participation or different types and qualities of schooling are crude at best.

A few studies consider changes in fertility over time, using either aggregate time series or retrospective family surveys. The difficulties of accounting for different responses in different cohorts have been discussed. In addition, little has been done to study the dynamic responses of families to changes during their lifetimes. This is obviously a serious problem when the explanation of the development process involves the determination of individual change.

The discussion of the evidence on fertility in the remainder of this section falls into the following eight categories:

- income, occupation, and socioeconomic status;
- education;
- female and child labor force activity and wages;
- migration, urbanization, and industrialization;
- childhood mortality;
- fecundity and family planning;
- marriage and family structure; and
- attitudes, roles, son preference, tastes, and institutions.

Income, Occupation, and Socioeconomic Status

In considering the effect of a family's income on its fertility, the focus here is on the "pure" income effect, that is, the effect of a rise in income with no related change in any prices of goods and services or the value of time of family members. Because in most areas of the world men are the primary income earners in a family and devote less time to child care than women, the simplifying assumption is made that the occupation and status of men are closely related to pure income. Although there are some changes in incentives when men get higher incomes or status, these secondary price effects have not been separated from the income effects in the empirical work.

The literature on the effects of income in developed countries is extensive. Perhaps the best exposition is by J. Simon.[4] He shows that the negative association between fertility and income (often observed in historical or cross-sectional data) is not inconsistent with the positive relation observed in the short run (over the business cycle). The reason is that certain variables, such as education, infant survival, and urbanization, which have a negative effect on fertility, are correlated positively with income. Thus the gross negative correlation of income with fertility reflects the negative influence of these variables across time or in cross section. In cyclical swings, these variables do not change much; the positive pure income effect can emerge. Analogously, higher fertility for those with higher relative income[5] simply means that other crucial variables such as education and age are being held constant.

It is possible also that the "pure" income effect on fertility is positive, but not observed. If wealthier parents choose to have higher quality (more expensive) children, correspondingly they may reduce the number of children. But this does not mean that children are inferior goods. The relevant measure, which is difficult to quantify, is "quality-adjusted" children.

An example of the gross relation between income and fertility is shown in Table 3.1. The strong negative relation also holds when fertility is classified by occupational or socioeconomic status, since both of these variables are tied closely to the income of the husband. A few studies have observed positive gross relations between fertility and measures of wealth,[6] but in general it is the failure to hold other factors constant that produces the apparent negative relationship.

TABLE 3.1

Children Ever Born to 1959 Sample of Ever-Married Women
Aged 35-50 of Differing Incomes in Santiago

Income (Pesos)	Children Ever Born
Less than 9,000	5.9
9,000-14,999	3.7
15,000-20,999	3.0
21,000-26,999	2.6
27,000-39,999	2.2
40,000 and over	2.4
Domestic servant	3.3
No answer	3.2
Total sample	3.4

Source: Leon Tabah, "A Study of Fertility in Santiago, Chile," Marriage and Family Living 25, no. 1 (February 1963): 22, Table 1.

The results of multiple regressions, whether single equation models or simultaneous equation models and whether across countries or within a given country, show no consistent effect for income. The coefficients of per capita income, male income, male labor force participation, or male wages fluctuate in sign (with positive coefficients predominating) and only rarely are significantly different from zero when other variables are held constant in the regressions. One strong result is the I. Adelman finding[7] that per capita income has a strong positive effect on birth rates across countries for women aged 15 to 19. This is most plausible for this age group, which is just starting families. The relation is also harder to establish for older groups whose current income may differ from income in the past when family size decisions were being made. There is some evidence of increasing family planning effectiveness with rising income or status. Hanna Rizk[8] shows that in the U.A.R. in 1959 only wives of men in the highest social class had lower fertility when they attempted to use family planning methods.

The regressions of Schultz[9] suggest that recent changes in income have a positive effect on fertility. This result confirms the Western experience of procyclical variations at least in the timing of fertility.[10] David Heer[11] finds a positive coefficient across countries for change in per capita energy consumption, which he used as a proxy for changing national income. S. Friedlander and M. Silver[12] find a slight negative relation between changing income and fertility across countries. In justifying the negative sign, they interpret the change in income as a measure that picks up changing social and economic opportunities as well as simple changes in income.

The effects of mobility or speed of change itself, apart from any changes in income, are hard to isolate. Individual social and economic mobility often is associated with migration (discussed subsequently). But mobility due to changing social and economic opportunities is distinct in that it can take place without physical migration. Studies of occupational mobility are generally inconclusive. Monica Boyd[13] shows that in Latin American countries, fertility of families who change occupational status is intermediate between that of their original and their new occupational groups. This result is similar to those of B. Hutchinson[14] and S. Iutaka and his colleagues[15] for mobility of individuals and between generations in Brazil. In Mexico, however, Boyd finds that upward mobility carries with it an independent effect in reducing fertility. This question must be studied further, particularly to determine the effects of development on individuals over their lifetimes.

In summary, the evidence for the effect of income on fertility is not strong when other associated factors are held constant. The suggestion of a positive effect is not observed consistently by the studies. Socioeconomic or occupational status usually is linked closely to other characteristics of development, such as education, female labor force participation, and child mortality. These variables, which often have intermediate effects in raising incomes, are discussed subsequently.

Education

The increase in educational levels associated with economic development is hypothesized to lower fertility. The several channels through which education operates are discussed before the evidence is reviewed.

The compulsory education of children is a cost factor, which tends to lower fertility. Time spent in education reduces the opportunity for a child to work and contribute to the family income. Higher voluntary educational expenses, holding income constant, also are associated with a decrease in the number of children.

Education affects the market productivity, nonmarket productivity, and tastes and attitudes of adults. Market productivity refers to the fact that educated people command higher wages and thus higher potential income. Furthermore, higher wages mean that individuals value their time more highly in other activities. Education has different effects for males and females because the raising of children usually is the responsibility of the wife. Where men share less in childrearing, male education represents more of a "pure income" effect and is apt to have a positive effect on fertility. Because men generally spend little time on childrearing, an increase in the value of their time makes children less costly relative to other activities. For the wife, education is expected to represent mainly a "price" effect and thus encourage her to enter the labor force or other activities away from home at the expense of more children.

Nonmarket productivity refers to the benefits of education in improving efficiency at home. One of the most prominent factors is increased efficiency and use of family planning methods. More educated people are better able to obtain and evaluate new information. Another significant effect can be on the wife's competence in raising children. The educated mother is more successful in investing in the quality of her children, for example, in health and education.

The education process has an effect on tastes and attitudes, which are vital to fertility. Students are introduced to a broader and more heterogeneous community. The educational process diffuses knowledge about new ideas and goods and reduces the traditional value placed on children.

Education can change fatalistic attitudes and enhance belief in one's own ability to control events. Where social mobility is related to educational achievement, individuals are encouraged to improve themselves by this route. At the same time, they may seek fewer children, to increase their material consumption, to improve their children's lot, and to further invest in both themselves and their children. Where rising education is associated with more independence for women, it increases the wife's role in decision making and her choice of activities.

Finally, there may be an association of education with fertility, not because of any causal relationship but because of the implied selection process. The fact that some people get more education than others simply could reflect the fact that they are more able and more progressive in all endeavors.

The gross association of fertility with education is strongly negative. This negative association also holds when some of the other relevant variables are held constant. Tables 3.2 and 3.3 include some representative data for fertility and female education in two developing countries.

The data show that fertility remains virtually constant at the lowest levels of education (up through four years of school or its equivalent) and then begins to fall: There is also some suggestion in other tables of R. Carleton[16] and in Israeli data of Y. Ben-Porath[17] that at lower general levels of education for older women the shift to lower fertility begins with even lower educational achievement. That is, educational differentials in fertility may be partly indicative of selection of individuals who are more innovative in all respects. Holding constant marital status and age or marriage duration (as well as for labor force activity in Puerto Rico), there is a difference of two to four children between the lowest and highest educational groups.

Cross-country regression studies relying on aggregate data have found a significant negative relation between various measures of fertility and education.[18] The difficulty of finding comparable measures of education and other variables across countries has impelled researchers to use data for areas within countries. These studies include G. Farooq and B. Tuncer,[19] M. Gendell, M. Maraviglia, and P. Kreitner,[20] Drakatos,[21] Iutaka, Bock, and Varnes,[22] Schultz,[23] Heer and Turner,[24] and Repetto.[25] Where data on female literacy or educational attainment have been available, the coefficient of male educational attainment has vacillated in sign and significance, for example, in the work of Schultz in Colombia[26] and Ben-Porath for Arabs in Israel.[27] The weakness of male education can be attributed to the relative balance of the two opposite effects

TABLE 3.2

Relationship of Fertility to Female Education in San Juan Standard Metropolitan Statistical Area
(children ever born per married woman aged 35-44, 1960 census)

Labor Force Status of Wife	School Grade Completed							
	0	1-4	5-6	7-8	9-11	12	13+	All Levels
All	5.8	5.6	4.5	3.5	3.0	2.4	2.3	4.1
Economically active	4.6	4.9	4.0	3.2	2.6	1.9	2.0	3.0
Nonactive	6.0	5.7	4.6	3.6	3.1	2.6	2.7	4.4

Source: R. Carleton, "Labor Force Participation: A Stimulus to Fertility in Puerto Rico?" Demography 2, no. 2 (May 1965): 237-38, Tables 4, 5.

TABLE 3.3

Live Births to Currently Married Women in Cairo
(1960 census)

Marriage Duration (years)	Illiterate	Barely Reads	Reads and Writes	Did Not Complete Intermediate	Completed Intermediate	Went Beyond Intermediate	Completed College or More	All Levels
0- 4.9	1.2	1.2	1.2	1.3	1.0	1.0	1.2	1.2
5- 9.9	3.4	3.6	3.4	3.2	2.8	2.6	2.5	3.3
10-19.9	5.9	5.8	5.5	4.6	3.7	3.7	3.3	5.7
20-29.9	8.0	7.6	6.5	5.6	4.3	3.6		7.6
30+	8.4	7.8	6.5	5.9	4.8	3.9		8.1

Source: J. Abu-Lughod, "The Emergence of Differential Fertility in Urban Egypt," Milbank Memorial Fund Quarterly 43, no. 2 (April 1965): 237, Table 1.

134

of raising wages by education--the higher income leading to more children and the higher cost of those children because of the income forgone when the husband helps rear them. Because the time cost of children is borne largely by the wife, her educational coefficient is more negative than that of the husband. When only adult education or literacy is included, the stronger education effect for the wife and the positive correlation between education of husband and wife yield a consistently negative sign.

Schultz studied adult education in both Colombia[28] and Puerto Rico[29] and finds strong negative effects. For Colombia the elasticity of "surviving fertility" (a measure similar to the child-woman ratio) with respect to percent of adults with some primary education is -0.08. In these two studies, as well as in those by Gendell, Maraviglia, and Kreitner[30] for Guatemala City, Heer and Turner[31] for Latin American countries, and Ben-Porath[32] for Arabs in Israel, the participation of women in the labor force is held constant. Thus the adult education variable largely represents the channels to lower fertility via increased use of contraception and changing tastes.

A final group of studies are simultaneously determined models of fertility and other variables. These include K. Maurer, R. Ratajczak, and Schultz[33] for Thailand, DaVanzo[34] for Chile, M. Nerlove and Schultz[35] for Puerto Rico, A. Harman[36] for the Philippines, P. Gregory, J. Campbell, and B. Cheng[37] across countries, H. Loebner and E. Driver[38] for India, and B. Rosen and A. Simmons[39] for Brazil. When female labor force participation or wages are included in the system as dependent variables, the effect of the exogenous education variable tends to be channeled indirectly through the labor force variables to fertility. The same tendencies are found, however, for the coefficients on child and adult education as in the single equation regressions cited earlier.

A few of the studies surveyed here have explored some of the paths from education to fertility other than through labor force activity. Education of either husband or wife is associated with more favorable attitudes toward the use of family planning methods. See E. Mueller,[40] R. Mitchell,[41] H. Schumann, A. Inkeles, and D. Smith,[42] Loebner and Driver,[43] and J. Williamson.[44] This survey has focused on fertility rather than contraception and thus has glossed over much of the literature on knowledge, attitudes, and practice of family planning (Knowledge, Attitudes, and Practices surveys). However, some typical figures on the use of family planning by education are given in Table 3.4 without holding any other variables constant. The effect of family planning on fertility is considered subsequently.

In addition, some evidence suggests that education plays a part in structuring the decision making of husband and wife, and the wife's

TABLE 3.4

Percentage of Latin American Legally or Consensually Married Women
Ever Using Family Planning, by Education, 1963-64

Area	None	Some Primary	Complete Primary	Some Secondary	Complete Secondary	Some University	Total
Large urban							
Buenos Aires	42.9	75.6	81.9	75.4	83.4	72.3	78.3
Rio de Janeiro	39.6	47.7	61.6	70.1	73.9	73.5	57.8
Caracas	35.5	53.5	70.8	76.9	66.7	77.8	60.0
San Jose	45.4	54.2	69.8	79.0	66.7	81.0	65.6
Bogota	14.5	28.6	40.1	59.1	74.5	73.9	39.8
Mexico	12.4	28.7	86.2	57.6	65.4	59.7	43.2
Rural--small urban							
Chile: Cauquenes	3.2	5.6	20.0	30.6	--	--	10.0
Chile: Mostazal	25.0	30.2	48.1	48.0	--	--	33.3
Colombia: Cartagena	8.3	10.7	20.0	33.3	--	--	11.5
Colombia: Neira	--	12.9	20.0	47.6	--	--	17.5
Mexico: Pabellon	2.4	3.9	25.0	--	--	--	5.0

Source: Carmen Miro and Walter Mertens, "Influences Affecting Fertility in Urban and Rural Latin America," Milbank Memorial Fund Quarterly 46, no. 3 (July 1968): 114, Table 11.

idea of her role. C. Oppong[45] finds in Ghana that as the wife's education rose relative to the husband's, their decision making was more shared, rather than dominated by either partner. R. Weller[46] finds no such effect in Puerto Rico. The Rosen and Simmons study for Brazil[47] sets out a structure where a wife's education increased the strength of her role in the family, which in turn decreased her ideal family size and actual family size.

Research is only beginning on the effects of parental education on efficiency in the home. Results by A. Leibowitz[48] for the United States show that parental education (especially that of the mother) and home instruction given by parents to their preschool children are crucial in raising children's intelligence quotient scores. This result should be more powerful in developing nations as educated parents become skilled at investing in proper nutrition at critical stages of child development.[49]

Child education has received less attention than female or adult education. Schultz[50] finds the expected negative sign in his study of Colombia, where the elasticity of surviving children with respect to the percentage of children in school is -0.05. The strong dampening effect of child education on fertility is supported by the time series results of S. Wat and R. W. Hodge[51] for Hong Kong. Contrary evidence of Schultz[52] for Jordan and that of Repetto[53] for Morocco seems to be due to inadequate data. It must be remembered, of course, that the education of children has not only current effects on their parents' behavior but also lagged effects on fertility. As children grow up and start their own families, they can be expected to follow a pattern of lower fertility than their uneducated peers.

In summary, education appears to be one of the most powerful and pervasive factors of development affecting fertility. The impact is largest and best documented in the case of women, who find that higher education opens opportunities to them. They thus can participate in activities not centered on the home or childrearing and undertake new economic and social responsibilities.

Female and Child Labor Force Activity and Wages

Labor force participation by women not only influences fertility but also is affected directly by it. Fecund women may attempt to limit their childbearing in order to work away from home. Subfecund women may tend to engage in outside activity because they have fewer home responsibilities. Women with large numbers of children may feel economic pressure to work. For older women with many children, it may be easier to work when older children can care for the younger ones.

The negative effect of labor force activity on fertility varies
with economic development. In traditional societies where production is oriented to the home, women can work (either paid or unpaid)
in agriculture and cottage industries without leaving the home. In
such a situation, childbearing or child care can be undertaken with
minimum increased effort; and women have less reason to reduce
fertility. Work outside the home, however, conflicts directly with
childrearing activities, particularly when children are too young to
attend school. Thus a woman may be forced to drop out of the labor
market for five to ten years or more. She not only loses the wages
she would have earned but also may have more difficulty in reenter-
ing the labor force later because of lost skills. As the economy
develops and labor force opportunities arise outside the home, women
sacrifice more and more earnings by choosing to stay at home.

The data support the distinction between work at home and
away from home. For example, Table 3.2 shows that Puerto Rican
married women economically active outside the home average 1.4
fewer children than nonactive women. The data in Table 3.5 illustrate the differential between working and nonworking Thai women.
In urban areas, where female employment is largely nonagricultural,
women in the labor force have fewer births. Furthermore, occupational differences in fertility are considerable, reflecting differing
amounts of conflict with the maternal role. Table 3.6 shows that in
Thailand fertility is highest for women working on farms or as sales
persons. These occupations require little training, pay low wages,
are usually carried out at or near the home, and, in addition, are
occupations in which children can become useful at an early age.
A. Jaffe and K. Azumi[54] report similar findings for both Japan and
Puerto Rico where women of comparable age, education, marital
status, and residence in the nonagricultural work force average 0.5
to 1.0 fewer children than women in traditional sectors or women
who do not work. J. Stycos[55] finds that women who are not employed
or are employed in service occupations have the highest registered
birth rates in Lima, Peru.

Multiple regression results show the same effect of paid, nonagricultural female labor force participation on fertility. The coefficient on labor force participation is consistently negative and
significant.[56] Education tends to have a stronger negative effect
than labor force participation but both are significantly negative.
Schultz's[57] estimate of the elasticity of fertility with respect to the
female labor force participation rate is -0.04, half of that with respect to education. Gendell, Maraviglia, and Kreitner[58] find that
women employed as domestic servants have even lower fertility than
other working women in Guatemala City. They suggest that as development proceeds and women shift from domestic service to other

TABLE 3.5

Children Ever Born to Ever-Married Women in Thailand,
by Labor Force Status, 1960

Area	Percent of Female Labor Force Working in Agriculture	All Women (Age Standardized)	
		In Labor Force	Housewife
Thailand	87	4.4	4.0
Bangkok	2	3.3	3.7
Other urban, nonagricultural	7	3.8	3.9
Urban, agricultural	65	4.0	4.1
Rural, nonagricultural	43	4.0	4.2
Rural, agricultural	97	4.5	4.3

Source: S. Goldstein, "The Influence of Labor Force Participation and Education on Fertility in Thailand," Population Studies 26, no. 3 (November 1972): 424, 426.

TABLE 3.6

Children Ever Born to Ever-Married Working Women
in Thailand, by Occupation, 1960
(age standardized)

Area	Farm	Crafts	Professional	Service	Sales
Thailand	4.5	3.6	3.5	3.6	3.9
Bangkok	2.7	2.8	2.4	2.9	3.7
Other urban, nonagricultural	4.0	3.1	3.1	3.8	4.0
Urban, agricultural	4.1	2.2	2.2	3.3	4.1
Rural, nonagricultural	4.1	3.9	3.4	4.1	3.9
Rural, agricultural	4.5	3.6	3.9	3.7	3.8

Source: S. Goldstein, "The Influence of Labor Force Participation and Education on Fertility in Thailand," Population Studies 26, no. 3 (November 1972): 429.

occupations, family size may in fact increase if there is not a large increase in the overall labor force participation rate. The validity of this hypothesis awaits testing by more refined occupational data. The simultaneous equation results bear out the single equation co-efficients, although there is some fluctuation in the coefficients.

Two studies note that labor force activity by women increases their influence in the household and their role as decision makers. Oppong[59] finds that in Ghana when women contribute significantly to family income there is less male domination of decisions. Rosen and Simmons[60] likewise find in Brazil that female participation in the labor force strengthens their role attitudes, which in turn lowers fertility. Roles would seem to be another case where the investiga-tion of simultaneous feedbacks is important. Not only are women with a modern role attitude more likely to work; but also the fact of working, their exposure to the market economy, and their contribu-tions to the household can change their role at home.

Some other indirect channels of labor force activity, such as possibly higher child mortality or morbidity when the mother works, have not been investigated in the literature.

The effect of children's labor force participation on fertility is positive in all the reviewed studies.[61] Where children are economi-cally productive, parents choose higher fertility. And where parents choose to have higher numbers of children rather than higher quality children, children receive less education and are sent to work at an earlier age.

In summary, the negative association of fertility with female economic activity outside the home is well established. Labor force participation is closely related to women's education, which trains women for nontraditional occupations. The opening up of new oppor-tunities with education means an increase in the real cost of children as women must forgo larger potential earnings in order to spend time in childrearing.

Migration, Urbanization, and Industrialization

Variables for urbanization, industrialization, and rural-to-urban migration have been used as measures for a whole host of changes that take place during economic development. They are associated with the value of children and women as income producers, cost of living, availability of goods, availability of information, in-come, and other variables.

Where detailed statistics have been hard to obtain, the percent-age of the labor force employed in agriculture has been used, gener-ally in regressions. The coefficients tend to be positive, and are significant in studies by Adelman,[62] Ekanem,[63] Friedlander and Silver[64] across countries, and by Drakatos[65] for Greece. Some of the other studies[66] have produced insignificant and even negative coefficients.

There has also been an attempt to break down the modernization process into two components. Urbanization is the first and represents the move from rural areas to more densely populated ones. The second component, industrialization, is distinct conceptually and represents the shift in the labor force from traditional subsistence activity to more complicated industrial structures. Tables 3.5 and 3.6 show urban-rural differentials in fertility. Regression results have not confirmed these urban-rural differentials. The negative coefficient on the urbanization variables has not been significant except in the study by Heer and Turner.[67] Population density has been used as an alternate variable to mirror the effect of more crowding and higher prices in the cities. The interpretation by Friedlander and Silver[68] that the positive coefficient on their housing adequacy variables reflects the easier use of contraceptives in homes with interior plumbing and fewer persons per room deserves more careful testing. Estimated coefficients are all negative, but only in cross-country studies by Adelman[69] and Heer[70] are they significant. With respect to industrialization, A. Zarate[71] finds no significant relation between fertility and proportion of workers in the secondary sector in urban areas. Rosen and Simmons[72] show that in Brazil fertility is lower in industrial cities than in nonindustrial ones, but no variables other than male occupational status are held constant.

The process of migration away from nonindustrial rural areas is explicitly examined in a few of the studies reviewed for this paper. One of the crucial questions is the degree to which migrants adapt to their new environment. Most of the studies compare the fertility of immigrants and natives within urban areas but do not compare the migrants with those left behind in rural areas. Nor do any studies treat the interesting question of whether there is a critical age by which social patterns are set and after which migration has little impact on behavior.

Short-term male migration to take a job and then return reduces fertility in Indian villages by about 0.5 children, holding class and marriage duration constant.[73] For permanent rural-urban migration, Iutaka, Bock, and Varnes[74] find in multiple regressions that men who have migrated to the cities have higher fertility than those who have always lived there. In addition, among migrants, those who came to urban areas before age 19 have lower fertility than those who arrived at older ages. Schultz[75] also finds higher fertility associated with the presence of migrants. The data for Puerto Rico, however, show just the opposite. Holding labor force participation constant, except for women above age 35, J. Macisco et al.[76] show that wives of recent migrants to San Juan have lower fertility, a result similar to that of G. Myers and E. Morris.[77] Part of the explanation may be that migration temporarily disrupts the family and inhibits childbearing. Or it may be that the men had married after coming to the city and thus had less time to establish a family. Finally, the Puerto Rican situation must be examined more carefully because the cities are not always the ultimate destination of migrants but often a way station to the United States. Thus the "nonmigrants" are not representative of the whole urban population but are those who choose not to move to the United States. S. Goldstein[78] finds a result similar to the Puerto Rican ones for recent migrants in Thailand. However, when comparing urban natives with others who had migrated to the city at any time during their lives, he finds no fertility differences. He suggests several possible reasons --the more innovative character of recent migration, selection of people with low fertility as migrants, and family disruption--but these cannot be tested without more detailed data.

Intercountry migration is considered by M. Nag[79] and Ben-Porath.[80] Permanent out-migration of males has helped reduce fertility in Barbados by lowering the sex ratio and thus the availability of marital partners.[81] From the point of view of the recipient country, Ben-Porath documents the higher fertility of migrants to Israel compared with natives. Among women of Asian and African origins, the excess fertility is lower for women who migrated at earlier ages. For women migrating to Israel from Western countries, excess fertility is lower for those migrating at older ages, possibly because many of these women were affected by the disruptions of World War II.

The overall evidence for the effects of urbanization, industrialization, and migration on fertility is weak and sometimes contradictory. The separate effects have not yet been isolated from each other or from other important variables that change with development. It appears that research emphasis should shift from the aggregates of urbanization or industrialization to describing and explaining the decisions of individual households to move and the effects of those decisions on fertility.

Childhood Mortality

With the falling mortality that accompanies development, fewer births are needed to achieve any given desired family size. Because of declining mortality rates, fewer resources are spent on children who die, so the cost per surviving child is lowered. Thus, parents may increase family size, increase the investment in each child for

higher quality, or both. It is even possible for desired family size
to increase sufficiently for more births to occur than before the fall
in mortality.* Family size, by affecting the amount of resources
available for each child, also influences mortality. In essence
parents face a quality-quantity trade-off. Lower child mortality is
one aspect of higher quality.

The biological mechanism of lactation tends to associate higher
mortality with higher fertility. Death of an infant, by terminating
lactation, exposes the mother to the risk of pregnancy sooner than
otherwise. This is, in effect, analogous to an increase in fecundity
(discussed following this subsection).

Although it is possible for lower mortality to raise fertility, the
evidence shows the opposite effect. Table 3.7 shows the strong positive association between the number of births and child mortality for
Jordan and Israel. In addition, S. Hassan[82] finds strong positive regression coefficients for child mortality in Egypt. In studies across
countries by Heer[83] and Weintraub[84] the infant mortality rate has a
positive coefficient in explaining births and, in fact, is the only variable that is significant in multiple regressions. In the simultaneous
equation study by P. Gregory, J. Campbell, and B. Cheng,[85] the
birth rate has a reduced form elasticity with respect to infant mortality of 0.18, second only to literacy (0.28). In the absence of reliable data for childhood mortality, several studies have used overall
mortality rates or life expectations instead, with signs and magnitudes of the coefficients similar to those for infant mortality.[86]

There is some evidence on the mechanisms by which parents
adjust to infant mortality. Harman[87] for the Philippines, Schultz
and DaVanzo[88] for East Pakistan, and Schultz[89] for Taiwan find, in
explaining age specific birth rates, that the older women (in the late
30s) have the strongest response to infant deaths. This suggests
that parents try to replace children who die, rather than to anticipate
future deaths with extra births. In the Philippines and Pakistan,
strong coefficients for the fertility of the youngest age groups as a
function of infant mortality may be due to the young wives' eagerness
to produce offspring and gain status.

---

*The exact condition for births to rise with a decline in infant
mortality, holding quality constant, is that the price elasticity of demand for children exceed unity. The result of falling mortality on the
overall growth rate of population depends not only on whether parents
reduce fertility but on the strength of this response. Donald J.
O'Hara in "The Microeconomics of the Demographic Transition,"
University of Rochester Discussion Paper, 1972, has shown that unless there is substitution of quality for quantity, the population
growth rate must rise.

TABLE 3.7

Child Deaths in Jordan and Israel by Number of Children Ever Born, 1961

Number of Children Ever Born	Percentage of Dead Children in Jordan by Mother's Age				Percentage of Non-Jewish Children in Israel Dying Before Age 5 for Mothers of All Ages		
	Ages 20–29	Ages 30–39	Ages 40–49	All Ages Over 13	Moslem	Druse	Christian
1	7	10	11	9	6	4	5
2	12	15	18	15	9	5	3
3	15	16	24	19	10	16	4
4	18	19	22	22	13	11	8
5	22	21	27	26	14	14	9
6	25	22	28	28	18	19	12
7	29	24	29	30	19	22	16
8	32	26	31	33	20	25	17
9	35	28	30	35			
10	39	45	33	38	29	25	25
11+	49	31	32	37			
All children	19	27	30	31	21	21	16

Source: T. Paul Schultz, Fertility Patterns and Their Determinants in the Arab Middle East, Rand Report no. RM-5978-FF, May 1970, pp. 420, 423.

Harman tests infant versus total reproductive mortality (including fetal, childhood, and young adult losses). He finds the stronger response for infant losses. It may be more difficult either biologically or emotionally for parents to replace older children than infants. Friedlander and Silver[90] find that infant mortality fluctuated in sign, but that childhood mortality (up to age 14) had a strong positive effect on fertility. Harman also finds that individual families had a positive and strong response to the infant mortality rate of their community of residence. Thus their expectations and consequent reproductive behavior were shaped not only by their own experience but also by the experiences of others in the same environment. The data for Puerto Rico[91] suggest that the lag in adjustment to changing mortality is not long. They find the strongest results when fertility is regressed on death rates of the preceding one to four years.

In summary, the response of births to child mortality is strongly positive, that is, families appear to adjust their fertility behavior quickly to changing mortality situations through the replacement mechanism.

Fecundity and Family Planning

Control of fertility depends on both fecundity and family planning. These two factors, along with mortality, determine the ease of attaining desired family size. They also affect the family size goal. For example, a woman who wants a large family may modify her goal if she is prone to miscarriages and must incur larger medical expenses and substantial periods of ill health to have more than one or two children. Couples who want small families may have extra children where effective contraception is unknown, rather than sacrifice sexual pleasure using birth control methods such as abstinence. The following discusses fecundity and family planning.

Fecundity

The general rise in the level of health may be very important in raising fertility at the initiation of economic development when populations are first provided with minimal health care facilities. Not only are couples in the childbearing ages more likely to complete the reproductive period, but they will also have a faster rate of childbearing.

Very few studies have related fertility to fecundity. Those by Heer[92] of altitude and Friedlander and Silver[93] of protein consumption suffer from poor controls for other important variables. Perhaps the most detailed studies are those by R. Henin[94] for the Sudan.

He compares women in nomadic tribes with women in tribes that recently had settled down to agricultural pursuits. With retrospective surveys he finds that the settlement leads to large increases in fertility, by up to two children in those tribes that had been settled longest. He only generally discusses the basic reasons for the change--rising income, higher value of children in a settled environment, less difficulty for women in bearing children than when they are nomadic. As for the immediate cause, he finds that changes in marital structure explained less than 50 percent of the rise. The rest he attributes to health improvements, which he details with scattered statistics. He finds that nomadic women have twice the incidence of miscarriage of settled women. Venereal disease and malaria affect at least 20 and 88 percent, respectively, of the adult nomads and are associated with fecundity impairments. The percentage of childless women is almost twice as high for nomads as for the longest settled tribe. Furthermore, it is only when tribes settled in one spot that they had access to regular health care, adequate sanitation, and regular food supplies. R. Barlow[95] mentions a similar initial rise in fertility in Ceylon after the eradication of malaria.

A final factor that may operate to increase fecundity is lactation. A. K. Jain et al.[96] find for intrauterine device accepters in Taiwan that higher education and urban residence were associated significantly with a reduction in breast feeding by mothers. The extent of the increased fertility due to reduced lactation is not clear, although historical studies such as E. A. Wrigley[97] and J. Knodel and E. Van de Walle[98] suggest that lactation is an important factor delaying conception.

Family Planning

The use of family planning methods helps parents control fertility. The spread of more effective contraceptives or availability of abortion makes it easier for them to exercise this control. Yet it must be noted that the transition to lower fertility took place in many industrialized countries even before modern mechanical contraceptives were available. Thus, the crucial element in reducing fertility is changing the family size goal. Provision of contraceptives can assist, but not substitute for this all-important element. Furthermore, it is possible that contraceptive use will increase without any effect on family size. As couples become aware of the reliability of modern contraception, they may use it simply to space children in a better way without changing the total number of children.

Although this survey has not made an extensive study of family planning programs, some evidence has been accumulated. Schultz[99]

finds that in Taiwan government provision of family planning and
health workers is associated with lower overall fertility. There is
also some indication of higher fertility for women aged 15 to 24,
suggesting that when reliable contraception was made available,
women chose to space children closer together without fear of errors
in later years. Schultz also finds that the impact of the family planning programs fell off over time. J. Reynolds[100] for Costa Rica
and Wat and Hodge[101] for Hong Kong show that family planning programs, while helping to meet increased demand for smaller families,
had little or no independent effect in creating that demand. These
results support the contention by H. Raulet[102] that family planning
programs have only a once and for all effect on fertility by informing
people about methods of control. Adoption of the methods can enable
them to avoid excess fertility but do little to reduce their desired
family size in the absence of important economic and social changes.
B. Hickman[103] also considered this issue.

Studies by Rele[104] and Harman[105] show positive association
between individual use of family planning and fertility. This result
need not imply that family planners have more children but simply
may indicate that the first adopters of family planning are women
who already have reached their desired family size. Western studies
show that effectiveness in the use of family planning methods increases as a couple approaches or exceeds their desired family size.
This conclusion also should hold in developing nations.

The influence of health improvements on fecundity and family
planning is probably unimportant for most nations today, though it
may loom large for countries at very low development levels. Family
planning programs are important in allowing people to limit their
family size. But they do not have much impact on desired family
size, which is still high in most areas. Thus, they are not a panacea
for population problems.

Marriage and Family Structure

The organization of households has important effects on fertility. Most of the fertility throughout the world occurs within marriage,
either legal or consensual. Since one of the reasons people marry is
to have children and since marriage brings exposure to pregnancy,
marriage is associated with higher fertility. Because marriage is
determined together with such variables as desired fertility and labor
force activity, it is responsive to many of the same factors that affect
them. A full explanation of fertility must explain marriage also as
part of this simultaneous system.

The marriage variable is tied in with the question of household structure. The type, stability, and prevalence of marriage have important implications for fertility. Consensual marriages, which are prevalent in Latin America, are associated with transitory arrangements and more family instability. Women tend to maintain closer ties to the labor market to reduce their dependence on their husbands. Without the long-term commitment of legal marriage as a means of support for themselves and their children, women may try to hold down fertility and maintain more independence than in traditional legal marriages. The prevalence of consensual versus legal marriages tends to change over the life cycle. Young adults may enter several temporary unions as a form of trial marriage before settling down to raise a family in a permanent legal marriage. Marriage stability also is affected by customs and laws concerning divorce. Where divorce is easily obtained, average marriage duration falls, with a negative impact on fertility. The proportion of adults married rises, however. People marry earlier and more frequently and search less for the optimal partner, knowing that they can change partners later.

Polygamy, which is prevalent in Moslem countries, is another form of marriage affecting fertility. It tends to increase the proportion of women married and thus boosts average fertility. It can lower the number of children born per married woman if there is less exposure to pregnancy (due, for instance, to more frequent visits of the wife to her parents or lower coital frequency). Thus the total effect of polygamy on average fertility of women (married and unmarried) is of ambiguous sign. The prevalence of marriage also is affected substantially by the ratio of men to women in adult ages. Differential migration patterns of men and women, usually connected with employment opportunities, alter the sex ratio and thus marriage and fertility.

Finally, the structure of the household, apart from the individual couple, should affect fertility. Extended families are thought to encourage high fertility by reducing the costs to the couple of an extra child, by providing housing and other resources so couples can marry earlier, and by delaying response to changing conditions because of the influence of older generations in the family.

The evidence reviewed here concerns first marriage and then family structure.

Marriage

When marriage (or the ratio of males to females, as a proxy for marriage) is entered as an explanatory variable in fertility equations, it has a strong positive effect. The impact tends to be larger for women in the early years of marriage. It tapers off in later years when couples begin to limit their fertility. Between legal and consensual marriages, the regression results clearly have shown lower fertility for consensual marriages, as expected, when other factors are held constant.[106] DaVanzo finds an elasticity of 0.75 for the response of the birth rate of women 45 to 49 with respect to legal marriage, compared with a 0.12 elasticity with respect to consensual marriage. C. Miro and W. Mertens[107] and Myers and Morris[108] find higher fertility in consensual marriages in some Latin American countries, but fail to hold constant factors such as age, labor force activity, or education. Unstable marriages may reduce fertility or lower fecundity may cause less stable marriages through less exposure to pregnancy. Van de Walle[109] cites evidence from Africa that once-married women have almost 30 percent higher fertility than women married five or more times. Van de Walle is also the sole source of evidence on polygynous marriages. Fertility of African women in polygynous unions is lower at all ages than that of women in monogamous unions. He attributes this to men with infertile first wives seeking second wives to have children. W. Goldschmidt[110] makes the point that where first wives are fertile, second and later wives are acquired to display wealth more than to produce large families. Even though the fertility of married women is clearly lower in a polygynous situation, the data are insufficient to determine whether average fertility of all women is higher or lower than in a nonpolygynous situation.

Family Structure

Studies of fertility in relation to family structure are inconclusive. The gross data, such as that for India in Table 3.8, show lower or unaffected fertility in joint families. A study by Nag[111] finds uniformly lower coital frequency for all ages and castes in joint families and suggests it was due to lack of privacy and stronger pressures for traditional behavior. Rele[112] and J. Palmore[113] suggest that couples with high fertility who live in joint families may be forced out of them because of conflicts and limited resources within the household. The data for West Malaysia in Table 3.9 shows that past as well as current residence is an important determinant of fertility. Those who previously lived in extended families have the highest fertility.

There is scattered evidence for other mechanisms by which family structure affects fertility. Harman[114] finds that in the Philippines, residence in a joint family is associated with delayed rather than earlier marriage. Presumably, joint family residence

TABLE 3.8

Children Ever Born to Women in Bengal, India,
by Family Type and Caste, 1960-61
(age standardized)

Caste	Simple Family	Joint Family
Hindu Brahmin	4.3	3.9
Hindu Satchasi and Ghose	4.0	4.0
Other Hindu	3.3	3.3
Sheikh Muslim	4.7	4.5
Non-Sheikh Muslim	3.0	2.8
Muslim Fishermen	2.3	2.4

Source: Kanti Pakrasi and Chittaranjan Malaker, "The Relationship Between Family Type and Fertility," Milbank Memorial Fund Quarterly 45, no. 4 (October 1967): Table 1.

TABLE 3.9

Children Ever Born to Women in West Malaysia
by Family Type and Age
(standardized for residence, age at first marriage,
times married, female education, and race)

Age of Wife	Now in Extended Family	Formerly in Extended Family	Never in Extended Family
All, 15-44	3.2	4.7	4.2
15-24	1.6	2.2	1.9
25-34	3.9	4.9	4.3
35-44	5.6	6.4	5.6

Source: James A. Palmore, "Population Change, Conjugal Status and the Family," in Population Aspects of Social Development, United Nations Asian Population Studies Series, no. 11, October 1972, Table 26.

is due to lack of means to set up an independent household as well as
the postponement of marriage. Palmore[115] cites evidence from
Korea that couples in extended families are less receptive to the use
of birth control, particularly induced abortion.

In summary, marriage is a powerful variable influencing fertility. There is some limited evidence on the effect on fertility of
different forms of marriage. The work on family structure so far
has been inconclusive and lacks adequate distinction among different
types of extended family situations.

Attitudes, Roles, Son Preference,
Tastes, and Institutions

This subsection presents evidence on a number of speculative
topics about which few facts have emerged.

Attitudes and Roles

Perhaps the most important of these speculative topics is the
effect of attitudes and roles on fertility. Williamson[116] finds evidence in Nigeria, Chile, East Pakistan, India, and Israel for more
favorable attitudes to birth control where subjective efficacy (belief
in one's ability to influence events) is high. Friedlander and Silver[117]
find that an index of achievement motivation is negatively related to
the birth rate. Studies by Weller,[118] Mitchell,[119] and Rosen and
Simmons[120] attempt to measure not just general modern attitudes,
but the specific roles of husband and wife. Weller finds for Puerto
Rican working women a negative relation between children ever born
and the strength of the wife's role in decision making. When he controls for marriage duration, however, the relationship evaporates,
suggesting perhaps that the decision making variable is just a proxy
for age, with older wives being less active in decisions and having
higher fertility. Rosen and Simmons in Brazil find that fertility fell
along with ideal family size as families adopted modern views of the
role of women in society and egalitarian decision making. Mitchell
finds that when couples asserted that they wanted no more children,
the use of family planning methods is greater by couples who have
either better husband-wife communication or more delegations of
authority to the wife. In addition, where partners disagree about
whether to have more children, the husband's view is more important
for the use of birth control. His findings are similar to those cited
by A. Michel[121] for Puerto Rico.

Although some evidence exists on the importance of attitudes
and roles for fertility, only Rosen and Simmons did a multivariate

study. More work is needed where the other determinants of fertility are held constant.

Son Preference

Most families in developing countries want children, either sons or daughters, to provide for them in their old age. In some countries, however, women as yet are not very active in market activities (for example, Middle Eastern countries); and in others sons are indispensable for religious reasons (such as India, where the population is largely Hindu). It is in these countries that some authors have tried to test the effect of the ratio of male to female children on fertility. Repetto[122] finds no relation between children ever born and the sex ratio of the first three children (or of all children) in India, but an unexpected and puzzling positive correlation in Morocco and East Pakistan. He tentatively concludes that families with an unusually high proportion of sons have higher incomes and thus do not feel the economic pressures of large families as soon as families with many daughters.

The work of Ben-Porath[123] and Ben-Porath and F. Welch[124] examines the propensity to have another child, or the interval to another child, holding parity constant, for East Pakistani women and some Israeli women of Asian and African origin. They find that families with balanced sex ratios tend to have fewer children or longer intervals to the next child than families with large proportions of either boys or girls. They also find some evidence that families with a predominance of daughters try to have more sons, particularly at the lower parities.

Schultz and DaVanzo[125] find that in Pakistan the positive response of fertility to infant mortality is stronger for the death of a son than for the death of a daughter. S. Chandrasekhar[126] reported that female infant mortality is 205 per thousand in the Indian Khanna study and 170 for males, the opposite of mortality experience in most industrialized nations.

Tastes and Institutions

Religious differences have been explicitly analyzed in some studies. Gregory, Campbell, and Cheng[127] and Russett et al.[128] find that the Catholic variable had a small and insignificant coefficient, contrary to expectations. Friedlander and Silver[129] had the same result, along with a positive but insignificant sign for the dominance of non-Western religions. L. Day[130] argues that the Catholic religion promotes fertility only in highly developed countries and only for political reasons, that is, where Catholics see themselves as an important but not dominant part of the population. The institution of the Catholic church has been important in determining the availability of family planning services and abortion, which affects control over family size rather than desired family size itself. The Moslem religion also has been associated with higher fertility, but the evidence is inconclusive.[131]

Tastes for consumer goods are analyzed by Freedman,[132] who finds that couples who successfully have planned their families differed significantly from others. They are more modern in their economic behavior and have more savings and consumer durables, even when other variables are controlled. Friedlander and Silver[133] find that radio ownership and contacts with other countries (measured by foreign mail) were associated with reduced fertility, but are not significant. Friedlander and Silver also have done the most extensive analysis of institutions. The extent of a social security system and the number of years of compulsory education are negatively related to fertility as expected, but the results are not strong. The existence of a Communist political system is negative and sometimes significantly associated with fertility. This result may indicate that Communist provision of social security, female education and employment opportunities, and birth control information outweigh pronatalist policies such as free education and child care. Further work appears to be needed on these and other institutional questions, especially in individual countries where institutions change only slowly over time. The hypothesis of G. Ohlin[134] that forms of inheritance affect fertility has not yet received any empirical treatment.

CONCLUSIONS

The state of knowledge about the determinants of fertility is reviewed here. The strengths and weaknesses in the empirical work are noted; and, finally, the author looks beyond the present work to outline some possible approaches for future research.

State of Knowledge

This review of the literature has pointed to the association of several factors with declining fertility. The relative importance of the different variables to the decline of fertility can be evaluated in two ways according to one's purpose. For the purpose of explaining fertility the appropriate ranking simply takes the variables in order of their elasticities in a multivariate analysis. For the purpose of evaluating policy, however, it is necessary to consider not only which variables have the biggest impact but also which variables are the easiest to change. The total effectiveness of policy on fertility depends on both conditions. Marriage is perhaps most highly correlated with fertility of the variables studied, but it presents very few opportunities for planners to bring about fertility changes. Child mortality is another important variable, since parents adjust their fertility to achieve their family size goals. Yet development strategists have little scope for using mortality as a tool to affect fertility.

Since the ultimate concern of this research is with policy prescriptions for the reduction of fertility, the ranking of the variables attempts to suggest the effectiveness of trying to influence a given variable. The previous section demonstrates that in order of size of elasticity, marriage would be the most powerful factor, followed by female education, female labor force participation, child mortality, and family planning programs. The influences of urbanization, agricultural activity, education or productive activity of children, income, preferences, and institutional factors have proved to be relatively small or have not yet been documented adequately and distinguished from the major factors. When account is taken of the potential for policy intervention, however, the variables that stand out are those that measure the status of women, and those relating to family planning activities.

The status of women has been measured most clearly by their education and nontraditional labor force opportunities. For education the gross differential between the fertility of women with the highest levels of education and those with no education is as high as two, three, or four children. The partial relationship is only slightly less strong than the gross one. When other variables (labor force activity, family income, husband's education, mortality, and such) are held constant, the education of women has a significant negative impact on fertility. In this partial formulation, education represents several causal relationships, which have not been separately documented. Education lowers fertility through such channels as the improved efficiency of contraceptive acquisition and use by educated women, by their improved ability to produce quality children in terms of health and cognitive investments with a simultaneous focus of these investments on a smaller number of children, by their own exposure to modern ideas and thus higher aspirations for their own and their children's standard of living, and by the increased opportunities for nontraditional activities that necessarily do not involve market work.

The clearest channel through which women's education operates is the opening up of new opportunities for labor force activity, which conflict with traditional home- and children-centered lives. As women's education and thus wages rise, staying at home to raise children involves larger sacrifices in terms of the income they could have earned by working. In addition, even for uneducated women, the substitution of industrial for agricultural or cottage industry work causes higher opportunity costs of children.

Family planning programs seem to be very important for a fertility decline when the process of economic development has led to both higher potential fertility and at the same time lower desired fertility. Although historical experience demonstrates the possibility of declining fertility with the spread of traditional means of contraception, governmental policies have been able to reduce the information lag as well as to introduce modern methods of family planning. Family planning activities, however, have not as yet been shown to have any large independent effect in the reduction of family size goals.

The other variables are considerably weaker in magnitude, in significance, or in potential for intervention. Variables measuring urbanization are not significant when the major factors are held constant. The extent of agriculture is sometimes, but not always, positively related to fertility. A more precise variable seems to be the education or labor force activity of children, which measures the productive value of children in both agricultural and industrial settings. Children's education and work is generally of strong concern to policymakers in developing nations. Income generally has a small coefficient of indeterminate sign in explaining fertility, suggesting that the shift to higher quality children may be an important part of the development process. The scanty evidence on institutional and taste factors suggests predictable influences, but ones that must be studied in the specific environment surrounding decision making.

It is difficult to generalize from the evidence reviewed here about the specific impact on fertility rates of a given expenditure on family planning programs or education in a particular country. Although specific estimates are available for some of the countries studied, there are serious problems of data comparability across countries. Not only have studies used different indicators of the same variable (for example, percent literate, median education, percent with a certain level of schooling to measure education), but also the same indicator may measure different things in different settings (for example, a year of schooling may be different in rural than in urban areas, in a culture stressing education by rote than in one stressing reasoning ability). The evidence presented here should be viewed as pointing the way for further work in a particular national and cultural setting.

Unanswered Questions

The study has left several broad questions unanswered. One is the question of the timing of fertility. The works examined here have focused almost exclusively on completed fertility. Even when age specific birth rates are the dependent variable there is little analysis to separate the changes in the timing of births from differences in fertility between different cohorts of women.

Second, because of data limitations, almost all the studies in developing countries have been of cross section rather than of time series data. Researchers have been unable to tackle the effects of slow secular changes on fertility. This omission has been particularly important with respect to environmental and taste factors, which may be relatively constant in a cross section and change only slowly with the process of development. There has been some improvement with the gathering of retrospective data in fertility histories.[135] If these studies can be combined with the collection of socioeconomic variables as well as demographic ones, some of the dynamic processes in fertility will become investigatable.

A related unanswered question is the response of individuals to the changes of economic development. For example, several studies have compared migrants with natives in urban areas. But they have not examined the changes in migrants that took place as they moved and adapted to the new urban environment. Nor have there ever been sufficient studies of migrants compared with nonmigrants who remained in rural areas. Until such studies are made, it is only possible to compare different individuals with different characteristics. It is difficult to predict what will happen when a given individual's characteristics (such as residence, labor force status, or income) are changed over time.

Another question deals with the existence of "thresholds." Several writers[136] have suggested that fertility will not decline until certain absolute levels of modernization (measured by education, social services, and such) are reached. The question of modernization thresholds, however, is linked with the question of distribution. If higher average income or education simply means more for a small upper class group, it is unreasonable to expect any change in the behavior of others. Since the upper classes tend to have the lowest fertility, changes that are limited to them and not distributed to the broad majority will have little impact on fertility. Thresholds that are expressed in terms of percentage of a country's population with a certain education, income, or occupation, for example, simply may indicate the extent of the effects of development and, thus, how many people will begin to alter their behavior.

A somewhat different interpretation of the word "threshold" is as a crucial level for individual family behavior. An example would be the statement that fertility behavior shifts dramatically only when a given level (say, four to six years) of education is reached. Few of the studies examined here have been organized to test such statements. Most of the studies have used statistical techniques, which assume that the response of fertility to explanatory variables is either linear or log-linear. Only the study by Gendell, Maraviglia, and Kreitner[137] allowed for discontinuities in any given effect or interactions between two different effects. The testing of these more complicated hypotheses requires more observations than aggregate data usually allow. With the growing use of either longitudinal or retrospective information for individual households, the question of thresholds can be addressed. The most likely threshold may be education. Tables 3.2 and 3.3 indicate a minimum of female education before fertility changes. But once the minimum is attained, the effect of education on fertility appears quite smooth with no abrupt shifts for increasing educational levels. Further testing must be made with other variables held constant to substantiate this result.

The evidence of fertility studies shows the importance of modern activity of women in education and in the labor force. The broadening of opportunities for women leads them to center their lives less on the household and more on other activities that compete for time and resources once devoted to children. Information about the exact magnitudes or functional forms of this relationship is regrettably sparse. For some individual countries, however, progress has been made in investigating the relationships peculiar to them.

Possible Uses and Future Work

For a nation trying to predict and influence its future path, the better it understands the causal relationships involved the more it will succeed. But since each factor that is accounted for requires more effort, more research, and more complexity, the policy maker must make trade-offs according to what he is trying to do. For some purposes a simplified description of the determinants of fertility may be all that is needed. On the other hand, where the policy maker is trying to influence fertility decisions, he must know the exact points at which intervention is most likely to be successful. In the following paragraphs several questions are considered in which the determinants of fertility might enter.

In general, planning models use established economic relationships to predict the outcome of changing certain exogenous variables. Countries typically try to plan expenditures on both economic and social goals. Yet many of these expenditures are made without thought to their long-run consequences for fertility. Examples are easy to find. In the case of economic policies, developing countries are faced with a choice of different modes of industrial development. They can opt for heavy industry, light industry, or cottage industries.

Although the main criteria on which these decisions are made are usually contributions to national output, planners should recognize that they have important effects on other social and economic variables. Light industries, which offer employment to women, will tend to draw women out of the home and give them incentives to reduce fertility. Heavy industry, which relies primarily on male labor, will not have the same impact. Cottage industries, by enabling women to combine work at home with family responsibility, may serve only to encourage existing high fertility patterns.

With respect to social policies, long-run planning models that simply project trends in fertility and mortality ignore the consequences and interactions of different policies with respect to education, labor force behavior, health, and other social services. An understanding of the determinants of fertility allows planners, for example, to justify education not just for the training of skilled workers but also for the fertility behavior changes it sets into motion. With opportunities for children's education, parents today will have fewer children. As the children reach adulthood, they too will have smaller families. In the field of labor policy[138] wholesale adoption of Western labor codes may produce unintended consequences. For example, employers who must pay maternity benefits and child allowances to women will prefer to hire men, perpetuating the home-centered role of women. The list of policies with indirect and sometimes very important consequences for fertility decisions could be extended almost indefinitely.[139]

In contrast with general planning models are those that focus on specific population problems and policies. Some of the macroeconomic relations can be aggregated to specify more effectively the demographic sector. The analysis of the determinants presented above is particularly important for the planner facing the problem of how to reduce fertility. The planner must be aware of the precise interactions of the relationships specified in this analysis as well as others that are probably the determinants of labor force activity and marriage. The planner in this case should not be thought of as a family planning minister with limited objectives and control of only part of the overall government budget. A family planning minister, for example, has no control over educational policy or budgets even though those factors may have important interactions with the success of family planning activities. The planner envisioned here should be at the highest echelon of government and should evaluate policies and goals within a national framework, not within the constraints of a specific ministry. The planner must ask questions such as, "How much is it possible to reduce fertility by the provision of family planning services? How much fundamental social and economic change is necessary before people reduce the number of children they want?" Perfect family planning could be worthless if every couple wanted and produced six children. The planner using a complete model of fertility has the tools to evaluate the implications of different policies. Estimates of the price elasticity of demand for children will permit the assessment of monetary incentives such as bonus payments in contrast with nonmonetary incentives for smaller families. Answers can be given to questions such as, "If government child care services are provided, will the potentially lower fertility due to drawing women into the labor force be offset by decreased costs of raising children?"

For this type of analysis the planner must, of course, look both to general relationships and to specific ones germane to the individual country. This study has described some of the relationships and data that will be crucial to a model of fertility. In these and other possible uses of fertility analysis it is important to stress two basic points. First, the fertility decision is one of a group of decisions taken simultaneously. Analyses of fertility must also consider these other decisions, particularly those of labor force participation and marriage. Finally, countries concerned with population growth must seek to understand not only fertility, but also migration and mortality. Although fewer relevant policy choices may be available with respect to mortality and migration, accurate planning and prediction requires an understanding of their determinants and of their interactions with fertility.

**FERTILITY AND
ECONOMIC DEVELOPMENT**
Paul R. Gregory
John M. Cambell, Jr.

INTRODUCTION

The pursuit of more specific knowledge about the ways in which fertility and economic development interact with each other has resulted in a potpourri of theories with various policy implications for raising a country's standard of living. Though most of the theories of the determinants of fertility add to the store of knowledge regarding the relationship between fertility reduction and economic development, no theory or combination of theories is presently accepted by all social scientists as an adequate description of the relationship between fertility and economic development. The absence of agreement among social scientists means that countries desiring to adopt policies for controlling fertility to increase their rate of economic growth must select from a variety of theories--economic, sociological, psychological, socioeconomic, and such, all claiming to identify the key determinants of fertility. The development of these theories without due regard for their policy relevance and the tendency to present them as mutually exclusive, have generated considerable uncertainty among policy makers over which approach, if any, truly leads to policy that optimizes perceived national welfare.*

*This uncertainty is reflected by the opposition of many LDCs to explicit fertility control programs expressed at the World Population Conference in Bucharest, Summer 1974.

The authors acknowledge the helpful comments of Michael Keeley and the late Stephen Enke for his advice on an earlier draft. The usual caveats apply.

The economic and sociological theories of the interaction between economic development and fertility differ primarily in the variables each has chosen to explain fertility. Economic theory is characterized by an emphasis on family income and the cost of children as the primary determinants of the demand for children, with the relative impact of income and child cost on fertility varying as a country passes through the stages of development. Income and child cost are generally presumed to have positive and negative effects on child quantity demand,[140] although G. Becker and H. G. Lewis[141] have shown that the child quantity income coefficient will be zero or negative under certain conditions.*

Opponents of the economic approach to fertility analysis include individuals from a variety of disciplines, all eschewing a number of different criticisms of the economic approach but agreeing on the importance of including changes in attitudes as an important determinant of fertility reduction and as an explanation of why fertility changes in the process of development.[142] The perceived importance of people's attitudes common to all these researchers is the reason for referring to this group as the sociological school of thought, even though its membership is interdisciplinary.

The economic and sociological theories thus agree that understanding the determinants of fertility and the relationship between fertility and economic development is a necessary condition for guiding policy formulation in developing nations. Economic theory emphasizes income and child cost as the primary determinants of fertility. The importance of attitudes and changes in attitude formation as a country develops are viewed as being at least as important by the sociological group as the income and child cost variables. Which view, economic or sociological, is correct and whether these positions necessarily are mutually exclusive represent two fundamental questions for which answers must be forthcoming if an effective, concerted population policy is to be developed.

The discussion here will demonstrate that the economic and sociological explanations of the interaction between economic development and fertility reduction actually can complement each other if each is interpreted in a flexible and comprehensive manner. By incorporating proxies for attitudes, which have been proposed and used by the sociological analysts, income and child costs are shown to explain a significant portion of the variation in fertility in a

---

*A more detailed discussion of the problems of measuring income and costs, and the conditions under which the income effect might be negative or zero can be found in the article by Anne Williams in the preceding section.

homogeneous group of developing countries. Furthermore, one finds
that empirically the income and child cost impact on fertility varies
over the course of modernization as the attitude proxy changes.
Thus, the general findings can be summarized as

● income and child cost explain a significant portion of the variation
  in observed fertility;
● the magnitude and sign of income and child cost can vary as a
  country develops; and
● these changes in sign and magnitude appear to represent, in part,
  the effect of changes in attitudes.

For these reasons, it is the contention here that existing studies
of the fertility-development trade-off are unsatisfactory for policy
planning because static model tests of the dynamic relationship between fertility and economic development, relying heavily on ceteris
paribus assumptions and partial relationships, have produced potentially erroneous conclusions regarding the fertility decision due to
their failure to capture intertemporal demographic, socioeconomic,
and attitudinal changes. For example, Schultz[143] demonstrates that
aggregate, single period, cross section models underestimate the
importance of slowly changing variables and overestimate the impact
of variables that are changing more rapidly because nonlinearities
inherent in the fertility process cause the intensity of each determining variable's impact on fertility to vary as underlying taste, cultural,
and other control variables change in the course of modernization.
Thus fertility policy prescriptions must be selected that are relevant
to the country's current stage of modernization and that possess the
flexibility needed to adapt to changing economic and social environments in the course of development.
In this paper, an economic model specifying a static fertility
model with income and child cost as the primary determinants is
compared with an interaction model, where changes in economic
development are incorporated directly into the impact (elasticity) of
income and child cost variables on fertility. The interaction model
identifies the impact of modernization on underlying economic relationships by illustrating the pattern of income and child cost elasticity
response to changes in economic development, including a specific
test of the variation of the child quantity income elasticity as the
country develops economically. The main interaction variable, the
variable responsible for causing the shifts in the income and child
cost variable's sign and magnitude, is somewhat arbitrarily chosen
to be the percent of the country's population residing in an urban
area (UP) because this variable has been accepted by the sociological
group as a proxy for the effect of attitudes upon fertility.[144] In

addition, economic theory suggests that urbanization or industrialization may influence income and price elasticities. Thus, the transformation of the basic economic model into an interaction model in which the interaction variable (UP) represents an accepted proxy for changes in attitudes due to economic development provides a preliminary evaluation of whether the level of modernization or urbanization influences the size and magnitude of the income and cost variables.

This interaction model is estimated initially using OLS regression techniques. Next, the Ordinary Least Squares (OLS) interaction results are checked against a Two-Stage Least Squares (2SLS) estimation of a two-equation model in which the impact of fertility on per capita income is endogenized; and it is shown that the basic OLS results are not affected seriously by simultaneous equation bias. The models are fitted to a cross section of 18 Latin American countries using data from 1950 and 1960. The sample is limited to Latin America to control for cultural and racial differences among groups, and a multiperiod sample is used to better capture secular trends in the fertility-economic development relationship. A list of variables and data sources follows. All data are drawn from readily available United Nations' publications. The authors do not pretend that the data measure perfectly the price, income, and modernization variables called for by the theory. Rather ad hoc proxies, which are commonly used as approximations of theoretical variables, are included; and the results must be interpreted with this important reservation in mind. Furthermore, it would have been desirable to deal with cross sections covering a longer time span, but data limitations prohibited this approach.

1. Crude birth rate (CBR) is the number of registered births per 1,000 population. Source of data: Demographic Yearbook (various years) (New York: United Nations).

2. Per capita product (PY) in 1960 constant U.S. dollars. Source of data: Yearbook of National Accounts, 1969 (New York: United Nations).

3. Infant mortality (IM) number of deaths of infants under one year of age per 1,000 live births. Source of data: Demographic Yearbook (various years) (New York: United Nations).

4. Percentage of urban population (UP): percentage of urban population over total population. Source of data: Demographic Yearbook (various years) (New York: United Nations).

5. Female labor population rate (FPR): the percentage of the female population that is economically active. Source of data: Demographic Yearbook, 1970 (New York: United Nations).

6. Illiteracy rate (IL): the percentage of illiteracy in the population 15 years of age or over. Source of data: Demographic Yearbook (various years) (New York: United Nations).

7. Total labor participation rate (TPR): the percentage of total population that is economically active. Source of data: Demographic Yearbook, 1970 (New York: United Nations).

8. Per capita energy consumption (EC): quantities in million metric tons of coal equivalent and in kilograms per capita. Source of data: Statistical Yearbook (various years) (New York: United Nations).

FERTILITY AND ECONOMIC DEVELOPMENT: AN OVERVIEW

The present unsettled state of opinion over the determinants of fertility and the relationship between fertility and economic development is a continuation of over a century of debate. Originally, Malthus argued that the world would always be at a "subsistence level" because any increase in real economic welfare always precipitates an upsurge in population growth through rising fertility and declining mortality, until the addition of new members to the population exactly offsets the original increase in economic welfare. However, the "subsistence level" theory ignores the possibility of technological advance and the lag between economic and population growth. Arguments for the retarding effect of fertility on economic development can be found in R. Nelson's "low level equilibrium trap"[145] and Enke's simulations,[146] which emphasize the adverse effect of rapid population growth on the rate of economic growth. However, Enke's work differs from the pessimistic pronouncements of Malthus in that Enke argues that fertility can be limited through family planning, bonus payments, or other government programs.

Central to the pessimistic conclusions of Malthus are the assumptions that income has a positive effect on family size (on both fertility and survival rates) and that the positive relationship remains positive at all stages of development. Additionally there is considerable evidence provided by Enke's simulations that rapid population growth has adverse effects on income per capita. A complete analysis of the effects of population growth on economic growth may be found in the paper in Chapter 1 by Keeley.

On the more optimistic side, J. Hansen[147] has argued that economic growth and increased fertility are not necessarily incompatible because the income effect on fertility is believed to be insignificant (thus breaking the necessary link in the Malthusian model) and constant over time--a finding supported by Y. Venieris and his colleagues[148]--and because population growth may be necessary to prevent "underconsumption" problems from retarding development. Hansen's contention that the quantity income elasticity is insignificant is consistent with the theory of the Chicago School (the "new home economics"), which argues that rising family income necessarily does not raise fertility because the income elasticity with respect to the quantity of children is low. Rather, rising income is diverted into child quality expenditures and not into the production of additional children. Furthermore, economic development retards fertility by increasing the opportunity costs of (time intensive) children as the value of parents' time rises. Relating the Chicago School theory to our immediate problem--the linkage between economic development and fertility--the necessary conclusion is an optimistic one: rising income necessarily does not lead to increased family size owing to the weakness of income effects and to the strength of the substitution effects.[149]

Opponents of the Chicago School approach also arrive at optimistic conclusions, at least in a long-term setting, emphasizing, however, the role of attitudinal shifts during economic development. Leibenstein[150] disputes the contention that insignificant income effects are swamped by strong price effects on the grounds that the price effect is "unlikely to be significant enough to explain the negative relation between significantly divergent economic groups and fertility." Leibenstein's alternative explanation also leads to similarly optimistic conclusions, namely, changes in social status associated with rising family income cause tastes to shift away from children and toward higher status commodities. In this manner, fertility declines as perceived utility costs of children begin to rise at a faster rate than relative income.

A third and related view of the linkage between fertility and economic development is proposed by various sociologists such as Coale[151] and Davis,[152] who argue that with modernization and urbanization come dramatic changes in attitudes toward children and the woman's role in the home, thus causing a secular decline in fertility. Importantly, the Theory of Demographic Transition argues that nations entering into the modernization process may find that fertility initially responds positively to rising income until the above-mentioned changes in attitudes predominate.[153]

Thus the consensus of population authorities seems to be that there is no long-term incompatibility between economic development and fertility in that the process of economic development serves to unleash strong forces in the form of substitution effects and attitudinal shifts, which in the absence of countervailing income effects, cause fertility to decline sufficiently for the rise in income to outpace the rise in population. The empirical underpinnings of this view are strong: the mass of secular evidence on declining fertility in the course of modern economic growth[154] and the considerable cross section evidence on the strength of substitution and weakness of income effects in industrialized countries.[155]

POPULATION PRESSURES AT LOW LEVELS
OF DEVELOPMENT

Viewed from the perspective of a low income country attempting to generate economic growth, such long-range optimism does not
seem comforting. Closer examination of the above theories suggests
one reason: if the attitudinal changes stressed by Leibenstein, Coale,
and Davis are slow in coming about during the early stages of modernization, rising infant and adult survival rates will not be offset by
declining fertility; and diminishing returns will be experienced.
Furthermore, the empirical findings here suggest that the income
effect on the quantity of children is indeed positive at low levels of
economic development, contrary to the findings of past empirical
research, which fails to incorporate the effects of modernization on
economic fertility determinants. In fact, the authors here find that
the response of fertility to changes in particular economic variables
varies substantially according to the degree of modernization. Therefore, the authors warn against drawing generalizations about population policies from the experiences of countries at different stages of
modernization without first incorporating vital preferential shift
factors into the general model.

AN OLS INTERACTION MODEL OF FERTILITY

The basic static demand model assumes that the demand for
births, as measured by CBR, is "explained" by income and substitution effects, holding the level of "modernization" constant as measured by the percent of UP and the IR. The percent of urban population has been used as a proxy for attitudes because it is the movement of traditional agrarian society into the city, faced with a new
lifestyle in the urban environment, which may stimulate changes in
attitudes.[156] Attitudes may respond to a variety of factors in the
urban environment: the shift in industrial structure away from agriculture and toward textiles and manufacturing leads to changes in the
work ethic, and the different lifestyle and family pattern encountered
in the city may induce the residents to adjust their attitudes to cope
with the breakup of a close knit family unit.* Additionally, variables
such as female labor force participation may have very different

---

*Psychologists refer to the adjustment in attitude in response
to a changing environment as "cognitive dissonance." For a more
thorough discussion of how this concept has been applied to fertility
analysis, see R. A. Easterlin (1975).

meanings in rural and urban settings. In fact, female labor force
participation and childrearing may not be incompatible in a rural
setting, whereas they usually are in an urban setting. The illiteracy
rate is used in conjunction with percent of urban population to include
another proxy for modernization that is commonly used to measure
economic growth in the economic growth literature.[157] However,
the emphasis is on percent of urban population.

Thus, the static demand-for births model is

$$CBR = f(PY, FPR, IM, IL, UP) \qquad (3.1)$$

where PY   denotes per capita income (1960 U.S. dollars),
    FPR   denotes the female labor participation rate,
    IM   denotes the rate of infant mortality,
    IL   denotes the illiteracy rate,
    UP   denotes the percent of urban population.

The rationale for including these various income and cost proxies
has been discussed elsewhere, but a brief discussion at this point
seems warranted. At this point a narrow economic interpretation
(through income and substitution effects) is applied to the variables
in equation (3.1), and other factors are incorporated later in the
interaction model.

The measure of fertility--the crude birth rate (CBR)-- is used
instead of a measure of completed fertility, because this measure
may be more accurate for low income countries where changes in
the timing of births seem to be of much less consequence in accounting for changes in birth rates over time. In this manner, the relationship between the stock and the flow tends to be fairly stable.
The authors also experimented with the general fertility rate (GFR)
as an alternative dependent variable but were forced to drop this
approach owing to suspect age distribution data. The authors recognize that the CBR measure is a poor measure of fertility; but, in
general, the correlation between the crude birth rate and other fertility measures (such as the GFR or the child-woman ratio) tends to
be high. Thus, the CBR measure should serve as an adequate fertility proxy.

As far as the cost and income variables are concerned, per
capita income (PY) is included in the model because one would expect fertility decisions to change with income, holding tastes, fertility control, and fertility costs constant. This income effect could
range from positive to negative depending on the magnitude of the
substitution and income elasticities. Infant mortality (IM) is positively related to births where a highly price inelastic demand for
surviving offspring exists. On the other hand, IM may be negatively

related to births through the price effect if demand is price elastic insofar as increases in child mortality may increase the cost of rearing a child to maturity. IM's net effect, therefore, will depend on which effect tends to dominate.

The percent of UP is expected to vary inversely with fertility if the costs of fertility (both the direct commodity costs and indirect opportunity costs of child bearing and raising) are positively related to the level of urbanization. Thus UP is postulated to act as a proxy for the price (cost) of children. Another cost proxy is the female labor participation rate (FPR). The reasoning behind its inclusion in the static demand-for-births model is the expected trade-off between fertility and female labor force participation as mothers must withdraw from the labor force to bear and rear (at least to nursery school age) their children. This withdrawal from the labor force will tend to generate costs, in addition to the immediate loss of earned income, in the form of lost experience and depreciation of human capital, which will lessen the wife's earning capacity.

The preferred opportunity cost measure in fertility analysis of developed countries has centered around a monetary measure of time value, usually an observed wage rate. Arguments for wage rates and against FPR generally rely on Mincer's accurate theorizing that FPR is the inverse of the birth rate in static demand analysis, and Willis' less accepted arguments for linearity between time value and observed wage rates. However, wage rates as a time value measure also contain some recognized deficiencies. For nonworking women, Gronau has shown that wage rates underestimate time value, while part-time female labor participant's time value also has been shown to be measured imperfectly by wage rates in Willis' work. Obviously, the researcher is left with two imperfect opportunity cost proxies.

Given this situation, we have opted for the FPR measure in a study that concentrates on modernizing countries because wage data restricted to industrialized laborers is believed to be a poorer proxy for opportunity costs of a mother's time than in developed country studies and because the wage rates effect on fertility will be captured when equation (3.2) is extended to account for the simultaneous relationship between fertility and income. Obviously, both measures are imperfect proxies. For the benefit of any individuals skeptical of proxies, it should be noted that econometric theory has developed some preliminary evidence, which shows that the loss of statistical precision resulting from specification error, such as leaving out opportunity costs, exceeds that from inadequate proxies except when the proxy measurement error is very large.

Finally, the illiteracy rate (IL) is a general proxy for education of parents. In the static model, education may affect directly fertility demand as a proxy for parents wages insofar as male and female wages are positively related to the level of education. It should be noted that a net wage effect is being proxied here as the wife's wage probably will be related negatively to fertility (a price of time-substitution effect), whereas the husband's wage rate would be related positively to fertility through the income effect. Third, education will tend to affect the wife's productivity in home activities and thus the shadow price of the wife's time in the home.

Again one should stress the relatively crude nature of the empirical model and the fact that it necessarily does not capture pure income and substitution effects. The income variable may pick up some price-of-time substitution effects; the IM variable may capture stock adjustment and substitution effects, and so on.

The basic demand model (3.1) is amended by the introduction of an interaction function g which incorporates the effects of modernization. The interaction function g is specified in two variants: $g_A(UP)$ and $g_B(UP, IL)$, where the complete model is

$$CBR = f(PY, \ FPR, \ IM, \ IL, \ UP) \cdot g_A(UP) \qquad (3.2)$$

or $\quad CBR = f(PY, \ FPR, \ IM, \ UP) \cdot g_B(UP, IL)$

For purposes of empirical estimation, both g and f are assumed linear* to yield the interaction models reported in Table 3.10. The most critical feature of the interaction model is that it allows the various income and cost effects of the demand model to vary with modernization.

Why would one expect significant interactions of this type? With modernization, significant changes in the nature of income and cost relationships may occur. For example, as urbanization proceeds, the "producer good" nature of children diminishes, thus changing the basic fertility cost calculus; and the opportunity cost of children in terms of forgone female earnings rises as formal ties to the industrial labor force must be broken (and human capital depreciated) to bear and rear children. Furthermore, if fertility

---

*A similar interaction model has been applied to U.S. time series data by M. L. Wachter, "A Time Series Fertility Equation: The Potential for a Baby Born in the 1970s," Working Paper, Department of Economics, University of Pennsylvania, 1974. The authors also experimented with nonlinear g functions. The introduction of such nonlinearities failed to improve the results described in this paper.

TABLE 3.10

OLS Interaction Model, Latin American Fertility, Combined
Time-Series/Cross Sections (1950 and 1960)
(dependent variable is CBR)

Model	Constant	PY	UP	FPR	IM	IL	IL UP	PY UP	FPR UP	IM UP	PY IL	FPR IL	IM IL	IL²	UP²
										Regression Coefficients with Respect to:					
1	42.1	0.22 (2.2)	-0.40 (2.5)	-0.35 (2.2)	0.09 (1.9)	0.10 (1.2)	--	--	--					--	--
										$R^{-2*} = 0.40$		SE = 7.0	F = 5.8		
2A	-33.4 (1.0)	1.03 (2.4)	1.58 (1.4)	1.05 (2.1)	0.16 (1.0)	0.48 (1.9)	-0.008 (1.5)	-0.02 (1.8)	-0.04 (2.8)	-0.002 (0.7)				--	-0.003 (0.3)
										$R^{-2} = 0.58$		SE = 5.9	F = 5.7		
2B	-81.3 (1.3)	1.42 (1.9)	2.23 (1.1)	0.53 (0.3)	0.57 (1.5)	1.26 (1.8)	-0.009 (0.6)	-0.02 (1.9)	-0.03 (1.3)	-0.007 (1.2)	-0.005 (0.5)	0.005 (0.3)	-0.006 (1.3)	-0.002 (0.3)	-0.005 (0.3)
										$R^{-2} = 0.55$		SE = 6.1	F = 6.1		

*R^2 is adjusted for degrees of freedom.

Note: t values in parentheses.

Source: Data supplied by the authors.

control, as proxied by the IR, improves in the course of modernization, then excess fertility* will decline.[158]

Finally, the pure income effect may vary with modernization,[159]
and, insofar as our per capita income measure also may capture
substitution effects (as a proxy for wages and the price of time), the
measured income effect may vary as the relative strength of income
and substitution effects change during modernization. The variation
in measured income arises because its basic component--the wage
rate--is also a proxy for the value of time;[160] and, therefore, increases in the wage rate produce an income effect in the form of rising measured income, hours worked being held constant, and a substitution effect as a result of the rising value of the worker's time.
Which effect dominates depends on each factor's relative weight.

Equation (3.2) is estimated using OLS and the results are recorded in Table 3.10. Model 2A, based upon the interaction function
$g_A(UP)$, provides the "best" results in terms of coefficient significance, and statistical and standard error. Model 2B, employing the
more complex interaction function $g_B(UP, IL)$, yields similar results.
For reference purposes, the noninteraction static demand model results are also recorded in Table 3.10.

Space constraints prevent dwelling on the table's results; the
principal concern is the variability of elasticities during modernization. It is perhaps sufficient to note that the OLS results, especially
equation (3.2), provide support for the interaction model in terms of
significance of interaction coefficients. Deserving of special men-
tion are the strong interactions of PY and FPR with UP. Comparison
of the two interaction models (2A and 2B) with the noninteraction results of equation (3.1) indicates significant reductions in unexplained
variance and improvements in standard errors as a consequence of
introducing the interaction terms.

MODERNIZATION TURNING POINTS: AN INVESTIGATION OF ELASTICITY VARIABILITY

In this section, the authors will concentrate on the variability
of income and substitution elasticities in response to changes in modernization. As noted previously, "modernization" is incorporated in
the model in the form of the interaction functions, $g_A(UP)$ and
$g_B(UP, IL)$. First, one calculates the elasticities of CBR with

---

*Excess fertility is defined as the number of actual births minus
the number of children that would be born if contraception were cost-
less.

respect to the explanatory variables in the interaction model (PY, FPR, IM, IL, UP), evaluated at the sample means. Second, one calculates "modernization turning points" (MTPs) from the partial derivatives of CBR with respect to PY, FPR, IM, IL, and UP. This is done by determining the values of UP (the principal modernization proxy) at which the various elasticities change sign, if at all. In this manner, one obtains crude summary measures of the pattern of elasticity change in the course of modernization and some rather stark detail on how societies in different stages of modernization respond differently to price and income changes. The mean elasticities and "modernization turning points" are recorded in Table 3.11. The figures in parentheses are derived from $g_B(UP, IL)$, and the non-parenthesized figures are derived from the "better" $g_A(UP)$ interaction results (Table 3.10). The g_A elasticities and the MTPs are stressed in the discussion below. The mean CBR elasticities are interpreted as the percent change in CBR brought about by a 1 percent change in the independent variable evaluated at the sample means. The interaction impact of "modernization" on the various income and substitution effects is incorporated directly into these mean elasticities (as evaluated at UP) insofar as the elasticities are functions of UP. Thus the mean CBR elasticities relate the response of CBR to changes in the various explanatory variables at an average level of "modernization."

TABLE 3.11

Mean Elasticities and Modernization Turning Points (MTPs)
for Latin American Fertility (CBR), OLS Results

Independent Variable	Mean CBR Elasticities	MTPs (UP Value at Which Elasticity Sign Changes)	Interpretation: Elasticity is
PY	0.30 (0.35)	69 (68)	-above 69 (68)
FPR	-0.23 (-0.28)	28 (22)	+below 28 (22)
IM	0.16 (0.07)	80 (47)	-above 80 (47)
IL	0.15 (0.11)	60 (54)	-above 60 (54)
UP	-0.22 (-0.26)	10 (20)	+below 10 (20)

Source: Data supplied by the authors.

The mean CBR elasticities provide no surprises: the PY income elasticity is a positive 0.3; the UP, FPR, and IL substitution elasticities have the expected signs (-0.22, -0.23, and 0.15, respectively--recall that education is measured inversely by IL); and the IM elasticity is positive (0.16), indicating a domination of the replacement demand effect over the substitution effect. These elasticities are functions of the level of modernization owing to the postulated interaction effects and, thus, will change during the process of modernization. Convenient summary measures of the pattern of elasticity change are the MTPs in Table 3.11, which are calculated to indicate at what UP value the above elasticities change sign, if at all, and thus the stability of the respective income and substitution effects during the course of modernization.

Looking at the MTPs in Table 3.11, we find considerable variability in elasticities: the PY elasticity changes from positive to negative at a relatively high UP value (UP = 69 and above)--a finding that seems to indicate a lessening of income effect on child quantity as high levels of modernization are achieved, possibly due to quality substitutions or to shifts in tastes. Most important, this finding suggests a significant direct impact of income on fertility at low levels of economic development, which diminishes thereafter.

The FPR elasticity changes from positive to negative at relatively low levels of modernization (UP = 28 and above). This elasticity shift can be explained readily by the fact that at low levels of urbanization the opportunity cost of children in terms of forgone earnings would be relatively small when the principal source of female employment is agriculture.* As urbanization proceeds, opportunity costs rise as mothers must withdraw from the industrial labor force as postulated above. In fact, the most significant modernization interaction is between UP and FPR, demonstrating the strength of this cost transition.

The IM elasticity changes sign only at quite high levels of urbanization (UP = 80 and above). This finding would seem to indicate that, ceteris paribus, the replacement effect of infant mortality tends to dominate its cost impact over the course of modernization, and only at quite high levels of modernization will the substitution effect dominate. Thus families in both rural and relatively highly urbanized societies seek to replace children lost due to child mortality even though the producer good effect would be higher in the rural society. The IL elasticity is positive up to UP = 60, after which it becomes negative. A possible explanation for this finding is that at

---

*For a more detailed discussion of the costs incurred by female employment, see the article by Williams in this chapter.

higher levels of modernization, reductions in IL will capture primarily income effects; whereas at lower levels of modernization, primarily substitution effects are captured. A more likely explanation is the variability of fertility control during modernization, where marginal increases in fertility control due to increasing literacy may be larger at lower levels of modernization; and the fact that modernization and contraceptive technology would be expected to be related positively. Finally, one notes that the UP elasticity is negative throughout almost all stages of modernization indicating its consistent negative impact on CBR through substitution effects and taste shifts.

AN INVESTIGATION OF ELASTICITY RANGES

The forgoing discussion attempts to pinpoint critical fertility elasticity turning points during the process of modernization. However, further calculations are required to determine over what UP ranges the respective elasticities are "small" and thus exert relatively unimportant impacts on fertility. In Table 3.12 the authors calculate [using the $g_A(UP)$ interaction function] the respective UP values, which yield elasticities of between +0.10 and -0.10 for the respective independent variables. In this manner, crude calculations are provided of modernization ranges over which the elasticity is small (adopting an arbitrary standard of less than 0.10 in absolute value for the various elasticities) and likely to appear as an unimportant explanatory variable when the absolute magnitude is fairly close to zero in regression models based on samples representing different stages of modernization.

TABLE 3.12

Elasticity Ranges for Various UP Values

Independent Variable	Mean Elasticity	Value of UP at Which Elasticity Is				
		0.10	0.05	0(MTP)	-0.05	-0.10
PY	0.30	60	64	69	72	76
FPR	-0.23	21	25	28	31	35
IM	0.16	58	69	80	90	100
IL	0.15	48	54	60	66	72
UP	-0.22	Negative	3	10	17	24

Source: Data supplied by the authors.

For example, the income (PY) elasticity is less than 0.10 in absolute value for urbanization ratios of between 60 and 76 percent, which suggests, when combined with the mean elasticity of 0.30, that significant (positive) income effects will be obtained only at low levels of urbanization. The FPR elasticity, on the other hand, is less than 0.10 in absolute value between 20 and 35 percent, suggesting significant FPR effects at relatively higher UP proportions. The IM elasticity is less than 0.10 in absolute value for urban proportions above 58 percent. Therefore, the IM impact seems to be relevant only at lower UP proportions. The other elasticity ranges are to be interpreted in the same manner.

FURTHER CALCULATIONS--2SLS RESULTS

The above OLS results may be subject to simultaneous equation bias due to the exogenous specification of PY, for PY may be related negatively to CBR for reasons outlined in the above literature survey.* For this reason, the authors have respecified the basic interaction model by endogenizing the PY variable, where PY is assumed to be a function of CBR and per capita capital, labor, and human capital inputs.[161] The 2SLS results are recorded below and are not discussed in detail due to space limitations. The 2SLS results are as follows

$$CBR = -27.37 + 0.85PY + 1.51UP + 1.00FPR + 0.131M$$
$$\quad\quad\quad (0.8)\quad\quad (1.6)\quad\quad (1.3)\quad\quad (2.0)\quad\quad\quad (0.8)$$

$$+0.48IL - 0.008IL \cdot UP - 0.011PY \cdot UP - 0.037FPR \cdot UP$$
$$\quad (1.8)\quad\quad (1.4)\quad\quad\quad\quad (1.2)\quad\quad\quad\quad\quad (2.7)$$

$$- 0.002IM\ UP - 0.005UP^2 \quad\quad R^{-2} = 0.57$$
$$\quad (0.4)\quad\quad\quad (0.5)\quad\quad S.E. = 5.9$$
$$\quad\quad\quad\quad\quad\quad\quad\quad\quad\quad\quad F\quad = 5.9$$

$$PY = 61.2 - 0.331CBR + 0.288EC + 0.030IL - 0.964TPR$$
$$\quad (2.4)\quad\quad (0.9)\quad\quad\quad (6.7)\quad\quad\quad (0.2)\quad\quad\quad (1.8)$$

$$R^{-2} = 0.58$$
$$S.E. = 12.7$$
$$F\quad = 13.0$$

where EC denotes energy consumption per capita (proxy for capital per capita); TPR denotes total labor force participation rate. Of

---

*Enke and Keeley in an earlier chapter discuss the importance of this issue to fertility analysis.

particular interest is the CBR coefficient in the PY equation, which captures the impact of CBR on PY. The coefficient has the expected negative sign but is not significant (roughly equalling its standard deviation). The lack of statistical significance is due in part to the static specification of the income equation: fertility actually affects income through the savings rate and labor force participation rate in a lagged manner, the lag being up to as much as 18 years or until children enter the labor force as Keeley documents in his earlier article in this book.

In Table 3.13 a second set of mean elasticities and MTPs calculated from the 2SLS structure model is provided. At issue is whether simultaneous equation bias significantly affects the OLS results.

TABLE 3.13

Mean Elasticities and MTPs, 2SLS,
Latin American Fertility

Independent Variable	Mean CBR Elasticities	MTPs
PY	0.33	76
FPR	-0.25	27
IM	0.15	77
IL	0.14	59
UP	-0.33	0

Source: Data supplied by the authors.

A cursory comparison of Tables 3.11 and 3.13 indicates the close correspondence between OLS and 2SLS results in terms of mean elasticities and MTPs. Thus the basic OLS results are shown to be not significantly affected by simultaneous equation bias. The mean CBR elasticities in Table 3.13 have the same signs as the Table 3.11 elasticities and are also similar in magnitude. The most significant elasticity change is the rise (in absolute value) of the UP elasticity from -0.22 to -0.33; other elasticity changes are marginal. The same can be said of the 2SLS MTPs. The most significant MTP change is the increase in the PY MTP from 69 to 76--a direct consequence of the endogenization of the PY variable.

POLICY IMPLICATIONS

A nonlinear interaction model of fertility is postulated to allow income and cost coefficients to vary explicitly with "modernization," as proxied by the degree of urbanization. The model is fitted using OLS to a combined time series cross section sample of Latin American countries (1950 and 1960), and it is shown that income and substitution effects on fertility do vary considerably during the course of urbanization. In fact, the majority of income and substitution elasticities change sign during modernization (urbanization); and these results are shown to hold in a simultaneous equation setting in which the reverse effect of fertility on income is endogenized. The variation in elasticities supports the position that the economic and sociological views regarding the relationship between fertility and modernization can be reconciled through the recognition of this variability during the course of modernization. For modernizing countries, the shift in sign and magnitude of the fertility determinants over the course of economic development suggests that caution must be exercised in applying the fertility experience of one country to another country at a different level of economic development. Fertility reduction policies based on the experiences of one country's economic development conceivably could increase fertility in the developing country if the relative strengths of the income and substitution effects are ignored. Furthermore, fertility policies should be designed to reflect the change in the relative weights as the country modernizes; otherwise an optimal fertility policy at one point in time may turn out to be a suboptimal approach to economic growth in a future time period.

As far as the prospects for significant fertility reduction during the early stages of modernization are concerned, the findings are not encouraging: at low modernization levels, the income effect is indeed positive, while many of the retarding substitution effects do not begin to operate in the expected manner until relatively high levels of modernization are attained. The potential of increased fertility to slow this role of economic growth in a modernizing country is the fundamental message in Enke's population research.[162] Thus countries with very low levels of modernization should not expect economic development per se to lead to reduced fertility. If such countries do desire to slow the rate of population growth, explicit population policies that increase the costs of children should be adopted since lowering income is not a politically viable nor socially desirable policy.

NOTES

Review and Evaluation
of the Literature
Anne D. Williams

1. Gary S. Becker, "An Economic Analysis of Fertility," in
Demographic and Economic Change in Developed Countries (New
York: Universities-National Bureau, 1960), pp. 209-31; "A Theory
of the Allocation of Time," Economic Journal 75, no. 299 (September
1965): 493-517; Ronald Freedman, "The Sociology of Human Fertility," Current Sociology 10/11, no. 2 (1961-62): 37-117; R. A.
Easterlin, "An Economic Framework for Fertility Analysis," Studies
in Family Planning 6, no. 3 (March 1975): 54-63; Robert J. Willis,
"A New Approach to the Economic Theory of Fertility Behavior,"
Journal of Political Economy 81, no. 2 (March/April 1973): S14-S64;
and T. Paul Schultz, "An Economic Model of Family Planning and
Fertility," Journal of Political Economy 77, no. 2 (March/April
1969): 153-80.
2. Robert A. Pollak and Michael L. Wachter, "The Relevance
of the Household Production Function and Its Implications for the
Allocation of Time," Journal of Political Economy 83, no. 2 (April
1975): 255-78.
3. Richard A. Easterlin, "Towards a Socioeconomic Theory
of Fertility: A Survey of Recent Research on Economic Factors in
American Fertility," in Fertility and Family Planning, ed. by S. J.
Behrman, Leslie Corsa, Jr., and Ronald Freedman (Ann Arbor:
University of Michigan Press, 1969); and Harvey Leibenstein, "An
Interpretation of the Economic Theory of Fertility: Promising Path
or Blind Alley?" Journal of Economic Literature 12, no. 2 (June
1974): 457-87.
4. Julian Simon, "The Effect of Income on Fertility," Population Studies 23, no. 3 (November 1969): 327-41.
5. Deborah S. Freedman, "The Relation of Economic Status
to Fertility," American Economic Review 19, no. 1 (October 1970):
25-48.
6. For example, W. Stys, "The Influence of Economic Conditions on the Fertility of Peasant Women," Population Studies 11,
no. 2 (November 1957): 136-48, for land holdings in Poland.
7. Irma Adelman, "An Economic Analysis of Population
Growth," American Economic Review 53, no. 3 (June 1963): 314-39.
8. Hanna Rizk, "Social and Psychological Factors Affecting
Fertility in the United Arab Republic," Marriage and Family Living
25, no. 1 (February 1963): 69-73.

9. T. Paul Schultz, Population Growth and Internal Migration in Colombia (Santa Monica: Rand Report no. RM-5765-RC/AID, July 1969).

10. Morris Silver, "Births, Marriages and Business Cycles in the United States," Journal of Political Economy 73, no. 3 (June 1965): 237-55.

11. David M. Heer, "Economic Development and Fertility," Demography 3, no. 2 (May 1966): 423-44.

12. Stanley Friedlander and Morris Silver, "A Quantitative Study of the Determinants of Fertility Behavior," Demography 4, no. 1 (February 1967): 30-70.

13. Monica Boyd, "Occupational Mobility and Fertility in Metropolitan Latin America," Demography 10, no. 1 (February 1973): 1-17.

14. Bertram Hutchinson, "Fertility, Social Mobility and Urban Migration in Brazil," Population Studies 14, no. 3 (March 1961): 182-89.

15. S. Iutaka, E. Bock, and W. Varnes, "Factors Affecting Fertility of Natives and Migrants in Urban Brazil," Population Studies 25, no. 1 (March 1971): 55-62.

16. Robert O. Carleton, "Labor Force Participation: A Stimulus to Fertility in Puerto Rico?" Demography 2, no. 2 (May 1965): 233-39.

17. Yoram Ben-Porath, Fertility in Israel, An Economic Interpretation: Differentials and Trends, 1950-1970 (Santa Monica: Rand Report no. RM-5981-FF, August 1970).

18. Barbara S. Janowitz, "An Empirical Study of the Effects of Socioeconomic Development on Fertility Rates," Demography 8, no. 3 (August 1971): 319-30; Heer, op. cit.; Adelman, op. cit.; David Heer and Elsa Turner, "Areal Differences in Latin American Fertility," Population Studies 18, no. 3 (March 1965): 279-92. Friedlander and Silver, op. cit.; and Bruce M. Russet, Hayward R. Alker, Jr., Karl W. Deutsch, and Harold D. Lasswell, World Handbook of Political and Social Indicators (New Haven: Yale University Press, 1964).

19. Ghazi M. Faroog and Baran Tuncer, "Provincial Fertility and Social and Economic Development in Turkey, 1935-1965" (New Haven: Yale University Economic Growth Center Discussion Paper no. 159, October 1972).

20. Murray Gendell, Maria N. Maraviglia, and Philip C. Kreitner, "Fertility and Economic Activity of Women in Guatemala City, 1964," Demography 7, no. 3 (August 1970): 273-86.

21. Constantine G. Drakatos, "The Determinants of Birth Rate in Developing Countries: An Econometric Study of Greece," Economic Development and Cultural Change 17, no. 4 (July 1969): 596-603.

22. Iutaka et al., op. cit.

23. Schultz, Population Growth and Internal Migration in Colombia, op. cit.; Fertility Patterns and Their Determinants in the Arab Middle East (Santa Monica: Rand Report no. RM-5978-FF, May 1970); "Explanation of Birth Rate Changes over Space and Time: A Study of Taiwan," Journal of Political Economy 81, no. 2 (March/April 1973): S238-S274.

24. Heer and Turner, op. cit.

25. Robert Repetto, "Son Preference and Fertility Behavior in Developing Countries," Studies in Family Planning 3, no. 4 (April 1972): 70-76.

26. Schultz, Population Growth and Internal Migration in Colombia, op. cit.

27. Ben-Porath, op. cit.

28. Schultz, Population Growth and Internal Migration in Colombia, op. cit.

29. Schultz, "An Economic Model of Family Planning and Fertility," op. cit.

30. Gendell et al., op. cit.

31. Heer and Turner, op. cit.

32. Ben-Porath, op. cit.

33. Kenneth Maurer, Rosalinda Tatajczak, and T. Paul Schultz, Marriage, Fertility and Labor Force Participation of Thai Women: An Econometric Study (Santa Monica: Rand Report no. R-829-AID/FF, April 1973).

34. Julie DaVanzo, Determinants of Family Formation in Chile, 1960 (Santa Monica: Rand Report no. R-830-AID, August 1972).

35. Marc Nerlove and T. Paul Schultz, "Love and Life Between the Censuses: A Model of Family Decision Making in Puerto Rico," Journal of Political Economy 82, no. 2 (March/April 1974): S200-S218.

36. Alvin J. Harman, Fertility and Economic Behavior of Families in the Philippines (Santa Monica: Rand Report no. RM-6385-AID, September 1970).

37. Paul Gregory, John M. Campbell, and Benjamin S. Cheng, "A Cost-Inclusive Simultaneous Equation Model of Birth Rates," Econometrica 40, no. 4 (July 1972): 681-87.

38. Hugh Loebner and Edwin D. Driver, "Differential Fertility in Central India: A Path Analysis," Demography 10, no. 3 (August 1973): 329-50.

39. Bernard C. Rosen and Alan B. Simmons, "Industrialization, Family and Fertility: A Structural Psychological Analysis of the Brazilian Case," Demography 8, no. 1 (February 1971): 49-69.

40. Eva Mueller, "Economic Motives for Family Limitation," Population Studies 26, no. 3 (November 1972): 383-403.

41. Robert E. Mitchell, "Husband-Wife Relations and Family-Planning Practices in Urban Hong Kong," Journal of Marriage and the Family 34, no. 1 (February 1972): 139-46.

42. Howard Schumann, Alex Inkeles, and David Smith, "Some Social Psychological Effects and Noneffects of Literacy in a New Nation," Economic Development and Cultural Change 16, no. 1 (October 1967): 1-14.

43. Loebner and Driver, op. cit.

44. J. Williamson, "Subjective Efficacy and Ideal Family Size as Predictors of Favorability Toward Birth Control," Demography 7, no. 3 (August 1970): 329-40.

45. Christine Oppong, "Conjugal Power and Resources: An Urban African Example," Journal of Marriage and the Family 32, no. 4 (November 1970): 676-80.

46. Robert Weller, "The Employment of Wives, Dominance, and Fertility," Journal of Marriage and the Family 30, no. 3 (August 1968): 437-42.

47. Rosen and Simmons, op. cit.

48. A. Leibowitz, "Home Investments in Children," Journal of Political Economy 82, no. 2 (March/April 1974): S111-S113.

49. Marcelo Selowsky, "An Attempt to Estimate Rates of Return in Investment in Infant Nutrition Programs," mimeographed, for International Conference on Nutrition, National Development, and Planning, October 1971; Alan Berg, The Nutrition Factor (Washington, D.C.: The Brookings Institution, 1973); and Berg, Nevin S. Scrimshaw, and David L. Call, Nutrition, National Development, and Planning (Cambridge, Mass.: Massachusetts Institute of Technology Press, 1973).

50. Schultz, Population Growth and Internal Migration in Colombia, op. cit.

51. Sui Ying Wat and R. W. Hodge, "Social and Economic Factors in Hong Kong's Fertility Decline," Population Studies 26, part 2 (November 1972): 455-64.

52. Schultz, Fertility Patterns and Their Determinants in the Arab Middle East, op. cit.

53. Repetto, op. cit.

54. A. Jaffe and K. Azumi, "The Birth Rate and Cottage Industries in Underdeveloped Countries," Economic Development and Cultural Change 9, no. 1 (October 1960): 52-63.

55. J. Stycos, "Female Employment and Fertility in Lima, Peru," Milbank Memorial Fund Quarterly 43, no. 1 (January 1965): 42-54.

56. Heer and Turner, op. cit.; Gendell et al., op. cit.; Schultz, op. cit.; Wat and Hodge, op. cit.; Repetto, op. cit.; and David S. Kleinman, "Fertility Variation and Resources in Rural

India (1961)," Economic Development and Cultural Change 21, no. 4 (July 1973): 679-98.

57. Schultz, Population Growth and Internal Migration in Colombia, op. cit.

58. Gendell et al., op. cit.

59. Oppong, op. cit.

60. Rosen and Simmons, op. cit.

61. John D. Kasarda, "Economic Structure and Fertility: A Comparative Analysis," Demography 8, no. 3 (August 1971): 307-17; Maurer et al., op. cit.; Da Vanzo, op. cit.; Harman, op. cit.; and Schultz, Fertility Patterns and Their Determinants in the Arab Middle East, op. cit.

62. Adelman, op. cit.

63. Ita I. Ekanem, "A Further Note on the Relation Between Economic Development and Fertility," Demography 9, no. 3 (August 1972): 383-98.

64. Friedlander and Silver, op. cit.

65. Drakatos, op. cit.

66. Schultz, op. cit.; Ben-Porath, op. cit.; Robert Weintraub, "The Birth Rate and Economic Development: An Empirical Study," Econometrica 40, no. 4 (October 1962): 812-17; and Heer and Turner, op. cit.

67. Ibid.

68. Friedlander and Silver, op. cit.

69. Adelman, op. cit.

70. Heer, op. cit.

71. Alvin Zarate, "Fertility in Urban Areas of Mexico: Implications for the Theory of Demographic Transition," Demography 4, no. 1 (November 1967): 363-71.

72. Rosen and Simmons, op. cit.

73. J. Rele, "Fertility Differentials in India," Milbank Memorial Fund Quarterly 41, no. 2 (April 1963): 183-99.

74. Iutaka et al., op. cit.

75. Schultz, Population Growth and Internal Migration in Colombia, op. cit.

76. John J. Macisco, Leon F. Bouvier, and Martha Renzi, "Migration Status, Education and Fertility in Puerto Rico, 1960," Milbank Memorial Fund Quarterly 47, no. 2 (April 1969): 167-87; and Macisco, Bouvier, and Robert H. Weller, "The Effect of Labor Force Participation on the Relationship Between Migration Status and Fertility in San Juan, Puerto Rico," Milbank Memorial Fund Quarterly 48, no. 1 (January 1970): 51-71.

77. George Myers and Earl Morris, "Migration and Fertility in Puerto Rico," Population Studies 20, no. 1 (July 1966): 85-96.

78. Sidney Goldstein, "Interrelations Between Migration and Fertility in Thailand," Demography 10, no. 2 (May 1973): 225-41.

79. Moni Nag, "The Influence of Conjugal Behavior, Migration and Contraception on Natality in Barbados," in Culture and Population, ed. by S. Polgar (Chapel Hill: University of North Carolina, 1971).

80. Ben-Porath, op. cit.; "Economic Analysis of Fertility in Israel: Point and Counter-point," Journal of Political Economy 81, no. 2 (March/April 1973): S202-S233; and "On Child Traits and the Choice of Family Size," mimeographed, Maurice Falk Institute for Economic Research in Israel, discussion paper 731 for XX International Meeting, The Institute of Management Sciences, June 1973.

81. Nag, op. cit.

82. Shafick S. Hassan, "Influence of Child Mortality on Fertility," Population Index 32, no. 3 (July 1966): 354; and "Religion versus Child Mortality as a Cause of Differential Fertility," Population Index 33, no. 3 (July-September 1967): 345.

83. Heer, op. cit.

84. Weintraub, op. cit.

85. Paul R. Gregory, John M. Campbell, and Benjamin S. Cheng, "A Cost-Inclusive Simultaneous Equation Model of Birth Rates," Econometrica 40, no. 4 (July 1972): 681-87.

86. Janowitz, op. cit.; DaVanzo, op. cit.; Schultz, "An Economic Model of Family Planning and Fertility," op. cit.; and Nerlove and Schultz, op. cit.

87. Harman, op. cit.

88. T. Paul Schultz and Julie DaVanzo, Analysis of Demographic Change in East Pakistan: A Study of Retrospective Survey Data (Santa Monica: Rand Report no. R-564-AID, September 1970).

89. T. Paul Schultz, "Explanation of Birth Rate Changes Over Space and Time: A Study of Taiwan," Journal of Political Economy 81, no. 2 (March/April 1973): S238-S274.

90. Friedlander and Silver, op. cit.

91. Nerlove and Schultz, op. cit.; Schultz, "An Economic Model of Family Planning and Fertility," op. cit.

92. David Heer, "Fertility Differences in Andean Countries: A Reply to W. H. James," Population Studies 21, no. 1 (July 1967): 71-73.

93. Friedlander and Silver, op. cit.

94. R. Henin, "Fertility Differentials in the Sudan," Population Studies 22, no. 1 (March 1968): 147-64; and "The Patterns and Causes of Fertility Differentials in the Sudan," Population Studies 23, no. 2 (July 1969): 171-98.

95. Robin Barlow, "The Economic Effects of Malaria Eradication," American Economic Review 57, no. 2 (May 1967): 130-48.

96. Anrudh K. Jain, T. C. Hsu, Ronald Freedman, and M. C. Chang, "Demographic Aspects of Lactation and Postpartum Amenorrhea," Demography 7, no. 2 (May 1970): 255-71.

97. Edward A. Wrigley, "Family Limitation in Pre-Industrial England," The Economic History Review 19, no. 1 (April 1966): 82-109.

98. John Knodel and Etienne Van de Walle, "Breast Feeding, Fertility and Infant Mortality: An Analysis of Some Early German Data," Population Studies 21, no. 2 (September 1967): 109-31.

99. Schultz, "Explanation of Birth Rate Changes Over Space and Time," op. cit.

100. Jack Reynolds, "Costa Rica: Measuring the Demographic Impact of Family Planning Programs," Studies in Family Planning 4, no. 11 (November 1973): 310-16.

101. Wat and Hodge, op. cit.

102. Harry M. Raulet, "Family Planning and Population Control in Developing Countries," Demography 7, no. 2 (May 1970): 211-34.

103. Bryan D. Hickman, Economic Incentives: A Strategy for Family Planning Programs (Santa Barbara: General Electric-TEMPO Report no. GE72TMP-33, October 1972).

104. Rele, op. cit.

105. Harman, op. cit.

106. DaVanzo, op. cit.; Edy Kogut, "The Economic Analysis of Demographic Phenomena: A Case Study for Brazil," Ph.D. dissertation, University of Chicago, September 1972; and Nerlove and Schultz, op. cit.

107. Carmen Miro and Walter Mertens, "Influences Affecting Fertility in Urban and Rural Latin America," Milbank Memorial Fund Quarterly 46, no. 3 (July 1968): 89-120.

108. Myers and Morris, op. cit.

109. Etienne Van de Walle, "The Relation of Marriage to Fertility in African Demographic Inquiries," Demography 2, no. 3 (August 1965): 302-8.

110. Walter Goldschmidt, "The Brideprice of the Sebei," Scientific American 229, no. 1 (July 1973): 74-85.

111. Moni Nag, "Family Type and Fertility," in Proceedings of the World Population Conference, United Nations (New York: United Nations, 1967), pp. 160-63.

112. Rele, op. cit.

113. James A. Palmore, "Population Change, Conjugal Status and the Family," in Population Aspects of Social Development, United Nations Asian Population Series, no. 11, October 1972.

114. Harman, op. cit.

115. Palmore, op. cit.

116. Williamson, op. cit.

117. Friedlander and Silver, op. cit.

118. Weller, op. cit.

119. Mitchell, op. cit.

120. Rosen and Simmons, op. cit.

121. Andree Michel, "Interaction and Family Planning in the French Urban Family," Demography 4, no. 2 (November 1967): 615-25.

122. Repetto, op. cit.

123. Ben-Porath, "On Child Traits and the Choice of Family Size," op. cit.

124. Yoram Ben-Porath and Finnis Welch, Uncertain Quality: Sex of Children and Family Size (Santa Monica: Rand Report no. R-1117-NIH/RF, revised October 1972).

125. Schultz and DaVanzo, op. cit.

126. Sripati Chandrasekhar, Infant Mortality, Population Growth, and Family Planning in India (Chapel Hill: University of North Carolina Press, 1972).

127. Gregory et al., op. cit.

128. Russett et al., op. cit.

129. Friedlander and Silver, op. cit.

130. Lincoln H. Day, "Catholic Teaching and Catholic Fertility," in United Nations Proceedings of the World Population Conference 1965 2 (1967): 249-50; "Natality and Ethnocentrism: Some Relationships Suggested by an Analysis of Catholic-Protestant Differentials," Population Studies 22, no. 1 (March 1968): 27-50.

131. See Dudley Kirk, "Factors Affecting Moslem Natality," in Family Planning and Population Programs, by Bernard Berelson et al. (Chicago: University of Chicago Press, 1966), ch. 46, for a general discussion; Loebner and Driver, op. cit., Table 8, for India; David Yaukey, "Some Immediate Determinants of Fertility Differences in Lebanon," Marriage and Family Living 25, no. 1 (February 1963): 27-34, for Lebanon; and Hassan, op. cit., for Egypt.

132. Deborah S. Freedman, "The Relationship of Family Planning to Savings and Consumption in Taiwan," Demography 9, no. 3 (August 1972): 499-505.

133. Friedlander and Silver, op. cit.

134. G. Ohlin, "Mortality, Marriage, and Growth in Pre-Industrial Population," Population Studies 14, part 3 (March 1961): 190-97.

135. See, for example, Harman, op. cit.; Henin, op. cit.; and Schultz and DaVanzo, op. cit.

136. Kirk, op. cit.

137. Gendell et al., op. cit.

138. Schultz, Fertility Patterns and Their Determinants in the Arab Middle East, op. cit.

139. Hickman, op. cit.

Fertility and Economic Development
Paul R. Gregory and
John M. Campbell, Jr.

140. Respectively, Becker, "An Economic Analysis of Fertility," op. cit.; and Willis, op. cit.

141. Gary S. Becker and H. Gregg Lewis, "On the Interaction between the Quantity and Quality of Children," Journal of Political Economy 81, no. 2 (March/April 1973): S279-88.

142. Ansley J. Coale, "Factors Associated with Development of Low Fertility: An Historic Summary," in Proceedings of the World Population Conference 1965, op. cit.; Kingsley Davis, Human Society (New York, 1949); Leibenstein, op. cit.

143. T. Paul Schultz, "A Preliminary Survey of Economic Analyses of Fertility," American Economic Review 53, no. 2 (May 1973): 71-78.

144. Leibenstein, op. cit.; and Coale, op. cit.

145. R. Nelson, "The Low-Level Equilibrium Trap," American Economic Review 46 (December 1956): 894-908.

146. Stephen Enke, "The Economic Consequences of Rapid Population Growth," Economic Journal 81 (December 1971): 800-11.

147. John R. Hansen, "Economic Consequences of Rapid Population Growth--A Comment," Economic Journal 83 (March 1972): 217-19.

148. Y. Venieris, F. Sebold, and R. Harper, "The Impact of Economic, Technological and Demographic Factors on Aggregate Births," Review of Economics and Statistics (November 1973): 55, 493-97.

149. Michael C. Keeley, "A Comment on an Interpretation of the Economic Theory of Fertility: Promising Path or Blind Alley?" Journal of Economic Literature 13, no. 2 (June 1975): 461-68; and Anne D. Williams, Determinants of Fertility in Developing Countries: Review and Evaluation of the Literature, Chapter 3 (1975).

150. Leibenstein, op. cit.

151. Coale, op. cit.

152. Davis, op. cit.

153. Simon Kuznets, "Quantitative Aspects of the Economic Growth of Nations," Economic Development and Cultural Change 15, no. 2 (January 1967): 1-14.

154. Ibid.

155. Schultz, "A Preliminary Survey of Economic Analyses of Fertility," op. cit.

156. Leibenstein, "An Interpretation of the Economic Theory of Fertility: Promising Path or Blind Alley?" op. cit.

157. Kuznets, op. cit.

158. M. L. Watcher, "A Time Series Fertility Equation: The Potential for a Baby Boom in the 1970s," Working Paper, Department of Economics, University of Pennsylvania, 1974.

159. Kuznets, op. cit.

160. Willis, op. cit.

161. Gregory et al. , op. cit.

162. Enke, op. cit.

OFFERING BONUSES TO REDUCE FERTILITY

Stephen Enke
Bryan D. Hickman

BACKGROUND

More than a dozen governments of LDCs have promoted and financed family planning services for over a decade. Even more LDC governments have initiated such birth control programs during the last ten years. Experience to date, though obviously varied, seems to indicate that even the most successful programs eventually "peak" at acceptance rates that are far below the fertility reductions needed to accelerate economic development significantly.[1] There are few official family planning programs today that are "protecting" more than 10 percent of all women aged 15 to 45, whether directly or through their male partners. Moreover, considering some of the older and more "successful" programs, such as those of India, Taiwan, and Korea, the proportion of fertile and exposed women who are protected appears not to be increasing. In most LDCs, desired population growth rates of around 1 percent a year would require an increase in contraceptive use of from three to five times, with perhaps one-half of all fecund and exposed women aged 14 to 45 (or perhaps all such women aged 25 to 45) practicing effective contraception for several years at a time.

All LDC official family planning programs emphasize, in terms of budgets, personnel, and materials, the supply of contraceptive

This is a revised version of an earlier article of the same title that appeared in the Journal of Biosocial Sciences, vol. 5, 1973. Some of the research on which this article is based was financed by the U.S. Agency for International Development's Office of Population.

information and means. Several of these programs provide small
incentive payments to "diffusers" (that is, those who introduce acceptors), vasectomy volunteers, doctors making IUD insertions,
and such; but to date there is only one program where incentive payments for such actions amount to as much as 20 percent of the program's total budget. * Family planning programs have been traditionally supply constrained in their early stages, and the initial
emphasis properly has been on supplying more clinics with equipment
and staff; more doctors, nurses, and other paramedics; and more
condoms, pills, and IUDs.

However, in those LDCs where the objective is a population
growth rate of 1 percent or less, an expanding family planning program inevitably will reach the stage where it is no longer supply
constrained but instead becomes demand constrained. Additional
clinics will be underutilized. Supplying more contraceptive devices
will not increase the number of acceptors. There may remain some
bottlenecks, such as lack of doctors to insert IUDs; but relative expansion ceases because there are not enough additional couples who
want to prevent pregnancies. At this point in their evolution, official LDC programs must expend resources and/or funds to increase
the demand for family planning services.

Broadly, there are two different approaches: those which increase the acceptance of family planning at any given price and
those which change the price of family planning. To accomplish the
former, the government can use resources to educate, promote,
and propagandize; using movies, radio, billboards, pamphlets, and
instructors, with the object of changing couples' attitudes toward
having children. To lower the price of family planning, it can make
payments to women who remain nonpregnant, to men who have
vasectomies, to diffusers who bring women to clinics for IUD insertions, and so on. The economic distinction between these two approaches is that the former uses scarce labor, capital and material
resources that would otherwise contribute to gross national product.
In contrast, bonuses are transfer payments and not resource costs,
so their payment does not subtract from national output (except for
costs of administration and economic costs of higher taxes).

---

*The Indian government's program for 1969-74 has bonus pay-
ments of all kinds equal to approximately one-fifth of the overall
budget. Expenditures in 1971-72, for instance, have been estimated
at $9.7 million. The Indian program is unique, however, in its
relative emphasis on bonus and is responsible for about three-
quarters of all family planning bonuses paid throughout the world. [2]

Some government programs already provide financial incentives. In India, a payment as high as 114 rupees ($15.20) occasionally has been paid to volunteers (for example, at recent vasectomy "festivals" such as Ernakulam*). However, according to calculations presented below, bonuses for having a vasectomy well could be many times larger than those offered by most government programs. Moreover, generous payments to women who remain nonpregnant also appear economical, but this type of bonus system has been introduced in only a very few instances.† The introduction of more kinds of bonuses, or paying more significant sums, would increase the number of acceptors; but the magnitude of the increase cannot be predicted without empirical research. It is becoming obvious, however, that present family planning programs with their emphasis on contraceptive supply rather than on creating contraceptive demand will not attain the acceptance rates that are deemed necessary by government planners.

Even among vigorous proponents of family planning, there are many who oppose the use of bonuses. A common view is that if birth control is in the self-interest of couples, they will practice it; if it is not, governments should not bribe them to do so. The arguments in favor of bonuses are several. Insofar as society provides many incentives in favor of high fertility (for example, lower taxes for large families or free schools), bonuses can be viewed as simply

---

*Several vasectomy "festivals" have yielded many thousands of operations over a period of weeks. The one in Ernakulam District has so far been the most successful. In addition to the cash bonus, a sari and a plastic bucket were provided as inducements (Krishnakumar, 1971). Vasectomy bonuses ordinarily available are less than half those offered at the largest "festivals." Critics of these publicized festivals complain that the wave of increased vasectomies that they produce is followed by a trough of very few volunteers.

†This type of bonus system has been introduced on tea estates in Southern India. These estates have long provided medical services on a paternalistic basis, and the women involved are well known to the estate management. In these experiments, women employees of the estate are given savings accounts in their own names, and monthly credits are made for as long as the women have less than three children. In the case of a third or subsequent birth, a substantial sum is forfeited, ostensibly to pay for maternity services. Any remaining balance is forfeited in the event of a fifth child being born. Otherwise the accumulated balance is paid to each woman when she has passed her childbearing years. Somewhat similar schemes have been proposed for certain areas in Malaysia.[3]

redressing the balance. Perhaps more important, the number of children that each couple typically wants may be greater than the number of children that is "best" for all couples to have, in which case society, through government, should reward those couples that limit their family size and so advance the general interest. As explained in what follows, bonuses are essentially the same as subsidies; it is hardly logical to favor subsidies but oppose bonuses, if bonuses are shown to be effective.

BONUSES VERSUS SUBSIDIES AND ADVERTISING

Bonus payments historically have been the last recourse adopted by family planning programs seeking to gain extra acceptors. Services will be subsidized, and promotion through advertising and education will be undertaken before bonuses are tried. However, all three means of increasing the number of acceptors can be used in various combinations, and a strong case can be made against including subsidies and advertising while excluding bonuses.

FIGURE 4.1

Bonuses, Advertising, and Subsidies

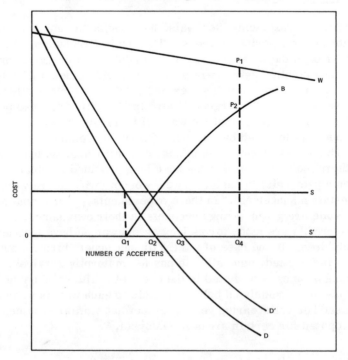

Figure 4.1 illustrates how these various methods interact with one another. The horizontal axis represents numbers of acceptors who are practicing effective birth control. This may be viewed as a proxy, albeit imperfect, for births prevented or reduced fertility, which are the real objectives of a family planning program. The vertical axis represents costs or worths in monetary terms. The D schedule represents the market demand curve for contraceptives or the worth that women acceptors place on effective birth control.* The S schedule shows the cost of supplying contraceptive services: in this instance, it is assumed that there are no economies or diseconomies of scale; and the schedule is horizontal. Assuming no subsidies and no bonuses, one would expect the number of acceptors to be $0Q_1$.

Subsidizing the services can increase the number of acceptors by making contraception cheaper for them. Full subsidization would lower the supply schedule from S to S', making birth control services "free" to users. In this extreme case, the number of acceptors would be $0Q_2$.

Advertising and education could be used in addition or instead. In either event, its effect is to increase acceptors' demands for contraceptive services. This is shown as a shift in the demand schedule to the right, say from D to D', depending on the intensity of the promotional effort.† (It also results in additional costs, not reflected in the supply curve S.) If such advertising were combined with complete subsidization, the expected number of acceptors would be represented by $0Q_3$. The number of acceptors with this degree of advertising, but without subsidization, would be determined by the intersection of the D' and S schedules.

Bonuses logically can be viewed as a sort of "subsidy" that exceeds the cost of the service. The real subsidy cannot exceed, of

---

*The negative inclination of the D (and D') schedule indicates that more women will pay a low contraceptive service cost than a high service cost. That the D schedule becomes negative means that beyond Q_2 additional acceptors have to be compensated in money or in kind for accepting contraception even though devices are free. That the D schedule is convex when viewed from the origin means that many more women will accept contraception for each unit increase in the bonus; or, stated conversely, for every unit increment in the cost of contraception, there is a progressively smaller decrease in the number of women who now will purchase it.

†Bonus payments to family planning field workers and other diffusers, as other promotional efforts, also have the effect of shifting the demand schedule to the right.

course, what the service in fact costs. However, if the service costs
$5 a year and the government wishes to spend $15 per acceptor to
induce more of them, it can either subsidize the service by $5 and
pay a $10 bonus or simply pay a $15 bonus without a subsidy. Prag-
matically, if subsidies are acceptable, bonuses that are "excess"
subsidies should be acceptable too. The main difference is that the
bonus beyond cost of service involves no resource costs, only transfer payments. The amount that government has to pay (in some
combination of bonuses and subsidies) to obtain acceptors is given
by the vertical distance between the supply curve S and the relevant
demand schedule (lying below it).

The amount that the government should pay for extra acceptors
to maximize social welfare depends on complex demographic-
economic interactions and externalities. The analysis of these factors is beyond the scope of this essay, but suffice it to say that the
social costs of additional births are likely to be higher than the private costs to the couples having them. It is, therefore, worthwhile
for government as representative of society as a whole to sponsor
family planning programs and to pay some level of bonuses. The
maximum amount that it can offer for successive increments of acceptors is shown in Figure 4.1 by the schedule designated W, which
is the social demand curve for births prevented. This schedule is
believed to be less negatively inclined than the private demand
schedule of acceptors designated D.

If government wanted $0Q_4$ acceptors, it could just afford to pay
P_1Q_4 per acceptor. The reflection of the demand curve into the
upper quadrant B shows that the government need only pay P_2Q_4,
securing a net gain for society of P_1P_2 per acceptor. If government
does not subsidize contraceptive services, the bonus can also be
P_2Q_4; and acceptors will use part of their bonus to pay the costs of
using contraceptives. If government pays service costs, the necessary bonus is P_2Q_4 minus SS'. To maximize social welfare, government should encourage contraceptive acceptance up to $0Q_5$ by
paying bonuses P_3Q_5 exclusive of contraceptive costs. At this point
the divergence between private and social benefits of preventing additional births is eliminated.

Any balanced family planning program is likely to depend on
subsidies, advertising, and bonuses, with the relative allocation of
funds depending on the relative effectiveness of each of these actions
on reducing fertility. Most important is undoubtedly the shape of
the acceptor demand schedules that exist with various degrees of
advertising. The more elastic these demand curves (that is, the
more responsive changes in quantity are to changes in price), the
more economical are subsidies and bonuses as compared with advertising, and the less so if they are instead inelastic. Also important

is the amount to which advertising expenditures add to the average supply cost in achieving a given shift of the demand curve. At the margin, the cost of obtaining an additional acceptor by shifting the demand curve through promotional efforts should be equated to the resource cost of obtaining an additional acceptor (of equivalent effect on fertility) by moving down the demand curve--either through bonuses or subsidies. Still another consideration is that bonuses alone are transfer payments from taxpayers to acceptors and involve no resource costs beyond administrative expenses incurred and the economic costs of higher taxes.

ALTERNATIVE BONUS SYSTEMS

Many different kinds of bonuses are possible. Some are alternatives in practice. Hence the overall design of a consistent program offering only compatible bonuses is not easy.

Bonuses can be paid for periods of zero fertility (for example, to women for remaining nonpregnant over several years) or for particular birth control acts (for example, a woman having an IUD insertion or a man volunteering for a vasectomy). Bonuses can be paid to acceptors or to "diffusers" who act as introducers. Supplementary bonuses could also be paid to certain close relatives of acceptors in an effort to gain their support.

Bonuses are logical, even when a family planning program is still supply constrained, for the adoption of a preferred method of contraception. A vasectomy, for example, is a superior birth control method, in cost-effectiveness terms, to the so-called rhythm method. In such cases, a bonus of some magnitude is warranted to secure the adoption of a method that statistically will prevent a given number of births at less cost.

Bonuses can be paid now or later. Thus several difficult-to-administer proposals have been advanced to give bonds to young couples that will mature when they attain some age (for example, 60 years) if they have had only small families (for example, no more than three live births).[4] However, the incentive effect of delayed rewards may be limited, even if such late maturing bonds include inflation adjustments. Nor do all couples in a traditional society trust the government to keep its promises several decades later. Moreover, poorer couples may have strong time preferences (for example, 25 percent a year) that exceed the productivity of government investments (for example, 15 percent), in which case earlier payments for performance are more effective as incentives and less expensive to government in terms of accomplishment.

Bonuses can be paid in money or in goods and services. Ordinarily $X in cash is more highly valued by acceptors than particular goods provided to them by government that cost it $X to supply. However, there may be some especially scarce goods and services, such as certain kinds of health care, that cost government less than their worth to some acceptors. Also there probably are couples who would prefer to receive certain socially acceptable benefits rather than cash "bribes." A possible compromise is payment in negotiable scrip or "stamps," where such scrip includes claims not only on appliances (for example, flashlights and radios) and materials (for example, cement and fertilizer) but also on specific quantities of food staples (rice and wheat) of immediate and known monetary value.

Another possible reward is not to pay a money bonus but instead to accord "contracepting" couples special priority claims on scarce public services such as health and education.[5] Government is unable in most LDCs to provide all the medical care and schooling that local families want. Thus a father who has a vasectomy before a certain age might be assured of so many years of education for a selected child. Rewards through according prior claims cost government almost nothing for they are essentially "paid" by families not practicing contraception that, as a result, lose government services. Priority reward systems must become less effective, however, as desired government services become more generally available or as more fecund and exposed couples become contraceptors.*

Bonuses for providing contraceptive services are another form of reward. Doctors, for instance, can be given a bonus for each IUD insertion or vasectomy that they perform, as in Korea. The commercial distribution of condoms and contraceptive pills can be subsidized by government supplying them at zero cost to wholesalers, so the final price to users becomes the distributors' gross profit margin. However, even if condoms and pills become as available in village stores as soap and matches, there may be little customer demand without an effective system of generous payments for remaining nonpregnant. It is probably necessary both to subsidize contraceptive supplies and user demands.

Most LDC governments that have experimented with bonuses have done so modestly. They may have offered a variety of incentives, but none have been so large that one might expect a severalfold increase in birth control practice. Vasectomy bonuses in India, for

---

*The "allocation" of health services provided by government in most developing countries tends to be capricious. More explicit and defensible criteria are needed to determine who gets priority attention and care.[6]

example, generally have approximated to two weeks' coolie wages. However, where LDC governments wish to halve fertility, innovations including large bonuses for continued nonpregnancy need to be tried. Unfortunately, the design of effective bonus systems is complex because cheating and other difficulties become more serious as bonuses to individuals become large, causing administrative costs to rise.

DIFFICULTIES IN PRACTICE

The basic idea of compensating with bonuses those women and men who practice birth control is obvious enough. But there are many practical difficulties in the administration of bonus systems. Any government that offers bonuses wishes to ensure that, in fact, it is obtaining the fertility reductions for which it ostensibly is paying.

In principle, bonuses should not be paid to adults who do not as a result have fewer children than they would otherwise, as, for example, if bonuses were paid to unexposed or infertile women for remaining nonpregnant. There is a relatively small but increasing minority of educated and urban couples who from perceived self-interest would practice birth control in the absence of any bonus for family planning. How large a bonus should be given for an IUD insertion if the woman's male consort previously used condoms? "Double payments," for example to a woman for remaining non-pregnant and to her spouse for having a vasectomy, should not be given. Large and "unearned" bonus payments must be avoided, if possible, even though such "wasted" expenditures may still leave bonus systems economical on balance; otherwise political ridicule could prove disastrous.

Governments should attempt not to pay large bonuses to women and men who would practice birth control even if offered only small bonuses. Older couples with already large families, who are less able or willing to have more children, may need little monetary incentive not to have children. It is unnecessary to pay them the scale of bonuses that might be needed to induce a 30-year-old mother (or father) with only two living children to have an IUD insertion (or vasectomy).

Governments should thus discriminate selectively by age or parity or, in some cultures, by civil status. Younger couples should receive larger bonuses than older couples because they ordinarily have higher fertility rates and fewer children. Where pregnancy outside marriage is considered reprehensible, young single girls already are motivated and so might be accorded smaller bonuses than married women of the same age. Couples with more daughters than sons might be paid larger bonuses than couples with mostly sons.

However, except perhaps in small villages, characteristics such as numbers and sexes of progeny are hard to check. The simplest basis of discrimination is probably age. (Where a woman's birth records are missing, an official estimate of her age can be made accurate to within a few years.)

A necessary feature of any bonus program is that it be reasonably "cheat-proof. " If bonuses are sufficiently large, women may seek to collect multiple rewards for multiple IUD insertions, themselves paying to have each removed in turn. Or, if women who remain nonpregnant for several years receive large bonuses, they may be motivated to register at several different inspection clinics and so try to receive multiple rewards. "Cheat-proofing" is possible, but it incurs administrative costs. These resource costs are likely to increase as bonus transfer payments increase in amount.

The response of eligible men and women to more substantial bonuses is, of course, uncertain. Nevertheless, it can be assumed that larger bonuses will induce more people to practice effective birth control for, at ever lower "prices, " more couples will take the trouble to obtain contraceptives. They will be more willing to forgo children who otherwise might provide them with immediate pleasure and subsequent support in old age. Conversely, small bonuses primarily motivate those couples who are less likely to have more children anyway, and who, therefore, provide less of a "service" to society for the compensation they receive from government. More birth prevention is usually obtained from those who will practice contraception only for higher rewards. These latter couples are presumably sacrificing more, whether it be personal convenience or wanted children, which is why it costs more to obtain their cooperation.

DESIRABLE INNOVATIONS

A really significant and efficient family planning program, one that perhaps includes one-half of all exposed and fecund couples and reduces gross reproduction rates by well over a third, in the future may have to include the following bonus-related features.

Nonpregnancy Payments

Future programs may have to stress such novel schemes as payments to exposed women of fertile age who remain nonpregnant. *

---

*At present, only Taiwan and India have experimental schemes to induce women to remain nonpregnant. In both instances cheating is

Such programs could mean the voluntary registration of almost half of all women aged 15 to 45 years. A small payment could be made on registration as compensation for inconvenience and to overcome inertia. To prevent a woman registering at more than one clinic, and thereby later earning several bonuses, a minute coded identification mark could be tattooed where it ordinarily would be covered by clothing. *

Registered women would then receive a bonus each six months on submitting to a superficial examination by a paramedic and being found nonpregnant. The amount of the semiannual bonus should increase with successive and "favorable" examinations. The amount of these payments would be related inversely to age.

In sparsely populated rural areas, mobile clinics would be used, visiting each village at predetermined dates each six months. Advance "diffusers" could recruit new registrants at a modest fee for each. Economies of scale would be realized because all local registrants could be served during the same few days.

Registration and examination clinics would be staffed with family planning advisors. Children of registered mothers would be examined on request by the doctors in charge. Payments for remaining nonpregnant would be made on the spot upon a favorable examination.

Emphasis on payments for nonpregnancy has several merits. Society is paying for performance, namely, a reduction in otherwise expected fertility. Couples of fecund age are afforded more incentives and more financial wherewithal to practice effective contraception.

Commercial Distribution of
Subsidized Contraceptives

If women are receiving up to $50 a year for remaining nonpregnant, they will be more anxious to seek and pay for contraceptives,

---

difficult. In Taiwan, where an educational bond is used as an incentive, there is usually reliable birth registration. In the South Indian tea estates, the women involved are employees and hence easily identified.

*Colored dots that can only be seen under certain light or with a magnifying glass might instead be tattooed on a registrant's fingers. The location could even be used as a binary code. Given four fingers on each hand and three joints per finger, enough combination of dots exist to record a great deal of information about the registrant and her family.

especially if the prices of such devices are low because they are
subsidized by government.

Many more couples, as well as single men and women, will
use condoms and pills if readily available and inexpensive. This
means that they must be obtainable not only at a few government
clinics but also in most village and local stores.* Such widespread
commercial distribution probably depends, however, on government
supplying condoms and pills at zero cost to distributors and on contraceptors knowing that the low retail cost to them will be more than
covered by the next semiannual nonpregnancy payment.

Government should place a maximum price on condoms and
pills that have subsidized commercial distribution. This price should
be printed on the wrapper. Otherwise merchants may seek to increase
their profits by raising retail prices, and thus reduce the use of these
contraceptives. Government also may subsidize distributors directly
or piggyback the distribution of contraceptives on the distribution of
other goods (for example, soap or matches) to assure wide distribution.

IUD Insertion Bonuses

IUD insertions should be increased by paying special extra fees
to paramedics and doctors for each insertion. A modest "inconvenience" payment might be made to the acceptor upon insertion. These
bonuses should not be so large as to encourage multiple IUD insertions and removals for the same women. To the extent that IUD insertions are especially cost-effective, this inconvenience payment
would serve as an inducement to discard some other inferior method.
The bonus should be slightly higher for younger women. However
(but only assuming substantial payments for remaining nonpregnant)
bonuses to women for accepting IUDs should be modest.

----

*India is currently the only country stressing commercial and
subsidized distribution of contraceptives, notably condoms. Given
the small number of family planning clinics relative to population in
all countries and especially in rural areas, it is difficult to imagine
how rural fertility is to be reduced except through commercial and
subsidized distribution. Such distribution of contraceptive pills
will never become significant, however, until the time that they are
available without prescription in local stores.

Bonuses for Vasectomies

Viewed in isolation, vasectomies for men with access to women of fertile age are highly cost-effective, and several national programs offer bonuses to evoke more volunteers. However, if women are receiving nonpregnancy payments, large bonuses for male sterilization are undesirable when considered within the context of a total program. It is administratively difficult to prevent a wife from obtaining nonpregnancy payments while married to a husband who has been sterilized. Moreover, because sterilization is ordinarily irreversible, it may be individually and socially unacceptable for men under, say, 35 years. However, if nonpregnancy payments are initially available only to younger women (for example, aged 15 to 30 years), vasectomy bonuses still could be paid to somewhat older married men (for example, aged 35 to 50 years). Such bonuses should be inversely related in amount to the man's age.

Bonus Eligibility and System Capacity

If a country has few paramedics and administrative personnel, little clinical equipment, and poor internal transportation and communication, bonuses should be designed to attract only contraceptors of the most fertile ages. Initially, for instance, the registration and examination of women for nonpregnancy payments might be limited to women under 30 years. In this case, only men over 35 would be eligible for vasectomy bonuses on the assumption that their women ordinarily would not be under 30. In this way, the number of "double payments" would be reduced. As national capacity to register and examine women increased, the maximum age for nonpregnancy payments and the minimum age for vasectomy bonuses might be increased year for year.

Summarizing, the envisaged program would emphasize considerable payments to registered women who remain nonpregnant, being larger for younger women and increasing as the term of nonpregnancy is prolonged. The commercial distribution of condoms and pills would be subsidized, even though the market demand for them is being increased by nonpregnancy payments. Inserters of IUDs would also receive bonuses, but IUD acceptors should receive only a modest bonus. Vasectomy bonuses would be continued, but only to men under 50 but over 35 years, to avoid double payments. Where clinic facilities are limited, nonpregnancy examinations and payments initially should be restricted to younger women (for example, under 30 years). "Diffusers" should receive payments whether they induce a younger

woman to register or a somewhat older man to volunteer for a
vasectomy.*

EVALUATING A SYSTEM OF BONUSES

If bonuses are to be used to make a family planning program
more effective, it is necessary to define "effective." What sort of
changes in couples' behavior are valuable in terms of the objectives
and constraints of the overall system? How can family planning programs and the bonus systems that, in turn, affect their performance
be best evaluated?

The objective of government programs should not be seen as
simply to increase the number of officially assisted contraceptors,
which has too often been the case, but rather to slow the rate of
population growth through reduced fertility. Birth control incentives
should prevent as many births as possible at a given cost. This cost
should include the provision of contraceptive advice and devices,
and educational programs to encourage acceptance, as well as the
financial incentives themselves.

Such ostensible monetary or budget costs may need some adjustments. The use of public health doctors, for example, who are
often employed by government in family planning programs at salaries
that do not reflect the full value of their time if directed instead to
healing and preserving life, should be "costed" into such programs
at their true cost.† Conversely, bonuses are transfer payments and
not resource costs; hence bonus payments should not be "costed" at
their full monetary value.

The extent to which bonus payments can be disregarded by
policy makers because they are mere transfer payments depends on
the level of decision making. For an administrator of a family planning program with a fixed money budget, bonuses cost him dollar for
dollar as much as do advertising or contraceptives. For a minister

---

*The most common form of bonus in those countries that have
them is for diffusers. They are paid in Indonesia, India, Korea,
Taiwan, Mauritius, Pakistan, and other countries. This tendency to
give a bonus to a diffuser rather than to an acceptor may reflect a
reluctance to bribe directly the woman or man who is to have, respectively, an IUD insertion or a vasectomy. Or it may reflect a
belief that, because a diffuser can earn many payments in connection
with many women and men, diffusers can be more strongly motivated.[7]

*How much higher these opportunity values are depends on the
ages and kinds of people whom doctors treat in their practice.[8]

of finance, who has to obtain funds through taxation, borrowing, or inflation, the expenditure of large funds on bonuses may mean fewer government expenditures for other purposes: in this case bonuses increase private claims and decrease public claims on national output. However, for the economy at large, changing contraceptive behavior through bonuses rather than by advertising leaves more GNP for beneficial consumption and investment. *

The timing of birth control performance and system cost are also important. Productive resources can be invested in LDCs at rates of return that may average from 10 to 20 percent a year. At 15 percent, a birth prevented five years from now is only worth half that of a birth prevented now, just as equal value resources expended in a family planning program today cost twice as much in present value terms as they would if deferred for five years. Thus contraceptive methods that involve a relatively high initial resource cost, but little or no subsequent costs, are not quite as effective as they may seem in undiscounted terms. Postponement of "marriage" and coitus is economically advantageous in that it defers resource costs of contraception and/or rearing children. †

A bonus system cannot be evaluated in isolation but only as part of an overall program. A preferred bonus system is one that most improves net "outputs" provided by the total program after deducting costs from benefits, all in present value terms. The cost is the present discounted value of future budgets after adjustments for lost opportunity costs and transfer payments (as indicated above). The effectiveness is the discounted reduction in births, based on the present discounted social value of a birth prevented, that can be expected to result from the costs incurred. Thus an optimum program is one that maximizes the present value of benefits minus costs, and this ordinarily will be a much larger and more costly program than one that maximizes the ratio of benefits to costs. ‡

When so evaluated, bonus-stimulated family planning programs can be improved in many ways. Deferring the average age at which

---

*The accounting of GNP includes the costs of advertising. Hence, if resource employment is constant, more advertising means fewer other (nonadvertising) kinds of GNP are available for consumption and investment. This argument is weakened obviously if more advertising means more employment and more GNP (with less leisure).

†"Marriage" here means sexual connection and not legal marriage.

‡The optimum-sized program, the one that maximizes any net surplus, is the one in which extra resources and funds have been expended until the marginal benefit value equals the marginal cost.

mothers give birth, that is, widening the generation interval, provides a benefit. So, of course, does reducing the net reproduction
rate. Persuading particular couples to use a more cost-effective
method is worth some bonus. Inducing younger couples to use contraceptives, because they ordinarily have a higher fertility, is worth
a considerable bonus. Securing adoption of contraceptive procedures
that minimize the use of overqualified doctors deserves a bonus.
Methods that involve a considerable initial resource cost, such as
sterilization of females, must have a fertility reduction effect sufficiently great to earn as high a return on the investment as do other
methods. Bonuses requiring a high money expenditure, being transfer payments, really may cost less in usable GNP than apparently
cheap educational campaigns.

The preferred role of bonuses depends very much on the stage
a family planning program has reached. During early years, when
more couples want assistance than can be supplied, bonuses should
be used, if at all, to induce couples to use more cost-effective methods. Paradoxically, if the constraint in these early years is not the
number of people who want fewer children but the availability and
distribution of contraceptive devices, the greatest fertility reduction
per unit expenditure may be realized by publicizing biologically inferior methods (such as withdrawal) and the general advantages of
planned parenthood. Later, when the ratio of available funds to acceptors increases markedly, it is worth spending resources and
bonuses to persuade acceptors to use more effective methods. And
during the later stages of an evolving and expanding program, when
the whole operation would otherwise be demand constrained, the
number of acceptors should be increased through bonuses, if economical.

Without more experimentation, it is impossible to predict
exactly what size bonuses will have a given effect in reducing fertility. The theoretical question of the size bonus that society should
pay is a complicated one. Society should be willing to spend resources on fertility reduction up to the point that the marginal social
cost is equal to the marginal social benefit--but determining this
level is difficult. The question of how much transfer society is willing to make to generate a real benefit to all citizens is largely political and often is decided by policy makers in the country facing the
decision. The economics underlying this decision is beyond the
scope of this essay. However, if a country is going to spend any
resources on family planning (however the decision on level of expenditures is made), bonuses should be considered along with all
other expenditures as an integral part of the program.

A quick calculation can be made of the probable order of magnitude of a bonus program in a typical LDC and the likely impact on

the economy's resources and the government budget. Imagine a fairly typical LDC with an income per capita of $200 a year. The population is assumed to be 10 million. The gross national product is hence $2 billion a year. The government's annual budget is $300 million a year, or 15 percent of GNP. The number of men and women aged 15 to 45 years is assumed to be 4 million. If about half these couples in each age cohort or, more practically, one million fecund women or men are practicing effective birth control, the population growth rate might fall from about 3 percent to 1 percent a year. What would this cost?

The total resource and money costs of bonus-assisted family planning programs depends, of course, on the number of acceptors of different methods. Suppose, for simplicity, that family planning bonuses are only paid for remaining nonpregnant. On average, one million women are assumed to register and receive bonuses. Whether they remain nonpregnant through IUD insertions, contraceptive pills, or their consorts using condoms or having a vasectomy does not matter. Only performance of acceptors matters.

Assume that bonuses average $37.50 a couple a year.* These could be paid in semiannual installments and could vary according to the amount of time since the woman last gave birth. Thus the first payment after six months might be only $10, but a younger woman aged 22 might receive as much as $50 on her seventh payment. An annual payment of $37.50 may seem too small to be very influential, but in an LDC where income per capita is $200, a work-age adult typically earns only about $400 per year. Thus the average bonus would be a month's earnings, and the high bonus for continued nonpregnancy could be one and a half month's earnings. Over 20 years, a couple could earn $750 and might have as many as four fewer children.

Assume also that the resource costs involved in administering a bonus program were $12.50 a couple, or about a third the amount of the bonus. If a million couples were receiving bonuses on average, the costs of the program would be $50 million, of which $12.5 million were resource costs and $37.5 million were transfer payments. The resource costs would be just over 0.6 percent of GNP. About 1.8 percent of GNP would be transferred to couples with small

---

*If government is also providing contraceptive devices free, these amounts should be reduced slightly. Suppose, for example, that women are remaining nonpregnant by using pills that the government supplies or distributes free. If the cost to government of pills is 25 cents per monthly cycle, the semiannual nonpregnancy payment would be $1.50 less than indicated above.

families from couples with large families. The impact on the budget would be significant, but not formidable. The resource costs of $12.5 million would represent about 4.2 percent of the budget, and the transfers would represent another 12.5 percent of the budget. An expenditure of this size would require additional taxation, but the political costs of the taxation would be offset in part by the payouts under the bonus program.

Total costs and benefits but not rates of return depend, in fact, on the response of acceptors by method to various bonuses. The position and shape of these acceptor demand schedules, such as D in Figure 4.1, are most uncertain. If they are not elastic over the ranges of concern, governments will find it hard not to pay large bonuses. In all probability, these demand schedules will shift to the right over time.* Accordingly, and partly because vasectomy volunteers and others may bitterly resent larger bonuses being paid later to others, governments should start with high bonuses and lower them later. Speculative effects are then favorable to contraceptive programs (for example, prospective vasectomy volunteers will not "hoard" their fertility). This might call for governments to offer the full maximum bonus at the outset. Later, as ever larger fractions of the eligible subpopulation accept birth control, less of the potential gain for society may have to be shared with acceptors.

The potential gain from bonus-augmented family planning programs and the justifiable bonus per acceptor also depend in part on the cost of providing contraceptive services. Unfortunately, the costs of birth control programs are not well known, and the marginal costs of serving more acceptors are especially uncertain. The costs that are reported are ordinarily average costs. These per acceptor costs are likely to be exaggerated for several reasons.† The lower

---

*This is because of changes in attitudes resulting from increased acceptance and knowledge of various methods of contraception. It takes time to reduce ignorance, for villagers to see how others who do use contraceptives have fared, and for traditional attitudes to be eroded. One argument for high initial bonuses is that the very gaining of acceptors will permit lower bonuses to be equally effective later.

†Estimates of per acceptor costs are likely to be overstated for several reasons. First, the numerator includes an allocation of overhead costs, many of which are associated with maternal health and child care services provided by the same clinic; because of foreign assistance to reduce fertility, some developing countries can be expected to "load" their joint overheads against family planning. Second, again because foreign assistance is available for family

they really are, and particularly if marginal costs are below average costs because of economies of scale, the higher the bonuses that can be justified.

SUMMARY

The performance of population programs suggests that even the more successful ones have acceptance rates that are only a fifth or so of what is needed to reduce population growth rates to the 1 percent a year that permits significant improvements in income per capita. Nor are large bonuses for reduced fertility or the adoption of contraception being used, except in one or two experimental programs, although several programs are using small bonuses. There is no guarantee that large bonuses will produce the number of acceptors that are needed, but it is fairly evident that without larger bonuses there will not be enough acceptors.

Briefly, if bonuses are to become an effective and acceptable feature of national family planning programs, they must meet at least the following requirements.

1. the various bonuses must be an integral part of an evolving and expanding system, and such bonuses must be evaluated in terms of the same criteria used to evaluate the overall family planning program;

2. bonus qualification and administration should be reasonably cheat-proof, and the majority of couples using contraceptives should not be able to collect more than one kind of bonus;

3. selective discrimination among acceptors, at least by age, should be attempted by government to reduce payments of unnecessarily large bonuses to those who would practice effective contraception for a smaller bonus;

---

planning, there is a tendency to add redundant people to the payroll, thereby demonstrating zeal and providing employment to friends and relatives. Third, where family planning programs are becoming demand constrained, an excessive clinic capacity means excessive costs. Fourth, the denominator used to determine per capita costs is sometimes not the number of current users of contraception but of new acceptors during the year. Fifth, the cost numerator may include all costs since the start of the program, including start-up costs. A rational and fairly standard set of accounts that would be adopted by most family planning programs and be subject to audit by at least host government officials is badly needed.

4. bonuses may be used to gain the acceptance of more cost-
effective methods or of more fertile couples, even during early
stages when a family planning program is generally supply constrained.

Finally, because bonuses are transfer payments and do not incur the large resource costs of more customary fertility reduction
programs, bonuses can be quite substantial in size. Indeed, they
should be preferred over other activities that do incur resource costs
up to the point that the resource costs associated with bonuses are
equal to those of more traditional expenditures that are equally effective in terms of reducing births. As such bonuses are really a
form of compensation, paying for valuable services undertaken at
some inconvenience and sacrifice; there is nothing morally reprehensible in paying them. Moreover, inasmuch as poorer people are
most likely to respond, there is a favorable income redistribution
effect and, of course, a prospect of higher average incomes because
of the fertility reduction.

CHILD SPACING STRATEGIES, OLD AGE SECURITY, AND POPULATION GROWTH

Donald J. O'Hara
Richard A. Brown

BIRTH LIMITATION AND BIRTH SPACING

"Family planning" involves both the number and the timing of a couple's children. Yet, especially in LDCs where the rate of population growth is a major concern, most family planning programs concentrate on reducing the number of births, sometimes to the extent of relying primarily on sterilization, which is of no use in altering the spacing of births. Even where contraceptives are offered widely, their usefulness in limiting births rather than spacing births is emphasized. This emphasis affects the portion of the population on which recruiting efforts are concentrated (women who are old enough to have had a number of children) as it conditions the measures used as indicators of success (continuation rates); and it leads to the view that a reduction in desired family size, through exhortation or incentives, must occur before the number of couples wanting to use contraceptives will be large enough to reduce the population growth rate substantially.

Donald O'Hara originally developed the idea of applying sequential decision making to old age security and presented it in his 1972 paper, "Mortality Risks, Sequential Decisions on Births, and Population Growth." Stephen Enke and Richard Brown presented some elaborations of this basic idea in their 1972, "Old Age Security With Fewer Children." This paper represents a further evolution. Michael Keeley commented on this version, although the views presented and any errors are the sole responsibility of the authors. The U.S. Agency for International Development provided financial support for some of the early development work under contract AID-CFD 2611.

The results presented below suggest, however, that a wider appreciation of the timing and spacing aspects of family planning could reduce substantially the population growth rates in LDCs even without a change in desired family size. A family planning program that gave birth spacing an emphasis equal to that of birth limitation no doubt would have to devote considerable energy and resources to explaining the usefulness of contraceptives for spacing, and it would want to recruit among younger women. Continuation rates among these women necessarily would be lower, for the essence of spacing is planned discontinuation. These factors might tend to increase the direct costs per participant; working in the opposite direction, however, is the fact that couples need not be persuaded to change their family size goals. Indeed, couples are attracted to spacing because it enables them to attain their desired family size with less risk of having too few or too many surviving children.

Only a small part of the reduction in the population growth rate that is possible with spacing is due to the direct effect of increased spacing, that of spreading a given number of births per woman over a long period, thereby increasing the interval between generations. Most of the reduction in the population growth rate comes from a reduction in the average number of births per woman. As explained below, the use of contraceptives for what is (from the viewpoint of the individual family) birth spacing results for the population as a whole in a substantial reduction in the number of births. The ability to space births enables couples to avoid some of the births that otherwise would be required as "insurance" against infant and child mortality. The effects discussed below are, therefore, of greatest importance where mortality is still moderately high or where parents believe this to be the case. Under such conditions, the indirect reduction in births that comes from spacing may be as important as the direct reduction that comes from birth limitation, because a large fraction of the population will be attracted to spacing substantially before they would be attracted to birth limitation.

It might be asked, at this point, why couples are not already practicing spacing if it is as attractive as it is said to be. One answer is that eventually spacing would be practiced widely even without encouragement from family planning programs, but that most couples have not yet discovered that spacing is an appropriate adaptation to two recent changes in their environment: a decline in mortality and access to highly effective modern contraceptives. As the results reported below show, it is only at intermediate mortality levels that the family formation strategies implied by birth spacing differ substantially from those implied by birth limitation. And it is only with highly effective contraceptives that spacing and limitation become separate alternatives; with primitive contraception, efforts to limit births result merely in uncertain increases in spacing.

The remainder of the paper discusses the interpretation of "family size" in a regime of moderately high mortality levels and discusses the relationship between family size, mortality levels, and population growth rates. The next section describes a model embodying a detailed specification of family formation patterns, with desired family size derived from parental desires for old age support, and reports the implied population growth rates under a variety of assumptions about the practice of spacing and the effectiveness of contraceptives. Then the authors interpret these results in terms of other possible determinants of desired family size and give some concluding remarks.

DESIRED FAMILY SIZE, MORTALITY, AND POPULATION GROWTH

Desired family size is defined as the family size that a couple views as most desirable, taking into account all the costs and rewards associated with having and raising children. Thus, desired family size depends on the parents' tastes (or attitudes and values) and on a whole range of more or less objective circumstances such as the lifetime earnings prospects of both parents, the extent of job opportunities outside the home for the wife, and the costs of feeding, clothing, housing, and educating children. All these may vary across a population or over time, with a resulting variation in desired family size. However, both kinds of variation are ignored in the analysis below, which considers only a "representative family."

Because conception (and contraception) and survival are uncertain, couples cannot be certain of achieving their desired family size. The couple only can alter the probabilities of obtaining various family sizes. In general, one would expect that parents' utility would decrease as the deviation between the actual family size and the desired family size increased. The specific model investigated in the next section incorporates this property incompletely and asymmetrically: all deviations below desired family size are assumed to be equally bad (and, in fact, extremely undesirable), and deviations above desired family size are increasingly less desirable as the deviation increases, though they are never so serious as deviations below.

When infant and child mortality are moderately high, it is important to distinguish between desired family size and births. Desired family size refers to survivors, not to births; if anything, births, rather than having a value per se, are a cost of obtaining survivors. In the most general treatment, the contribution of a child to "family size" would be a function of the age to which he survived.

One can calculate the average number of births required to obtain a particular family size under stipulated mortality conditions. If

one-quarter of all children die before age 20, couples who desire
three survivors to age 20 will require an average of four births per
couple to obtain this family size. One strategy would be for every
such couple to have exactly four births. Many couples would achieve
a family size of three, but a substantial fraction would have more
survivors than their desired family size, and some would have less.
Alternatively, if spacing were possible, each couple could have only
three births initially and wait at least a few years before deciding
whether to have subsequent children. Couples who experienced the
death of one or more children at early ages would replace them, and
even some of those whose first three children all survive the early
years of childhood may want a fourth child as "insurance" against
subsequent child mortality. The strategy of having three children
and then waiting may have both advantages and disadvantages from
the parents' viewpoint; the primary advantage is that it increases the
probability of achieving their desired family size. The importance
of this depends on the costs of deviations from their desired family
size. Disadvantages may include the fact that the fourth child, if
they eventually decide to have one, will be more separated in age
from the others and, perhaps, more costly to have and to raise than
if he had been born earlier.

    The number of couples whose first three children survive the
early years of childhood but who eventually decide a fourth, "insurance" birth is not necessary influences the population growth rate.
Although the number of "insurance births" depends in part on attitudes toward too many versus too few children, the ability to space
births may increase greatly the number of parents who are satisfied
with three children because the chances of each child's survival increase greatly over the first few years of life and thus the need for
insurance declines, perhaps to the point where it is no longer worth
the cost.

    One of the costs of achieving the desired family size is the cost
imposed by child mortality--the cost of bearing and partially raising
children who do not survive. Where mortality rates are moderately
high, this can be a substantial cost in expected value terms. As
mortality declines, this cost declines; and one would expect that desired family size would tend to increase. There is also a force working in the opposite direction: lower mortality makes investment in
the quality of a child (education, for example) more attractive; and
if parents substitute quality for quantity sufficiently, desired family
size may decline. [9] Any feedbacks, positive or negative, from mortality level to desired family size are ignored in this paper, however,
in the interest of simplicity.

    It is of some interest to explore the relationship between mor-
tality level and population growth rate, holding desired family size

constant. Stable population theory implies that, if family size is defined in terms of survivors to some age less than the average age at
motherhood (27 to 30 in most populations), then a constant family
size will result in a higher population growth rate as mortality declines. The reason is that a constant number of survivors to the
limiting age results in a larger number of survivors to the average
at motherhood, or a larger net reproduction rate. Figure 4.2 shows
another implication of this proposition, namely that family size must
decline as life expectancy increases to maintain a constant population
growth rate. Family sizes in LDCs have not declined as life expectancy increased; in fact, realized family sizes have increased
substantially. Although it is possible that desired family size increased, another possibility is that realized family size now exceeds
desired family size because the new lower mortality levels have not
been incorporated in fertility behavior. This could result from a lag
in the awareness of the mortality decline, or from a lack of confidence
that observed survival rates are anything more than a temporary run
of good luck, or from a lag in adjusting behavior to the new situation.
One such adjustment is the discovery and acceptance not merely of
birth limitation, which has apparently been practiced in all societies
to some degree, but of birth spacing, which becomes more important
at lower mortality levels and which requires modern contraceptives
to be fully effective at reasonable cost and effort.

DESIRED FAMILY SIZE AND OLD AGE SECURITY

This section reports fertility rates, intrinsic growth rates,
and other population characteristics that result with and without the
practice of spacing, under particular assumptions about the way in
which the "representative family's" desired family size is derived
from the parents' desires to have old age support from their children.
Although no one would assert that a desire for old age support is the
only reason parents have children, it is often asserted that family
sizes in LDCs are substantially larger than they otherwise would be
because parents have no satisfactory alternative sources of old age
support and because relatively large family sizes are required to in-
sure a satisfactory probability of surviving children.

The method of analysis used in this paper is dynamic programming. It is used to find the optimal solution for each set of conditions or "strategies" specified in this paper. The conditions include
such facts as mortality, the probability of conception, the probability
of contraceptive failure, and the probability of giving birth to a boy
for each of 12, 2.5-year age intervals. For each time period and
state (a state is defined as the combination of ages of each living male

FIGURE 4.2

Family Size Required to Maintain Stated Intrinsic
Growth Rates as Mortality Risks Decline

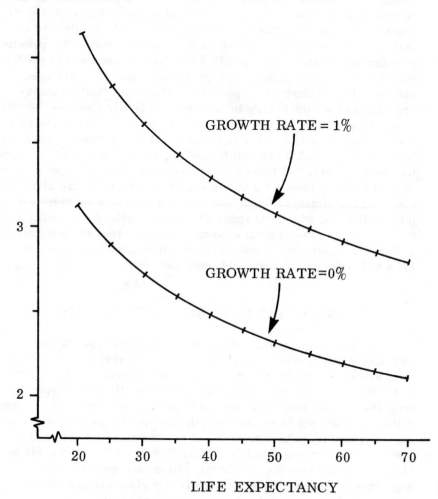

FAMILY SIZE*

GROWTH RATE = 1%

GROWTH RATE = 0%

LIFE EXPECTANCY

*In terms of the number of children.

Source: calculated from A. J. Coale and P. Demeny, Regional Model Life Tables and Stable Populations (Princeton: Princeton University Press, 1966), West, Females, TFR = 2.05 x GRR(29);
Family Size = $\dfrac{\text{TFR} \cdot {}_{15}L_0}{15}$

child), a calculation is made to determine whether the couple should try to give birth, use reversible contraception, or be sterilized. A strategy is a set of decisions associated with each possible state and time period. Each state must be considered separately to determine whether another child is optimal. The goal is to minimize the number of births while achieving a given probability of having at least one living son when the father is aged 65.

A detailed mathematical description of dynamic programming as it is used in this application appears in O'Hara.[10] The method starts with the last time period and proceeds backwards. First, an optimal decision set is found for all possible states in the last time period. Next, based on the results of the last time period, an optimal set of decisions is found for the next to the last time period. This process continues until all time and state decisions are found.

For each possible state and time period, deciding whether it is optimal to have another child may be thought of as a two-step process. First, it is determined whether existing sons give the required 90 percent probability. If the answer is yes, the decision is to refrain from having an additional child. If the answer is no, the decision is not automatically to have an additional child. Instead another step is required. In this step, it is determined whether the expected number of additional children required to achieve the objective will be less: (1) if an additional child is born now; or (2) if no child is born now, but one is born at some later point, perhaps only if one of the existing sons dies in the interim. The total number of contingencies that must be considered in this step is very large if there is even a moderate number of remaining decision points.

The structural characteristics of the model and their relationship to each strategy are explained in the table on page 218. The specific parameters chosen for the dynamic programming model are detailed below.

It assumed that births can occur at 2.5-year intervals, beginning when the wife is age 18 and the husband is age 21. Decisions on whether to have a child must be made 18 months earlier, which in many cases means that the couple's youngest existing child is only one year old. A maximum of 12 births per woman are permitted. It is assumed that fecundity declines as the wife ages.[11] As a consequence of this assumption, the spacing of births is somewhat riskier, and hence less attractive, than it otherwise would be. The ratio of male births to all births is assumed to be 0.513, which corresponds to a male/female birth ratio of 1.05.

Structural Characteristics of the Dynamic
Programming Model

Objective function: minimize the expected number of births per
woman (total fertility rate)

Subject to the following constraints
used in all cases:
- (1) achieve a fixed probability of having a living son when the father is age 65
- (2) a prescribed survival schedule (for males and females)
- (3) a prescribed sex ratio at birth
- (4) a prescribed fecundity schedule (for each of 12 birth intervals)

Optional depending on the specific strategy:
- (5a) an imperfect contraceptive with a prescribed failure ratio is available
- (5b) a perfect contraceptive is available
- (6) a requirement that the couple does not use contraceptives unless they have at least one living son
- (7) a requirement that the only available method of birth control is sterilization
- (8) a requirement that the first birth be delayed five years
- (9) a requirement that no birth control method be used

Optional constraints used in each strategy

Strategy	Description	Optional Constraints Used
A	no birth control	9
B	postpone marriage	8, 9
C	sterilization only	7
D	always a son (imperfect contraception)	5a, 6
E	always a son (perfect contraception)	5b, 6
F	latest date children	5b

Source: Data supplied by the authors.

Finally, all the results reported below assume that a 0.9 probability of having at least one son alive when the father reaches age 65 is sufficient for old age security through children. A 0.9 probability of at least one surviving son implies (1) approximately a 0.95 probability of at least one surviving child of either sex, and (2) an expected number of surviving sons that is greater than one. The realized probability of a father aged 65 having a surviving son is 0.75 to 0.85 in most LDCs, so a 0.9 probability appears to be a reasonable goal after allowing for the fact that the realized probabilities reflect the incidence of subfecundity and widowhood, which are not incorporated in the present model.

By making alternative assumptions about the available techniques for limiting and/or spacing births, one can construct models in which the optimal strategies for achieving old age support differ markedly, with corresponding differences in population growth rates. The six sets of assumptions for which numerical results are reported here.

Strategy A: no birth control. It is assumed that no birth control techniques are available; average fertility matches the assumed fecundity. This strategy is primarily useful as a benchmark for comparison with other strategies, not as a realistic alternative.

Strategy B: postpone marriage. Marriage is postponed five years, so the mother is 23 when she first has a child. As with strategy A, no birth control methods are available.

Strategy C: sterilization only. It is assumed that sterilization is the only birth control technique available or, equivalently, that only birth limitation, but not birth spacing, is practiced. Couples have children according to the assumed fecundity schedule until the number and ages of their living sons are sufficient to provide a 0.9 probability that at least one will survive to the father's 65th birthday. They then have no further children, even if none of the sons subsequently dies.

Strategy D: always a son (0.7 contraceptive effectiveness). Couples without a living son have children according to the assumed fecundity schedule until a son is born. Couples with a living son use traditional contraceptives that have a 70 percent success rate over the 2.5-year birth interval; this contraceptive use is discontinued if the end of the mother's fertile years approaches and mortality conditions are such that the existing son does not provide the required 0.9 probability of old age support.

Strategy E: always a son (perfect contraception). The same as strategy D, except that modern contraceptives, such as pills or IUDs, with an assumed effectiveness of 100 percent, are used.

Strategy F: latest date children. Parents have access to 100 percent effective contraceptives and use them to postpone and space births in a way that achieves the required 0.9 probability of old age support with as few births as possible. In practice, since the later a son is born the less time he has to survive to provide old age support, the smallest (expected) number of births is achieved by postponing childbearing until a combination of infant and child mortality risks, declining fecundity, and the approaching end of the wife's childbearing years make it necessary to begin having children to achieve the required probability of old age support. This "latest date children" strategy is again primarily a benchmark for comparison, especially with strategies E and F, and not a realistic alternative.

These various results are presented in Table 4.1, which is arranged by life expectancy. Accordingly, for any country approximating one of these life expectancies, it is possible to compare the results of different parental strategies directly.

The most important relations that emerge are those between the intrinsic growth rate and the strategy followed for a given life expectancy. It is evident, as depicted in Figure 4.3, that the intrinsic growth rate is very sensitive to differences in mortality levels and to the specific strategy used.

The failure rate, presented in Table 4.1, is never more than 10 percent, which means that for all life expectancies and strategies a success rate of 90 percent is achieved. The reason that the failure rate is below 10 percent for strategy F is that births are integral events (that is, one cannot have a fraction of a baby); and, since the failure rate has to be less than or equal to 10 percent for success, an extra birth often places the failure rate substantially below 10 percent.

The annual intrinsic rate of natural increase, as noted above, varies directly with the net reproduction rate and inversely with the interval between generations denoted by average age of motherhood. For every strategy, except A, B, and D, the net reproduction rate declines with increased life expectancy at birth. For delayed birth strategies, the average age at motherhood increases with longer life expectancies, still further reducing the intrinsic rate of natural increase.

In all instances, strategy A (no birth control) provides one extreme. It is noteworthy that for this strategy (and strategy B), the failure rate declines as the growth rate rises. The average age of motherhood rises slightly with life expectancy. Understandably, regardless of life expectancies considered, the intrinsic growth rate is higher with "no birth control" than under any other strategy. At a typical LDC life expectancy of approximately 50 years the intrinsic

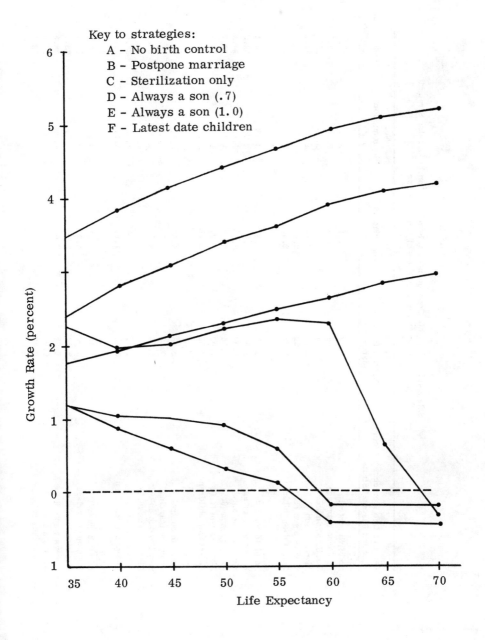

FIGURE 4.3

Population Growth Rates Under Different Strategies
at Various Mortality Levels

Key to strategies:
A - No birth control
B - Postpone marriage
C - Sterilization only
D - Always a son (.7)
E - Always a son (1.0)
F - Latest date children

Growth Rate (percent)

Life Expectancy

TABLE 4.1

Selected Demographic Consequences of Specified Family Planning Strategies
at Various Levels of Life Expectancy

Level of Life Expectancy (Years) and Parental Strategy	Intrinsic Rate of Natural Increase (percent)	Gross Reproduction Rate	Net Reproduction Rate	Mean Age of Motherhood	Failure Rate
35.0					
No birth control	3.48	5.31	2.83	29.9	3.1
Postpone marriage	2.44	4.34	2.23	32.7	5.5
Sterilization only	2.26	3.86	1.76	25.1	7.9
Always a son (0.7)	1.78	3.11	1.67	28.9	8.2
Always a son (1.0)	1.22	2.60	1.41	28.2	9.6
Latest date children	1.22	2.60	1.41	28.2	9.6
40.0					
No birth control	3.85	5.31	3.18	30.1	1.8
Postpone marriage	2.81	4.34	2.52	32.9	3.7
Sterilization only	1.99	2.54	1.62	24.3	8.0
Always a son (0.7)	1.96	2.90	1.76	28.7	6.8
Always a son (1.0)	1.09	2.27	1.37	28.8	9.3
Latest date children	0.92	2.21	1.32	30.2	9.6
45.0					
No birth control	4.16	5.31	3.52	30.3	1.1
Postpone marriage	3.13	4.34	2.81	33.0	2.5
Sterilization only	2.06	2.35	1.64	24.1	6.1
Always a son (0.7)	2.15	2.75	1.85	28.5	5.5
Always a son (1.0)	1.05	2.01	1.35	28.6	8.8
Latest date children	0.63	1.86	1.22	31.6	9.9
50.0					
No birth control	4.43	5.31	4.85	30.4	0.6
Postpone marriage	3.40	4.34	3.09	33.1	1.7
Sterilization only	2.24	2.26	1.71	23.8	4.2
Always a son (0.7)	2.32	2.63	1.93	28.3	4.5
Always a son (1.0)	0.93	1.76	1.29	27.6	8.5
Latest date children	0.32	1.55	1.11	32.1	9.8

55.0					
No birth control	4.67	5.31	4.15	30.5	0.5
Postpone marriage	3.64	4.34	3.35	33.2	1.2
Sterilization only	2.37	2.14	1.74	23.4	2.9
Always a son (0.7)	2.49	2.55	2.01	28.2	3.5
Always a son (1.0)	0.58	1.45	1.16	25.7	8.5
Latest date children	0.15	1.31	1.04	27.9	8.7
60.4					
No birth control	4.90	5.31	4.48	30.6	0.2
Postpone marriage	3.87	4.34	3.62	33.3	0.7
Sterilization only	2.32	1.95	1.69	22.5	2.8
Always a son (0.7)	2.67	2.51	2.13	28.3	2.4
Always a son (1.0)	-0.20	1.10	0.96	21.5	8.3
Latest date children	-0.42	1.04	0.87	33.4	8.9
65.8					
No birth control	5.10	5.31	4.79	30.7	0.1
Postpone marriage	4.07	4.34	3.89	33.4	0.5
Sterilization only	0.66	1.24	1.15	20.6	7.4
Always a son (0.7)	2.84	2.47	2.24	28.4	1.5
Always a son (1.0)	-0.19	1.04	0.91	21.1	6.1
Latest date children	-0.41	0.97	0.86	35.8	8.6
70.2					
No birth control	5.24	5.31	5.02	30.8	0.0
Postpone marriage	4.21	4.34	4.08	33.4	0.3
Sterilization only	-0.32	0.98	0.94	20.5	6.3
Always a son (0.7)	2.95	2.46	2.32	28.5	0.9
Always a son (1.0)	-0.21	1.00	0.96	20.8	4.1
Latest date children	-0.44	0.91	0.85	38.1	10.0

Note: The age specific mortality rates associated with each of the life expectancies are those provided by UN mortality levels 30 through 100, corresponding, respectively, to life expectancies 35.0 through 70.2 years: for example, life expectancy of 50 years corresponds with UN mortality level 60. The difference between the two "always a son" cases (0.7 v. 1.0) is the probability of contraceptive success during each two and one-half-year interval of the fertile age period of the couple.

Source: Data supplied by the authors.

growth rate is 4.4 percent a year; and the failure rate is 0.6 percent. Population would double in just 16 years.

Strategy B (postpone marriage age) involves a 5.0-year postponement of the first child. The mother has her first birth at age 23 instead of 18 and only has 10 rather than 12 ages at which she can have a live birth (with decreasing probability). Lower mortality levels bring no significant change in the average age of motherhood. At a life expectancy of 50 years, the intrinsic growth rate is 3.4 percent a year; and the failure rate is 1.7 percent. Population would double in 21 years.

Strategy C (no contraception until sterilization) has an approximately constant growth rate of life expectancies of 35 to 60 years, then the growth rate drops dramatically. This is partly because the average age of motherhood declines significantly and steadily with higher life expectancies. The annual growth rate is 2.2 percent, and the failure rate is 4.2 percent at a 50-year life expectancy. Population would double in 32 years.

Strategy D (always a son--0.7 probability of contraceptive success) is the first strategy to involve deliberate spacing, especially with longer life expectancies. This is indicated in part by the higher average age of motherhood which, for a 50-year life expectancy, is age 28.3 years under this strategy (compared with 23.8 years under strategy C). At a 50-year life expectancy, the intrinsic growth rate is 2.3 percent, and the failure rate is 4.5 percent. Population would double in 31 years.

Strategy E (always a son--perfect contraceptive) is the same as strategy D, except that the types of contraceptives used yield a high degree of certainty of birth prevention. The differences in population growth rates for the two strategies is very important. A low level of contraceptive failure is important to achieving low population growth rates through child spacing. At a 50-year life expectancy, strategy E has a population growth rate at 0.93 percent versus 2.3 percent for strategy D. The average age of motherhood is 27.6, and population doubles in 75 years.

Strategy F (latest date children) represents the opposite extreme from "no birth control." This strategy yields significantly lower gross reproduction rates, higher average ages of motherhood, and a slower intrinsic growth rate. However, for all life expectancies, this strategy is similar in outcome to strategy E (always a son --perfect contraception). Strategy F assumes perfect contraception, as does strategy E. Failure rates are comparatively high, almost 10 percent when life expectancies are below 60 years. At a life expectancy of 50 years, the failure rate is 9.8 percent; and the intrinsic growth rate is 0.3 percent. Population would double in 210 years.

Figure 4.3 indicates the effect on population growth rates of "spacing" (strategies D, E, and F), as contrasted with strategies A (no birth control), B (postponement of marriage), and C (sterilization). Although sterilization leads to a slower growth rate than does no birth control, it always yields faster growth rates than the two "spacing" strategies, where contraceptives are 100 percent effective.

COMPARISON OF RESULTS

Although the computer printouts of this simulation list several thousand timing and number of children outcomes for each of eight assumed UN mortality levels combined with each of the six parental strategies listed above, the mortality level and parental strategy combinations can be summarized in terms of

1. intrinsic rate of natural increase, the long-run population growth rate implied by the stipulated mortality schedule and the calculated fertility schedule;
2. gross reproduction rate, the average number of females born to women who survive their childbearing years;
3. net reproduction rate, the number of females expected in the next generation from each female birth;
4. average age at motherhood, the weighted average age of all mothers at the age of each birth; and
5. failure rate, the percentage of parents who do not have a surviving son when the father reaches age 65.

The above analysis explicitly assumes that an important motive for having children is old age insurance. Strategy F assumes that no other criteria are used in deciding when to have children, and hence it is the only pure old age strategy. However, if in fact parents have children deliberately, it may be for reasons such as having more children to produce income for the family or to "enjoy." Recognition of these common motivations necessarily does not vitiate the preceding argument. At short life expectancies, the number of births needed to provide old age insurance may exceed the number wanted for household production or enjoyment, in which case it is the insurance motivation that dominates. The present analysis indicates parents could reduce the number of births and still meet both goals.

At long life expectancies, the enjoyment factor may dominate, which means that governments striving to reduce fertility for purposes of economic development may have to use different appeals (such as promoting quality children through better education and health, rather than quantity). The analysis of this paper indicates that old age insurance is not the primary goal in such an instance if effective reversible contraceptives are being used. However, responsible governments can promote reduced fertility without jeopardizing the old age support of parents by their children. *

INTERPRETATION AND POLICY IMPLICATIONS

It was suggested that birth spacing would be attractive to couples because it would enable them to obtain their desired family size more often, with less probability of having too large or too small a family. It was further suggested that birth spacing and birth limitation became distinct courses of action only when highly effective modern contraceptives were available and that the quantitative importance of the distinction would be greatest at intermediate mortality levels.

The results reported above confirm these propositions, at least for the case in which desired family size is derived from desires for old age support in the manner specified. Strategy C (sterilization only) is a birth limitation strategy, but strategies D, E, and F are spacing strategies. Strategies D and E both place an "always a son" side condition on the basic old age support goal, but only strategy E permits the use of fully effective contraception. Strategy F (latest date children) also uses perfect contraception and focuses on the old age support goal without any side conditions. Consider now the results in Table 4.1 at the intermediate mortality levels, where life expectancy is 50 and 55 years.

With regard to obtaining desired family size, it is the failure rate column that is relevant. Desired family size is that family size that gives a 0.9 probability that at least one son will be alive when the father is age 65. If everyone achieved exactly the desired family size (which would involve fractional children), the failure rate would be 10 percent. Both perfect contraception spacing strategies (E and F), achieve failure rates of 8.5 to 10 percent, while the birth limitation strategy (C) and the imperfect contraception strategy (D) achieve

---

*Responsible governments also may wish to consider the "orphan" implications of these various parental strategies; that is, the absence of reverse support of young children by their parents. The absolute number of living males and females without living parents is greater in the case of strategy A than strategy F, simply because more children are born to each set of parents. And, with lower population growth rates, there are more adults in society for each orphan.

failure rates of less than 5 percent. These low failure rates represent family sizes that are too large, given the desired family size.
The magnitude by which family size is too large can be estimated
roughly by comparing twice the GRR for strategies C and E; there
are, on the average, about 1 to 1.5 more children per family with
birth limitation than with birth spacing. (Because of the asymmetri-
cal treatment of exceeding and falling short of the 0.9 probability
goal, instances of families that are too small are comparatively rare.)

With regard to the importance of modern contraceptives in making spacing substantially different from limitation, Figure 4.3 is
perhaps most illuminating. Strategy C is the birth limitation strategy, and strategy D is a spacing strategy with contraceptives of 0.7
effectiveness. Until life expectancy exceeds 60 years, the intrinsic
growth rate resulting from the two strategies are much the same.
In contrast, strategy E, which differs from strategy D only in that
it uses perfect contraceptives, achieves substantially lower growth
rates.

The above analysis has important policy implications. Some of
its results relate to family planning programs. Other findings indicate that certain government programs that often are considered incompatible are, in fact, consistent with one another.

According to the intrinsic growth rate criterion, birth control
measures that permit "spacing" should be stressed. Effective, reversible contraceptives and discretionary abortion, at least by this
standard, are preferable to irreversible sterilization.

As far as governments seek to persuade couples to practice
birth control, they should encourage couples to adopt spacing, perhaps in the form of the "always a son" strategy E. This strategy is
simple to explain and, at least for life expectancies typical of LDCs,
yields much lower intrinsic growth rates than presently experienced.
The "always a son" strategy is also in accord with most traditional
societies' values, for it means having children until a son is born
who survives, and hence, it would presumably be readily acceptable.

LDC governments as well as citizens can, and perhaps should
at present, rely on surviving children to support old parents. Insofar as security through children is practical, without threatening
other official objectives, governments could refrain from introducing
financial systems of old age support that are premature, given the
development stage of the national economy.

Old age security through children is compatible with the slow
population growth rates necessary for accelerated economic development, if a delayed birth strategy such as "always a son" is followed
and life expectancies at birth are not extremely low. Some LDCs
are even approaching life expectancies at which intrinsic growth rates
below 1.0 percent a year are compatible with security through children.

The "old age security" argument should not inhibit governments from promoting birth control for purposes of accelerating economic development.

Greater attention should be given to the education of young women (age 12 to 20) on the benefits of spacing. Such education will enable these women to seriously consider spacing before the first conception. In the past, family planning programs have placed far more emphasis on couples that had attained their desired family sizes.[12]

A national objective of lower mortality levels is compatible with national goals of reduced fertility for economic development and sufficient fertility for old age security. In fact, these last two goals become more compatible as life expectancies lengthen. However, to achieve the lower fertility that is made possible by reduced mortality, public health programs must be accompanied by family planning programs that emphasize "spacing."

NOTES

Offering Bonuses to Reduce Fertility
Stephen Enke and Bryan D. Hickman

1. R. J. Lapham and W. Parker Mauldin, "National Family Planning Programs: Review and Evaluation," Studies in Family Planning 3, no. 30 (1972): 29-52.

2. E. M. Rogers, "Incentives in the Diffusion of Family Planning Innovations," Studies in Family Planning 2, no. 12 (December 1971): 241-47.

3. R. G. Ridker, "Savings Accounts for Family Planning: An Illustration From the Tea Estates of India," Studies in Family Planning 2, no. 7 (July 1971): 150-52; and E. M. Rogers, "Field Experiments of Family Planning Incentives," Report prepared for U.S. Agency for International Development, May 1972.

4. R. G. Ridker, "Synopsis of a Proposal for A Family Planning Bond," Studies in Family Planning 1, no. 43 (June 1969): 11-16.

5. Thus in Taiwan, an "educational" bond is offered for limiting family size. O. D. Finnigan and T. H. Sun, "Planning, Starting and Operating an Educational Incentives Project," Studies in Family Planning 3, no. 1 (January 1972): 1-7.

6. S. Enke and R. A. Brown, "Economic Worth of Preventing Death at Different Ages in Developing Countries," Journal of Biosocial Sciences 4, no. 3 (July 1972): 299-306.

7. E. M. Rogers, "Incentives in the Diffusion of Family Planning Innovations," op. cit.

8. Enke and Brown, op. cit.

Child Spacing Strategies, Old Age
Security, and Population Growth
Donald J. O'Hara and Richard A. Brown

9. Donald J. O'Hara, "Mortality Risks, Sequential Decisions on Births, and Population Growth," Demography 9, no. 3 (August 1972): 485-98.

10. Ibid.

11. Robert G. Potter et al., "A Case Study of Birth Interval Dynamics," Population Studies 19 (1965): 81-96.

12. Bryan D. Hickman, "Economic Incentives: A Strategy for Family Planning Programs," General Electric-TEMPO Report, GE72TMP-33 (October 1972).

Abu-Lughod, Janet. "The Emergence of Differential Fertility in Urban Eghpt." Milbank Memorial Fund Quarterly 43 (April 1965): 235-53.

Adams, N. A. "Dependency Rates and Savings Rates: Comment." American Economic Review 61, no. 3, pt. 1 (June 1971): 472-75.

Adelman, Irma. "An Econometric Analysis of Population Growth." American Economic Review 53 (June 1963): 314-39.

_____, and Cynthia Morris. "A Quantitative Study of Social and Political Determinants of Fertility." Economic Development and Cultural Change 14 (January 1966): 129-57.

_____. "An Anatomy of Income Distribution Patterns in Developing Nations." Development Digest 9 (October 1971): 24-37.

Agency for International Development. Gross National Product: Rates and Trend Data. Washington, D.C.: USAID, 1970.

Allen, R. G. D. Macro-Economic Theory. New York: St. Martins Press, 1968.

Alvarez, Leonel. Proyeccion de la poblacion de Chile por sexo y grupos de edad, 1960-2000. Santiago: Centro Latinoamericano de Demografia (CELADE), series A, no. 84, 1966.

Barlow, Robin. "The Economic Effects of Malaria Eradication." American Economic Review 57 (May 1967): 130-48.

Becker, Gary S. "An Economic Analysis of Fertility." In Demographic and Economic Change in Developed Countries. Universities-National Bureau. New York: National Bureau of Economic Research, 1960.

_____. "Irrational Behavior and Economic Theory." Journal of Political Economy 70 (February 1962): 1-13.

_____. "A Theory of the Allocation of Time." Economic Journal 75 (September 1965): 493-517.

_____, and H. Gregg Lewis. "On the Interaction between the Quantity and Quality of Children." Journal of Political Economy 81 (March/April 1973): S279-S288.

Behrman, Jere R. "Sectoral Elasticities of Substitution Between Capital and Labor in a Developing Economy: Time Series Analysis in the Case of Postwar Chile." Econometrica 40 (March 1972): 311-26.

Behrman, S. J., Leslie Corsa, Jr., and Ronald Freedman. Fertility and Family Planning. Ann Arbor: The University of Michigan Press, 1969.

Bellman, Richard E. Dynamic Programming. Princeton, N.J.: Princeton University Press, 1957.

Bender, Donald R. "Population and Productivity in Tropical Forest Bush Fallow Agriculture." In Culture and Population, edited by Polanger. Monograph #9, Carolina Population Center, Chapel Hill: University of North Carolina, 1971.

Ben-Porath, Yoram. Fertility in Israel, an Economist's Interpretation: Differentials and Trends, 1950-1970. Santa Monica: Rand Report no. RM-5981-FF, August 1970.

_____. "Economic Analysis of Fertility in Israel: Point and Counter-point." Journal of Political Economy 81 (March/April 1973): S202-S233.

_____. "On Child Traits and the Choice of Family Size." Mimeographed. Maurice Falk Institute for Economic Research in Israel, discussion paper 731 for XX International Meeting, The Institute of Management Sciences, June 1973.

_____. "Fertility in Israel: A Mini-Survey and Some New Findings." Mimeographed. For conference on Economic Aspects of Population Growth, September 3-8, 1973, Valescure, France.

_____, and Finis Welch. Uncertain Quality: Sex of Children and Family Size. Santa Monica: Rand Report no. R-1117-NIH/RF, revised October 1972.

Berelson, Bernard. "Beyond Family Planning." Science, February 7, 1969, pp. 533-543.

_____, Richmond K. Anderson, Oscar Harkavy, John Maier, W. Parker Mauldin, and Sheldon J. Segal. Family Planning and Population Programs. Chicago: University of Chicago Press, 1966.

Berg, Alan. The Nutrition Factor. Washington, D.C.: The Brookings Institution, 1973.

_____, Nevin S. Scrimshaw, and David L. Call. Nutrition, National Development, and Planning. Cambridge, Mass.: Massachusetts Institute of Technology Press, 1973.

Berquo, Elza S., Rubens A. Marques, Maria L. Milanesi, Jose S. Martins, Eunice Pinho, and Imre Simon. "Levels and Variations in Fertility in Sao Paulo." Milbank Memorial Fund Quarterly 46 (July 1968): 167-88.

Blake, Judith. "Are Babies Consumer Durables? A Critique of the Economic Theory of Reproductive Motivation." Population Studies 22 (March 1968): 5-25.

_____. "Income and Reproductive Motivation." Population Studies 21 (November 1967): 185-206.

_____. "Reproductive Ideals and Educational Attainment Among White Americans, 1943-1960." Population Studies 21 (September 1967): 159-74.

Blandy, Richard. "The Welfare Analysis of Fertility Reduction." Economic Journal 84 (March 1974).

Bogue, Donald J., and J. A. Palmore. "Some Empirical and Analytic Relations Among Demographic Fertility Measures with Regression Models for Fertility Estimation." Demography 1 (1964): 316-38.

Boudon, Raymond. "A Method of Linear Causal Analysis: Dependence Analysis." American Sociological Review 30 (June 1965): 365-74.

Bourgeois-Pichat, Jean. "Relation between Foetal-Infant Mortality and Fertility." In United Nations, Proceedings of the World Population Conference 1965, Vol. 2. New York: United Nations, 1967.

Bowles, Samuel. Planning Educational Systems for Economic
    Growth. Cambridge, Mass.: Harvard University Press, 1969.

Boyd, Monica. "Occupational Mobility and Fertility in Metropolitan
    Latin America." Demography 10 (February 1973): 1-17.

Brito, Ronald. "Some Recent Developments in the Theory of Eco-
    nomic Growth: An Interpretation." Journal of Economic Litera-
    ture 11 (1973): 1344-66.

_____. "Steady-State Paths in an Economy with Endogenous Popula-
    tion Growth." Western Economic Journal 8 (December 1970):
    390-96.

Brown, Richard A. Survey of TEMPO Economic-Demographic
    Studies. Santa Barbara: General Electric-TEMPO Report no.
    GE74TMP-19, July 1974.

Burch, Thomas, and Murray Gendell. "Extended Family Structure
    and Fertility: Some Conceptual and Methodological Issues."
    Journal of Marriage and the Family 32 (May 1970): 227-36.

Burmeister, E., and A. R. Dobell. Mathematical Theories of Eco-
    nomic Growth. New York: Macmillan Co., 1970.

Cain, Glen G., and Adriana Weininger. "Economic Determinants of
    Fertility: Results from Cross-Sectional Aggregate Data."
    Demography 10 (May 1973): 205-23.

Caldwell, John. "Family Formation and Limitation in Ghana: A Study
    of the Residents of Economically Superior Urban Areas." In Fam-
    ily Planning and Population Programs, by Bernard Berelson et
    al., pp. 595-613. Chicago: University of Chicago Press, 1966.

Calhoun, John B. "Population Density and Social Pathology. Scien-
    tific American 206 (February 1962): 139-48.

Carleton, Robert O. "Labor Force Participation: A Stimulus to
    Fertility in Puerto Rico?" Demography 2 (1965): 233-39.

Chandrasekhar, Sripati. Infant Mortality, Population Growth, and
    Family Planning in India. Chapel Hill: University of North
    Carolina Press, 1972.

Cheung, Steven N. S. "The Enforcement of Property Rights in Children, and the Marriage Contract." The Economic Journal 82 (June 1972): 641-57.

Christ, Carl. Measurement in Economics. Stanford: Stanford University Press, 1963.

Clifford, William Bramwell II. "Modern and Traditional Value Orientations and Fertility Behavior: A Social Demographic Study." Demography 8 (February 1971): 37-48.

Coale, Ansley J. "Factors Associated with Development of Low Fertility: An Historic Summary." In Proceedings of the World Population Conference, 1965, Vol. 2. New York: United Nations, 1967.

_____, and P. Demeny. Regional Model Life Tables and Stable Populations. Princeton, N.J.: Princeton University Press, 1966.

_____, and E. M. Hoover. Population Growth and Economic Development in Low Income Countries: A Case Study of India's Prospects. Princeton, N.J.: Princeton University Press, 1958.

Cochrane, Susan Hill. "Mortality Level, Desired Family Size and Population Increase: Comment." Demography 8 (November 1971): 537-40.

Collver, O. Andrew. "Women's Work Participation and Fertility in Metropolitan Areas." Demography 5 (1968): 55-60.

_____, and Eleanor Langlois. "The Female Labor Force in Metropolitan Areas: An International Comparison." Economic Development and Cultural Change 10 (July 1962): 367-85.

Cooper, Charles A., and Sidney S. Alexander, eds. Economic Development and Population Growth in the Middle East. New York: American Elsevier, 1972.

Corsa, Leslie, Jr., and Deborah Oakley. "Consequences of Population Growth for Health Services in Less Developed Countries--An Initial Appraisal." In Rapid Population Growth, pp. 368-402. Washington, D.C.: National Academy of Sciences, 1971.

Dandekar, Kumudini. "Effect of Education on Fertility." In Pro-
    ceedings of the World Population Conference, 1965, Vol. 4.
    New York: United Nations, 1967.

Da Vanzo, Julie. Determinants of Family Formation in Chile, 1960.
    Santa Monica: Rand Report No. R-830-AID, August 1972.

Davis, Kingsley. Human Society. New York: 1949.

Day, Lincoln H. "Catholic Teaching and Catholic Fertility." In
    Proceedings of the World Population Conference, 1965, Vol. 2.
    New York: United Nations, 1967.

_____. "Natality and Ethnocentrism: Some Relationships Suggested
    by an Analysis of Catholic-Protestant Differentials." Population
    Studies 22 (March 1968): 27-50.

Demeny, Paul. "Demographic Aspects of Savings Investment, Em-
    ployment and Productivity." In Proceedings of the World Popu-
    lation Conference, 1965. New York: United Nations, 1967.

_____. "Investment Allocation and Population Growth." Demography
    2 (1965): 203-32.

Denison, Edward F. The Sources of Economic Growth in the U.S.
    and the Alternatives Before Us. New York: Committee for
    Economic Development, Library of Congress, 1962.

Denton, Frank T., and B. Spencer. "A Simulation Analysis of the
    Effects of Population Change on a Neoclassical Economy."
    Journal of Political Economy 81 (March/April 1973).

DeVany, Arthur, and S. Enke. Population Growth and Economic
    Development: Background and Guide. Santa Barbara: TEMPO,
    no. 119, 1968.

Drakatos, Constantine G. "The Determinants of Birth Rate in Devel-
    oping Countries: An Econometric Study of Greece." Economic
    Development and Cultural Change 17 (July 1969): 596-603.

Easterlin, Richard A. "An Economic Framework for Fertility Analy-
    sis." Studies in Family Planning 6 (March 1975): 54-63.

_____. "The Economics and Sociology of Fertility: A Synthesis."
    Philadelphia: Department of Economics, University of Pennsyl-
    vania, July 1973.

_____. "Towards a Socioeconomic Theory of Fertility: A Survey of Recent Research on Economic Factors in American Fertility." In Fertility and Family Planning, ed. by S. J. Behrman, Leslie Corsa, Jr., and Ronald Freedman. Ann Arbor: University of Michigan Press, 1969.

Eckert, Ross, and D. O'Hara. Manual for the Calculation of Government Expenditures for Selected Social Services. Santa Barbara: TEMPO, no. 121, 1968.

Ekanem, Ita I. "A Further Note on the Relation Between Economic Development and Fertility." Demography 9 (August 1972): 383-98.

Enke, Stephen. "Birth Control for Economic Development." Science, May 1969, pp. 798-802.

_____. "The Economic Aspects of Slowing Population Growth." Economic Journal 76 (1966): 44-56.

_____. Economic Benefits of Slowing Population Growth: Charts and Notes. Santa Barbara: TEMPO, no. 122, 1968.

_____. "The Economic Consequences of Rapid Population Growth." Economic Journal 81 (December 1971): 800-811.

_____. Economics for Development. Englewood Cliffs, N.J.: Prentice-Hall, 1963.

_____. "The Economics of Government Payments of Limit Population." Economic Development and Cultural Change 8 (1960): 339-48.

_____. "The Economics of Having Children." Policy Sciences 1 (June 1970): 15-29.

_____. "High Fertility Impairs Credit Worthiness of Developing Nations." In Spatial, Regional, and Population Economics: Essays in Honor of Edgar M. Hoover, ed. by Mark Perlman, Charles J. Leven, and Benjamin Chinitz, pp. 123-36. New York: Gordon and Breach, 1972.

_____. "Politico-Economic Global Systems." Macrosystems: Analysis, Instrumentation, and Synthesis of Complicated Systems. New York: Holt, Rinehart and Winston, 1971.

_____. "Reducing Fertility to Accelerate Development." Economic Journal 84 (June 1974): 349-66.

_____. "A Reply to Mr. Hansen." Economic Journal 82 (March 1973): 219-21.

_____. Using TEMPO II: A Budget Allocation and Human Resources Model. Santa Barbara: General Electric-TEMPO Report no. GE73TMP-12, April 1973.

_____. Zero U.S. Population Growth--When, How and Why. Santa Barbara: TEMPO, no. 35, 1970.

_____, and Richard A. Brown. "Economic Worth of Preventing Death at Different Ages in Developing Countries." Journal of Biosocial Science 4 (July 1972): 299-306.

_____, and Richard A. Brown. Old Age Insurance with Fewer Children. Santa Barbara: General Electric-TEMPO Report no. 72TMP-6, March 1, 1972.

_____, and R. G. Zind. "Effects of Fewer Births on Average Income." Journal of Biosocial Sciences 1 (January 1969): 41-55.

Faroog, Ghazi M., and Baran Tuncer. "Provincial Fertility and Social and Economic Development in Turkey, 1935-1965." New Haven: Yale University Economic Growth Center Discussion Paper no. 159, October 1972.

Faundes, Anibal, German Rodriguez-Galant, and Onofre Avendano. "The San Gregorio Experimental Family Planning Program: Changes Observed in Fertility and Abortion Rates." Demography 5 (1969): 836-46.

Finnigan, O. D., and T. H. Sun. "Planning, Starting and Operating an Educational Incentives Project." Studies in Family Planning 3 (1972): 1-7.

Francis, David R. "Review" of Rich. Christian Science Monitor, June 12, 1973.

Frederiksen, Harald. "Dynamic Equilibrium of Economic and Demographic Transition." Economic Development and Cultural Change 14 (April 1966): 316-22.

_____. "Feedbacks in Economic and Demographic Transition."
Science, November 14, 1969, pp. 837-47.

Freedman, Deborah S. "The Relation of Economic Status to Fertility." American Economic Review 53 (June 1963): 414-26.

_____. "The Relationship of Family Planning to Savings and Con-
sumption in Taiwan." Demography 9 (August 1972): 499-505.

_____. "The Role of the Consumption of Modern Durables in Eco-
nomic Development." Economic Development and Cultural
Change 19 (October 1970): 25-48.

Freedman, Ronald. "The Sociology of Human Fertility." Current
Sociology 10/11 (1961-62): 37-117.

_____, and Lolagene Coombs. "Economic Considerations in Family
Growth Decisions." Population Studies 20 (November 1966):
197-222.

_____, Lolagene Coombs, and Judith Friedman. "Social Correlates
of Fetal Mortality." Milbank Memorial Fund Quarterly 44 (July
1966): 327-44.

Frieden, Alan. "A Model of Marriage and Fertility." Ph.D. dissertation, University of Chicago, 1972.

Friedlander, Stanley, and Morris Silver. "A Quantitative Study of
the Determinants of Fertility Behavior." Demography 4 (1967):
30-70.

Gendell, Murray. "Fertility and Development in Brazil." Demography 4 (1967): 143-57.

_____. "The Influence of Family-Building Activity on Women's Rate
of Economic Activity." In Proceedings of the World Population
Conference, 1965, Vol. 4. New York: United Nations, 1967.

_____, Maria N. Maraviglia, and Philip C. Kreitner. "Fertility
and Economic Activity of Women in Guatemala City, 1964."
Demography 7 (August 1970): 273-86.

Goldschmidt, Walter. "The Brideprice of the Sebei." Scientific
American 229 (July 1973): 74-85.

Goldstein, Sidney. "The Influence of Labor Force Participation and Education on Fertility in Thailand." Population Studies 26 (November 1972): 419-36.

_____. "Interrelations Between Migration and Fertility in Thailand." Demography 10 (May 1973): 225-41.

Goubert, Pierre. "Legitimate Fecundity and Infant Mortality in France during the Eighteenth Century: A Comparison." Daedalus 97 (Spring 1968): 593-603.

Gregory, Paul R., John M. Campbell, and Benjamin S. Cheng. "A Cost-Inclusive Simultaneous Equation Model of Birth Rates." Econometrica 40 (July 1972): 681-87.

_____, John M. Campbell, and Benjamin S. Cheng. "A Simultaneous Equation Model of Birth Rates in the United States." Review of Economics and Statistics 54 (November 1972): 374-80.

_____, and J. Griffin. "Secular and Cross-Section Industrialization Patterns: Some Further Evidence on the Kuznets-Chenery Controversy." Review of Economics and Statistics 56 (August 1974): 360-68.

Griliches, Zui. "Comment on Nerlove's Paper." Journal of Political Economy 82 (March/April 1974): S219-S221.

Gronau, Reuben. "The Effect of Children on the Housewife's Value of Time." Journal of Political Economy 8 (March/April 1973): S168-S199.

Gupta, K. L. "Dependency Rates and Savings Rates: Comment." American Economic Review 61, no. 3, pt. 1 (June 1971): 469-71.

Guthrie, Harold W., Guy H. Orcutt, Steven Caldwell, Gerald E. Peabody, and George Sadowsky. "Microanalytic Simulation of Household Behavior." Annals of Economic and Social Measurement 1 (April 1972): 141-69.

Hansen, John R. "Economic Consequences of Rapid Population Growth--A Comment." Economic Journal 82 (March 1973): 217-19.

Harberger, Arnold, and Marcelo Selowsky. "Key Factors in the Economic Growth of Chile." Cornell University Conference on

The Next Decade of Latin American Development, April 1966.
Abridged version appears in Cuadernos de economia, no. 10
(Santiago: Universidad Catolica, December 1966).

Hardin, Garrett. "The Tragedy of the Commons." Science, December 13, 1968, pp. 1234-48.

Harman, Alvin J. Fertility and Economic Behavior of Families in
the Philippines. Santa Monica: Rand Report no. RM-6385-AID,
September 1970.

Hassan, Shafick S. "Influence of Child Mortality on Fertility."
Population Index 32 (July 1966): 354.

_____. "Religion versus Child Mortality as a Cause of Differential
Fertility." Population Index 33 (July-September 1967): 345.

Hawthorn, Geoffrey. The Sociology of Fertility. London: Collier-
Macmillan, 1969.

Heer, David M. "Economic Development and Fertility." Demography
3 (1966): 423-44.

_____. "Fertility Differences in Andean Countries: A Reply to
W. H. James." Population Studies 21 (July 1967): 71-73.

_____, and John Boynton. "A Multivariate Regression Analysis of
Difference in Fertility of United States Countries." Social
Biology 17 (September 1970): 180-94.

_____, and Dean O. Smith. "Mortality Level, Desired Family
Size, and Population Increase." Demography 5 (1968): 104-21.

_____, and Dean O. Smith. "Mortality Level, Desired Family
Size and Population Increase: Further Variations on a Basic
Model." Demography 6 (May 1969): 141-49.

_____, and Elsa Turner. "Areal Differences in Latin American
Fertility." Population Studies 18 (March 1965): 279-92.

Henin, R. "Fertility Differentials in the Sudan (with Reference to
the Nomadic and Settled Populations)." Population Studies 22
(March 1968): 147-64.

_____. "The Patterns and Causes of Fertility Differentials in the Sudan (with Reference to Nomadic and Settled Populations)." Population Studies 23 (July 1969): 171-98.

Herrick, Bruce, and Ricardo Moran. Declining Birth Rates in Chile: Their Effects on Output, Education, Health, and Housing. Santa Barbara: General Electric-TEMPO, Publication no. 71 TMP-56, 1972.

Hickman, Bryan D. Economic Incentives: A Strategy for Family Planning Programs. Santa Barbara: General Electric-TEMPO Report no. GE72TMP-33, October 1972.

Hill, C. Russell. "Education, Health and Family Size as Determinants of Labor Market Activity for the Poor and Nonpoor." Demography 8 (August 1971): 379-88.

Hsu, Francis L. Psychological Anthropology. Cambridge, Mass.: Schenkman Publishing Company, 1972.

Husain, I. Z. "Educational Status and Differential Fertility in India." Social Biology 17 (June 1970): 132-39.

Hutchinson, Bertram. "Fertility, Social Mobility and Urban Migration in Brazil." Population Studies 14 (March 1961): 182-89.

Instituto de Economia y Planificacion, Universidad de Chile. La economia de Chile en el periodo 1950-1963, 2 volumes. Santiago: Instituto de Economia, 1963.

International Economic Report of the President, 1973. Washington, D.C.: U.S. Government Printing Office, 1974.

International Labor Office. 1963 Yearbook of Labor Statistics. Geneva: ILO, 1964.

_____. 1967 Yearbook of Labor Statistics. Geneva: ILO, 1968.

International Union for the Scientific Study of Population. Contributed Papers of the Sydney Conference. Australia, 21-5 August 1967. Canberra, Australia: Department of Demography, National University, 1967.

Iutaka, S., E. Bock, and W. Varnes. "Factors Affecting Fertility of Natives and Migrants in Urban Brazil." Population Studies 25 (March 1971): 55-62.

Jaffe, A., and K. Azumi. "The Birth Rate and Cottage Industries
  in Underdeveloped Countries." Economic Development and Cultural Change 9 (October 1960): 52-63.

Jain, Anrudh K., T. C. Hsu, Ronald Freedman, and M. C. Chang.
  "Demographic Aspects of Lactation and Postpartum Amenorrhea."
  Demography 7 (May 1970): 255-71.

Jain, S. P. "Fertility Trends in Greater Bombay." In Contributed
  Papers of the Sydney Conference, International Union for the
  Scientific Study of Population. Australia, 21-5 August 1967.
  Canberra, Australia: Department of Demography, Australian
  National University, 1967.

Janowitz, Barbara S. "Cross-Section Studies as Predictors of
  Trends in Birth Rates: A Note on Ekanem's Results." Demography 10 (August 1973): 479-81.

_____. "An Empirical Study of the Effects of Socioeconomic Devel-
  opment on Fertility Rates." Demography 8 (August 1971): 319-30.

Johnson, James, and Bryan D. Hickman. A Cost Analysis of Two
  Family Planning Delivery Systems: Commercial Stores and
  Clinics. Santa Barbara: General Electric-TEMPO, 1974.

Kamerschen, David. "The Determinants of Birth Rate in Developing
  Countries: Comment." Economic Development and Cultural
  Change 20 (January 1972): 310-15.

Kasarda, John D. "Economic Structure and Fertility: A Comparative Analysis." Demography 8 (August 1971): 307-17.

Keeley, Michael C. "A Comment on an Interpretation of the Economic Theory of Fertility: Promising Path or Blind Alley?"
  Journal of Economic Literature 13 (June 1975): 461-68.

_____. "A Model of Marital Formation: The Determinants of the
  Optimal Age at First Marriage." Ph.D. dissertation, University
  of Chicago, August 1974.

Kelley, Allen C. "Population Growth, the Dependency Rate, and the
  Pace of Economic Development." Population Studies 27 (November 1973).

_____. "The Role of Population in Models of Economic Growth."
American Economic Review, Papers and Proceedings 64 (May
1974): 39-44.

Keyfitz, Nathan. Introduction to the Mathematics of Population.
Menlo Park, Calif.: Addison-Wesley Publishing Company, 1968.

Kim, S. et al. Dual Careers: A Longitudinal Study of Labor Market
Experience of Women. New York: Columbia University Press,
1972.

Kirk, Dudley. "Factors Affecting Moslem Natality." In Family
Planning and Population Programs, by Bernard Berelson et al.,
pp. 561-79. Chicago: The University of Chicago Press, 1966.

_____. "A New Demographic Transition." In National Academy of
Sciences, Rapid Population Growth, pp. 123-47. Baltimore:
Johns Hopkins Press, 1971.

Kleinman, David S. "Fertility Variation and Resources in Rural
India (1961)." Economic Development and Cultural Change 21
(July 1973): 679-98.

Knodel, John. "Infant Mortality and Fertility in Three Bavarian
Villages: An Analysis of Family Histories from the 19th Century." Population Studies 22 (November 1968): 297-318.

_____, and Etienne Van de Walle. "Breast Feeding, Fertility and
Infant Mortality: An Analysis of Some Early German Data."
Population Studies 21 (September 1967): 109-31.

Kogut, Edy. "The Economic Analysis of Demographic Phenomena:
A Case Study for Brazil." Ph.D. dissertation, University of
Chicago, September 1972.

Krishnakumar, S. "A Report on the Massive Family Welfare Festi-
val Ernakulam District," July 1 to July 31, 1971. Cochin,
Kerela, India. District Mimeographed Report, 1971.

Krishnamurty, K. "Economic Development and Population Growth
in Low Income Countries: An Empirical Study for India." Economic Development and Cultural Change 15 (October 1966): 70-75.

Kunz, Phillip. "The Relation of Income and Fertility." Journal of
Marriage and the Family 27 (November 1965): 509-13.

Langer, William L. "Checks on Population Growth: 1750-1850."
     Scientific American 226 (February 1972): 92-99.

Lapham, R. J., and W. Parker Mauldin. "National Family Planning
     Programs: Review and Evaluation." Studies in Family Planning
     3 (1972): 29-52.

Leasure, J. "Factors Involved in the Decline of Fertility in Spain."
     Population Studies 16 (March 1963): 271-85.

Leff, Nathaniel S. "Dependency Rates and Savings Rates." Ameri-
     can Economic Review 61 (December 1969): 886-96.

Leibenstein, Harvey. "The Economic Theory of Fertility Decline."
     Harvard Institute of Economic Research, April 1973.

_____. "An Interpretation of the Economic Theory of Fertility:
     Promising Path or Blind Alley?" Journal of Economic Litera-
     ture 12 (June 1974): 457-87.

_____. "Pitfalls in Benefit-Cost Analysis of Birth Prevention."
     Population Studies 23 (July 1969): 161-70.

Leibowitz, A. "Home Investments in Children." Journal of Political
     Economy 82 (March/April 1974): S111-S131.

Lloyd, P. J. "A Growth Model with Population and Technological
     Change as Endogenous Variables." Population Studies 23 (1969):
     463-78.

Loebner, Hugh, and Edwin D. Driver. "Differential Fertility in
     Central India: A Path Analysis." Demography 10 (August 1973):
     329-50.

Lorimer, Frank. Culture and Human Fertility. Paris: UNESCO,
     1954.

_____. "The Economics of Family Formation under Different Con-
     ditions." In Proceedings of the World Population Conference,
     1965, Vol. 2. New York: United Nations, 1967.

McCall, J. J. "Economics of Information and Job Search." Quar-
     terly Journal of Economics 84 (February 1970): 113-26.

McFarland, William E. Description of the Economic-Demographic
    Model. Santa Barbara: General Electric-TEMPO, 1968.

_____. Population, Land, and Economic Development. Santa
    Barbara: General Electric-TEMPO, Report no. GE74TMP-29,
    July 1974.

_____. Sensitivity Analysis of the Economic-Demographic Model.
    Santa Barbara: General Electric-TEMPO, no. 52, 1969.

_____, James P. Bennett, and Richard A. Brown. Description of
    the TEMPO II Budget Allocation and Human Resources Model.
    Santa Barbara: General Electric-TEMPO Report no. GE73TMP-
    13, April 1973.

_____, and D. O'Hara. Guatemala: The Effects of Declining Fer-
    tility. Santa Barbara: General Electric-TEMPO, no. 50, vol.
    2, 1969.

_____. Turkey: The Effects of Falling Fertility. Santa Barbara:
    General Electric-TEMPO, no. 50, vol. 1, 1969.

Macisco, John J., Leon F. Bouvier, and Martha Renzi. "Migration
    Status, Education and Fertility in Puerto Rico, 1960." Milbank
    Memorial Fund Quarterly 47 (April 1969): 167-87.

_____, Leon F. Bouvier, and Robert H. Weller. "The Effect
    of Labor Force Participation on the Relationship Between
    Migration Status and Fertility in San Juan, Puerto Rico." Mil-
    Bank Memorial Fund Quarterly 48 (January 1970): 51-71.

Markle, Gerald E., and Charles B. Nam. "Sex Predetermination:
    Its Impact on Fertility." Social Biology 18 (March 1971): 73-83.

Marshall, John F., Susan Morris, and Steven Polgar. "Culture and
    Natality: A Preliminary Classified Bibliography." Current
    Anthropology 13 (April 1972): 268-77.

Martin, Edwin W. Development Co-operation: Efforts and Policies
    of the Members of the Development Assistance Committee.
    Paris: Organization for Economic Cooperation and Development,
    1972.

Mauldin, W. Parker, Nazli Choucri, Frank W. Notestein, and Michael
    S. Teitelbaum. "A Report on Bucharest." Studies in Family
    Planning 5 (1974): 357-96.

Maurer, Kenneth, Rosalinda Ratajczak, and T. Paul Schultz. Marriage, Fertility and Labor Force Participation of Thai Women: An Econometric Study. Santa Monica: Rand Report no. R-829-AID/RF, April 1973.

Michael, Robert A., and Robert J. Willis. "Contraception and Fertility: Production under Uncertainty." Mimeographed. National Bureau of Economic Research, November 1973.

Michael, Robert T. "Education and the Derived Demand for Children." Journal of Political Economy 81 (March/April 1973): S128-S164.

Michel, Andree. "Interaction and Family Planning in the French Urban Family." Demography 4 (1967): 615-25.

Mincer, Jacob. "Market Prices, Opportunity Costs, and Income Effects." In Measurement in Economics, by Carl Christ, pp. 67-82. Stanford: Stanford University Press, 1963.

Miro, Carmen, and Walter Mertens. "Influences Affecting Fertility in Urban and Rural Latin America." Milbank Memorial Fund Quarterly 46 (July 1968): 89-120.

Mitchell, Robert E. "Husband-Wife Relations and Family-Planning Practices in Urban Hong Kong." Journal of Marriage and the Family 34 (February 1972): 139-46.

Morales, Julio. Chile: Nuevas proyecciones de poblacion por sexo y grupos de edades, 1960-2000. Santiago: Centro Latinoamericano de Demografia (CELADE), series A, no. 99, 1969.

Mueller, Eva. "Economic Motives for Family Limitation." Population Studies 26 (November 1972): 383-403.

Munroe, Robert L., Ruth H. Munroe, and Robert A. Levine. "Africa." In Psychological Anthropology, edited by Francis L. Hsu, pp. 71-120. Cambridge: Schenkman Publishing Co., 1972.

Myers, George, and Earl Morris. "Migration and Fertility in Puerto Rico." Population Studies 20 (July 1966): 85-96.

Nag, Moni. "Anthropology and Population: Problems and Perspectives." Population Studies 27 (March 1973): 59-69.

_____. Factors Affecting Human Fertility in Nonindustrial Societies: A Cross-Cultural Study of Human Reproduction. New Haven: Yale University Press, 1962.

_____. "Family Type and Fertility." In Proceedings of the World Population Conference, 1965, Vol. 2. New York: United Nations, 1967.

_____. "The Influence of Conjugal Behavior, Migration and Contraception on Natality in Barbados." In Culture and Population: A Collection of Current Studies, edited by Steven Polgar, pp. 105-23. Chapel Hill: University of North Carolina, Monograph No. 9, Carolina Population Center, 1971.

National Academy of Sciences. Rapid Population Growth, Vol. 2. Edited by Roger Revelle. Baltimore: The Johns Hopkins University Press, 1971.

Nelson, R. "The Low-Level Equilibrium Population Trap." American Economic Review 46 (December 1956): 894-908.

Nerlove, Marc. "Household and Economy: Towards a New Theory of Population and Economic Growth." Journal of Political Economy 82 (March/April 1974): S200-S218.

_____, and T. Paul Schultz. Love and Life Between the Censuses: A Model of Family Decision Making in Puerto Rico. Santa Monica: Rand Report no. RM-6322-AID, September 1970.

Newcombe, Howard B., and Philip O. W. Rhynas. "Child Spacing Following Stillbirth and Infant Death." Eugenics Quarterly 9 (May 1962): 25-35.

Office of International Science, AAAS. Culture and Population Change. Washington, D.C.: AAAS, August 1974.

O'Hara, Donald J. Changes in Mortality Levels and Family Decisions Regarding Children. Santa Monica: Rand Report no. R-914-RF, February 1972.

_____. "The Microeconomics of the Demographic Transition." Mimeographed. University of Rochester, Department of Economics Discussion Paper, August 1972.

_____. "Mortality Risks, Sequential Decisions on Births, and Population Growth." Demography 9 (August 1972): 485-98.

Ohlin, G. "Mortality, Marriage, and Growth in Pre-Industrial Population." Population Studies 14 (March 1961): 190-97.

Oppong, Christine. "Conjugal Power and Resources: An Urban African Example." Journal of Marriage and the Family 32 (November 1970): 676-80.

Orcutt, Guy H., and Alice M. Rivlin. "An Economic and Demographic Model of the Household Sector: A Progress Report." In Universities-National Bureau, Demographic and Economic Change in Developed Countries, pp. 287-318. New York: National Bureau of Economic Research, 1960.

Pakrasi, Kanti, and Chittaranjan Malaker. "The Relationship Between Family Type and Fertility." Milbank Memorial Fund Quarterly 45 (October 1967): 451-60.

Palmore, James A. "Population Change, Conjugal Status and the Family." In Population Aspects of Social Development. United Nations Asian Population Studies Series, no. 11, October 1972.

Pareek, Udai, and V. Kothandapani. "Modernization and Attitude Toward Family Size and Family Planning: Analysis of Some Data from India." Social Biology 16 (March 1969): 44-48.

Paydarfar, Ali, and Mahmood Sarram. "Differential Fertility and Socioeconomic Status of Shirazi Women: A Pilot Study." Journal of Marriage and the Family 32 (November 1970): 692-99.

Pearson, Lester B. Partners in Development: Report of the Commission on International Development. New York: Praeger Publishers, 1969.

Phelps, Edmund S. "Population Increase." Canadian Journal of Economics 1 (August 1968).

_____. "Second Essay on the Golden Rule of Accumulation." American Economic Review 55 (September 1965): 793-814.

Polgar, Steven, ed. Culture and Population: A Collection of Current Studies. Chapel Hill: University of North Carolina, Monograph No. 9, Carolina Population Center, 1971.

Pollak, Robert A. , and Michael L. Wachter. "The Relevance of the Household Production Function and Its Implications for the Allocation of Time." Journal of Political Economy 83 (April 1975): 255-78.

Population Reference Bureau. 1972 World Population Data Sheet. Washington, D.C.: PRB, 1972.

Potter, Robert G. "Birth Intervals: Structure and Change." Population Studies 17 (November 1963): 155-66.

_____, John B. Wyon, M. New, and J. E. Gordon. "Fetal Wastage in Eleven Pujab Villages." Human Biology 37 (September 1965): 262-73.

_____, John B. Wyon, Margaret Parker, and John E. Gordon. "A Case Study of Birth Interval Dynamics." Population Studies 19 (1965): 81-96.

Pugo, Jose et al. "Efectos de la aplicacion y difusion de sistemas de control de natalidad en el area hospitalaria norte de Santiago de Chile y en mujeres tratadas en la clinica obstetrica de la Universidad de Chile." Revista chilena de obstetricia y ginecologia 32 (1967): 220-27.

Rainwater, Lee. And the Poor Get Children. Chicago: Quadrangle Books, 1960.

Raulet, Harry M. "Family Planning and Population Control in Developing Countries." Demography 7 (May 1970): 211-34.

Rele, J. "Fertility Differentials in India." Milbank Memorial Fund Quarterly 41 (April 1963): 183-99.

Repetto, Robert. "Son Preference and Fertility Behavior in Developing Countries." Studies in Family Planning 3 (April 1972): 70-76.

Reynolds, Jack. "Costa Rica: Measuring the Demographic Impact of Family Planning Programs." Studies in Family Planning 4 (November 1973): 310-16.

Rich, William. Smaller Families through Social and Economic Progress. Washington, D.C.: Overseas Development Council Monograph, no. 7, January 1973.

Ridker, R. G. "Savings Accounts for Family Planning: An Illustration from the Tea Estates of India." Studies in Family Planning 2 (1971).

_____. "Synopsis of a Proposal for a Family Planning Bond." Studies in Family Planning 1 (1969): 11-16.

Ridley, Jeanne Clare, Mindel C. Sheps, Joan W. Linger, and Jane A. Menken. "The Effects of Changing Mortality on Natality." Milbank Memorial Fund Quarterly 45 (January 1967): 77-97.

Rizk, Hanna. "Social and Psychological Factors Affecting Fertility in the United Arab Republic." Marriage and Family Living 25 (February 1963): 69-73.

Roberts, Robert E. "Modernization and Infant Mortality in Mexico." Economic Development and Cultural Change 21 (July 1973): 655-69.

Robinson, Warren. "Urbanization and Fertility: The Non-Western Experience." Milbank Memorial Fund Quarterly 41 (July 1963): 291-308.

Rogers, E. M. "Field Experiments of Family Planning Incentives." Report prepared for U.S. Agency for International Development, May 1972.

_____. "Incentives in the Diffusion of Family Planning Innovations." Studies in Family Planning 2 (1971): 241-47.

Rosen, Bernard C., and Alan B. Simmons. "Industrialization, Family and Fertility: A Structural Psychological Analysis of the Brazilian Case." Demography 8 (February 1971): 49-69.

Russett, Bruce M., Hayward R. Alker, Jr., Karl W. Deutsch, and Harold D. Lasswell. World Handbook of Political and Social Indicators. New Haven: Yale University Press, 1964.

Sabagh, Georges. "Differential Fertility in an Arab Country." Milbank Memorial Fund Quarterly 41 (January 1963): 100-106.

Sato, K. "On the Adjustment Time in Neoclassical Growth Models." Review of Economic Studies 3 (July 1966): 263-68.

Sato, R. "Fiscal Policy in a Neoclassical Growth Model: An Analysis of the Time Required for Equilibrating Adjustment." Review of Economic Studies 30 (February 1963): 16-23.

Scanzoni, John, and Martha McMurry. "Continuities in the Explanation of Fertility Control." Journal of Marriage and the Family 34 (May 1972): 315-21.

Schiefelbein, Ernesto. El sistema educacional chileno. Santiago: Ministerio de Educacion Publica, Superintendencia de Educacion, 1970.

Schultz, T. Paul. "An Economic Model of Family Planning and Fertility." Journal of Political Economy 77 (March/April 1969): 153-80.

_____. "An Economic Perspective on Population Growth." In National Academy of Sciences, Rapid Population Growth. Washington, D.C.: National Academy of Sciences, 1971.

_____. Evaluation of Population Policies: A Framework for Analysis and Its Application to Taiwan's Family Planning Program. Santa Monica: Rand Report no. R-643-AID, June 1971.

_____. "Explanation of Birth Rate Changes Over Space and Time: A Study of Taiwan." Journal of Political Economy 81 (March/April 1973): S238-S274.

_____. Fertility Patterns and Their Determinants in the Arab Middle East. Rand Report no. RM-5978-FF, May 1970. Reprinted in Charles A. Cooper and Sidney S. Alexander, eds., Economic Development and Population Growth in the Middle East, pp. 399-500. Santa Monica: RAND Corporation, 1970.

_____. Population Growth and Internal Migration in Colombia. Santa Monica: Rand Report no. RM-5765-RC/AID, July 1969.

_____. "A Preliminary Survey of Economic Analyses of Fertility." American Economic Review 53 (May 1973): 71-78.

_____, and Julie DaVanzo. Analysis of Demographic Change in East Pakistan: A Study of Retrospective Survey Data. Santa Monica: Rand Report no. R-564-AID, September 1970.

Schultz, T. W. "The Value of Children: An Economic Perspective." Journal of Political Economy 81 (March/April 1973): S2-S13.

Schumann, Howard, Alex Inkeles, and David Smith. "Some Social Psychological Effects and Noneffects of Literacy in a New Nation." Economic Development and Cultural Change 16 (October 1967): 1-14.

Scientific American, September 1974. "The Human Population."

Selowsky, Marcelo. "An Attempt to Estimate Rates of Return in Investment in Infant Nutrition Programs." Mimeographed. For International Conference on Nutrition, National Development and Planning, October 1971.

Sheps, Mindel C. "An Analysis of Reproductive Patterns in an American Isolate." Population Studies 19 (July 1965): 65-80.

Silver, Morris. "Births, Marriages and Business Cycles in the United States." Journal of Political Economy 73 (June 1965): 237-55.

_____. "Births, Marriages, and Income Fluctuations in the United Kingdom and Japan." Economic Development and Cultural Change 14 (April 1966): 302-15.

Simmons, G. B. "The Indian Investment in Family Planning." Occasional paper of the Population Council, 1971.

Simon, Julian L. "The Effect of Income on Fertility." Population Studies 23 (November 1969): 327-41.

_____. The Effects of Income on Fertility. Chapel Hill, North Carolina: Carolina Population Center, 1974.

_____. "The Role of Bonuses and Persuasive Propaganda in the Reduction of Birth Rates." Economic Development and Cultural Change 16 (April 1968): 404-11.

Singer, S. Fred, ed. Is There an Optimal Level of Population? New York: McGraw-Hill, 1971.

Solow, Robert. "A Contribution to the Theory of Economic Growth." Quarterly Journal of Economics 70 (February 1956): 65-94.

Stoeckel, John, Alauddin Chowdhury, and Wiley Mosley. "The Effects of Fecundity on Fertility in Rural East Pakistan (Bangla-
desh)." Social Biology 19 (June 1972): 193-201.

Stone, Richard. Demographic Accounting and Model-Building.
Paris: Organization for Economic Cooperation and Development, 1971.

Stycos, J. "Education and Fertility in Puerto Rico." In Proceedings
of the World Population Conference, 1965, Vol. 4. New York:
United Nations, 1967.

_____. "Female Employment and Fertility in Lima, Peru." Mil-
bank Memorial Fund Quarterly 43 (January 1965): 42-54.

_____, and Robert Weller. "Female Working Roles and Fertility."
Demography 4 (1967): 210-17.

Stys, W. "The Influence of Economic Conditions on the Fertility of
Peasant Women." Population Studies 11 (November 1957): 136-48.

Swan, T. W. "Economic Growth and Capital Accumulation." Economic Record 32 (November 1956): 334-61.

Sweet, James. "Family Composition and the Labor Force Activity
of American Wives." Demography 7 (May 1970): 195-209.

Tabah, Leon. "A Study of Fertility in Santiago, Chile." Marriage
and Family Living 25 (February 1963): 20-26.

Tabbarah, Riad. "Toward a Theory of Demographic Development."
Economic Development and Cultural Change 19 (January 1971):
257-77.

Taeuber, Irene B. "Discussion of Berquo et al." Milbank Memorial
Fund Quarterly 46 (July 1968): 186-88.

Taylor, Carl E. "Nutrition and Population." In Nutrition, National
Development and Planning, by Alan Berg, Nevin S. Scrimshaw,
and David L. Call, pp. 74-80. Cambridge, Mass.: Massachusetts Institute of Technology Press, 1973.

_____, and Marie-Francoise Hall. "Health, Population, and Eco-
nomic Development." Science 157 (August 11, 1967): 651-57.

Thomas, Harold A., Jr. "Population Dynamics of Primitive Societies." In Is There an Optimal Level of Population? by S. Fred Singer. New York: McGraw-Hill, 1971.

Tobin, James. "Comment on T. Paul Schultz." Journal of Political Economy 81 (March/April 1973): S275-S278.

Tsubochi, Yoshihiro. "Changes in Fertility in Japan by Region: 1920-1965." Demography 7 (May 1970): 121-34.

United Nations. The Determinants and Consequences of Population Growth. New York: United Nations, 1953.

_____. 1964 Demographic Yearbook. New York: United Nations, 1965.

_____. UNESCO, Statistical Yearbook. New York: United Nations, 1971.

_____. Yearbook of National Accounts Statistics. New York: United Nations, 1973.

_____, Department of Economic and Social Affairs. Methods for Population Projections by Sex and Age. New York: United Nations, 1956.

_____, Department of Economic and Social Affairs. Proceedings of the World Population Conference 1965. New York: United Nations, 1967.

U.S. Department of Commerce, Social and Economic Statistics Administration, Bureau of the Census. LRPM2: A System of Perspective Planning Submodels. Washington, D.C.: Socioeconomic Analyses Staff Paper no. 72-3, May 1972.

Universities-National Bureau Committee for Economic Research. Demographic and Economic Change in Developed Countries. Princeton: Princeton University Press, 1960.

Van Den Ban, A. W. "Family Structure and Modernization." Journal of Marriage and the Family 29 (November 1967): 771-73.

Van de Walle, Etienne. "The Relation of Marriage to Fertility in African Demographic Inquiries." Demography 2 (1965): 302-308.

Venieris, Yiannis P. , Frederick D. Sebold, and Richard D. Harper. "The Impact of Economic, Technological and Demographic Factors on Aggregate Births." Review of Economics and Statistics 155 (November 1973): 493-97.

Viel, Benjamin, and S. Lucero. "Analysis of Three Years' Experience with IUDs Among Women in the Western Area of the City of Santiago." American Journal of Obstetrics and Gynecology 106 (March 1970): 765-75.

Walsh, B. T. Economic Development and Population Control. New York: Praeger Publishers, 1971.

Wat, Sui Ying, and R. W. Hodge. "Social and Economic Factors in Hong Kong's Fertility Decline." Population Studies 26 (November 1972): 455-64.

Watcher, M. L. "A Time Series Fertility Equation: The Potential for a Baby Boom in the 1970s." Working Paper, Department of Economics, University of Pennsylvania, 1974.

Weintraub, Robert. "The Birth Rate and Economic Development: An Empirical Study." Econometrica 40 (October 1962): 812-17.

Welch, Finis. "Education in Production." Journal of Political Economy 78 (January/February 1970): 35-59.

Weller, Robert. "The Employment of Wives, Dominance, and Fertility." Journal of Marriage and the Family 30 (August 1968): 437-42.

_____. "The Employment of Wives, Role Incompatibility and Fertility." Milbank Memorial Fund Quarterly 46 (October 1968): 507-27.

Wickens, M. R. "A Note on the Use of Proxy Variables." Econometrica 40 (July 1972): 759-62.

Williams, Anne D. "Fertility and Infant Mortality." Thesis prospectus, University of Chicago, October 1973.

Williamson, John B. "Subjective Efficacy and Ideal Family Size as Predictors of Favorability Toward Birth Control." Demography 7 (August 1970): 329-40.

Willis, Robert J. "A New Approach to the Economic Theory of Fertility Behavior." Journal of Political Economy 81 (March/April 1973): S14-S64.

Wray, Joe D. "Population Pressure on Families: Family Size and Child Spacing." In National Academy of Sciences, Rapid Population Growth. Washington, D.C.: National Academy of Sciences, 1971.

Wrigley, Edward Anthony. "Family Limitation in Pre-Industrial England." The Economic History Review 19 (1966): 82-109.

_____. Population and History. New York: McGraw-Hill, 1969.

Wynne-Edwards, V. "Self-Regulating Systems in Populations of Animals." Science 147 (March 1965): 1543-48.

Yaukey, David. "Some Immediate Determinants of Fertility Differences in Lebanon." Marriage and Family Living 25 (February 1963): 27-34.

Youssef, Nadia H. "Social Structure and the Female Labor Force: The Case of Women Workers in Muslim Middle Eastern Countries." Demography 8 (November 1971): 427-39.

Zaiden, G. "Population Growth and Economic Development." Studies in Family Planning 1 (May 1969): 1-5.

Zarate, Alvan. "Fertility in Urban Areas of Mexico: Implications for the Theory of the Demographic Transition." Demography 4 (1967): 363-71.

_____. "Some Factors Associated with Urban-Rural Fertility Differentials in Mexico." Population Studies 21 (November 1967): 283-93.

MICHAEL C. KEELEY is presently an economist at the Center for the Study of Welfare Policy, Stanford Research Institute. He was formerly an economist with General Electric-TEMPO where his work on this book was done. He is author of several works on the economics of marital formation, the economic theory of fertility, and the interrelationships between demographic variables and economic development.

STEPHEN ENKE managed the General Electric-TEMPO Washington Operation for five years until his untimely death in 1974, directing studies in population, manpower, defense strategies, and other public policy issues. He was director of the Logistics Department of RAND Corporation in the late 1940s and early 1950s, taught at Yale and Duke Universities, and was assistant to the president of the Institute for Defense Analysis. His government positions included serving as Deputy Assistant Secretary of Defense (Systems Analysis) under Robert McNamara, Assistant to the Administrator of the Agency for International Development, and consulting positions with the White House, National Security Council, and numerous government agencies. He wrote several books, including Economics for Development, International Economics (with Salara), and Defense Management, as well as over a hundred published articles on a wide variety of issues.

RICHARD A. BROWN is the manager of Population Studies at General Electric-TEMPO. He has overall responsibility for TEMPO's economic-demographic research contracts. He has been involved in a number of policy studies at TEMPO. The areas studied include: the TEMPO I and TEMPO II economic-demographic models, pension reform, the social security system of the United States, and the United States all-volunteer army. He has published in journals and numerous internal TEMPO documents.

J. M. CAMPBELL, JR. is a research associate at the University of Chicago and Vice-President of John M. Campbell and Co. The author's article was prepared while he was an economist at General Electric-TEMPO. He is the author of numerous works on the economics of population and fertility, education, housing, and the petroleum industry, including articles in Econometrica, the

Journal of Political Economy, the Review of Economics and Statistics, Journal of Economic Inquiry, and others, and a book on the petroleum industry.

PAUL R. GREGORY is a full professor of economics at the University of Houston. He is the author of numerous works on population, economic development, and Soviet economics, including several books in each subject category. His journal publications include Econometrica, Review of Economics and Statistics, Journal of Political Economy, Economic Development and Cultural Change, Soviet Studies, Quarterly Journal of Economics, and others. His books include Soviet Economic Structure and Performance (New York: Harper and Row, 1974) and Socialist and Non-Socialist Industrialization Patterns (New York: Praeger, 1970).

BRUCE HERRICK is Associate Professor of Economics at the University of California, Los Angeles and a consultant to General Electric-TEMPO. He has been visiting professor at the University of Chile and San Andres University (La Paz, Bolivia), as well as serving as adviser to the Venezuelan Manpower Planning Office and the World Bank. His publications include articles and reviews in the fields of economic development, economic demography, and labor economics, as well as Urban Migration and Economic Development in Chile (MIT Press, 1965).

BRYAN D. HICKMAN is manager of the Social Programs group at General Electric-TEMPO, working in the areas of development economics, health planning, manpower, and population policy. He served as consultant to the White House Council on International Economic Policy reviewing U.S. foreign assistance programs, and participated in the reforms of the Selective Service System leading to the introduction of the lottery system and the end to most deferments.

DOUGLAS L. MAXWELL is currently with the population unit of General Electric-TEMPO. He was formerly assistant professor at State University of New York at Binghamton. He is the author of works on income tax policy, and demographic, economic, and educational growth in developing countries.

DONALD J. O'HARA is an assistant professor of economics at the University of Rochester. He was formerly a research economist at General Electric-TEMPO, where he participated in economic-demographic analyses of developing countries. He is the author of articles on economics and population in the Journal of Political Economy, Demography, and Studies in Family Planning.

ANNE D. WILLIAMS is assistant professor in the economics department and research associate of the Population Studies Center at the University of Pennsylvania, Philadelphia. She is also a consultant for the Population Group at General Electric-TEMPO, where she undertook the research for this article, and for Wharton Econometric Forecasting Associates, Philadelphia. She has written articles on population problems and econometrics and is currently researching the interactions of fertility and reproductive loss.

RELATED TITLES
Published by
Praeger Special Studies

THE MICRO-ECONOMICS OF DEMOGRAPHIC
CHANGE: Family Planning and Economic Well-Being
Theodore K. Ruprecht
and Frank I. Jewett

RESPONSES TO POPULATION GROWTH IN INDIA:
Changes in Social, Political, and Economic Behavior
edited by Marcus F. Franda

FOOD, POPULATION, AND EMPLOYMENT: The
Impact of the Green Revolution
edited by Thomas T. Poleman
and Donald K. Freebairn

DEVELOPMENT WITHOUT DEPENDENCE
Pierre Uri

MA